AI
Self-Driving Cars
Imminence

Practical Advances in
Artificial Intelligence and Machine Learning

Dr. Lance B. Eliot, MBA, PhD

Disclaimer: This book is presented solely for educational and entertainment purposes. The author and publisher are not offering it as legal, accounting, or other professional services advice. The author and publisher make no representations or warranties of any kind and assume no liabilities of any kind with respect to the accuracy or completeness of the contents and specifically disclaim any implied warranties of merchantability or fitness of use for a particular purpose. Neither the author nor the publisher shall be held liable or responsible to any person or entity with respect to any loss or incidental or consequential damages caused, or alleged to have been caused, directly or indirectly, by the information or programs contained herein. Every company is different and the advice and strategies contained herein may not be suitable for your situation.

ISBN: 978-1-95-738600-3

DEDICATION

To my incredible daughter, Lauren, and my incredible son, Michael.

Forest fortuna adiuvat (from the Latin; good fortune favors the brave).

CONTENTS

ACKNOWLEDGMENTS

I have been the beneficiary of advice and counsel by many friends, colleagues, family, investors, and many others. I want to thank everyone that has aided me throughout my career. I write from the heart and the head, having experienced first-hand what it means to have others around you that support you during the good times and the tough times.

To Warren Bennis, one of my doctoral advisors and ultimately a colleague, I offer my deepest thanks and appreciation, especially for his calm and insightful wisdom and support.

To Mark Stevens and his generous efforts toward funding and supporting the USC Stevens Center for Innovation.

To Lloyd Greif and the USC Lloyd Greif Center for Entrepreneurial Studies for their ongoing encouragement of founders and entrepreneurs.

To Peter Drucker, William Wang, Aaron Levie, Peter Kim, Jon Kraft, Cindy Crawford, Jenny Ming, Steve Milligan, Chis Underwood, Frank Gehry, Buzz Aldrin, Steve Forbes, Bill Thompson, Dave Dillon, Alan Fuerstman, Larry Ellison, Jim Sinegal, John Sperling, Mark Stevenson, Anand Nallathambi, Thomas Barrack, Jr., and many other innovators and leaders that I have met and gained mightily from doing so.

Thanks to Ed Trainor, Kevin Anderson, James Hickey, Wendell Jones, Ken Harris, DuWayne Peterson, Mike Brown, Jim Thornton, Abhi Beniwal, Al Biland, John Nomura, Eliot Weinman, John Desmond, and many others for their unwavering support during my career.

And most of all thanks as always to Lauren and Michael, for their ongoing support and for having seen me writing and heard much of this material during the many months involved in writing it. To their patience and willingness to listen.

INTRODUCTION

This is a book that provides the newest innovations and the latest Artificial Intelligence (AI) advances about the emerging nature of AI-based autonomous self-driving driverless cars. Via recent advances in Artificial Intelligence (AI) and Machine Learning (ML), we are nearing the day when vehicles can control themselves and will not require and nor rely upon human intervention to perform their driving tasks (or, that allow for human intervention, but only *require* human intervention in very limited ways).

Similar to my other related books, which I describe in a moment and list the chapters in the Appendix A of this book, I am particularly focused on those advances that pertain to self-driving cars. The phrase "autonomous vehicles" is often used to refer to any kind of vehicle, whether it is ground-based or in the air or sea, and whether it is a cargo hauling trailer truck or a conventional passenger car. Though the aspects described in this book are certainly applicable to all kinds of autonomous vehicles, I am focused more so here on cars.

For this book, I am going to borrow my introduction from those companion books, since it does a good job of laying out the landscape of self-driving cars and my overall viewpoints on the topic.

INTRODUCTION TO SELF-DRIVING CARS

This is a book about self-driving cars. Someday in the future, we'll all have self-driving cars and this book will perhaps seem antiquated, but right now, we are at the forefront of the self-driving car wave. Daily news bombards us with flashes of new announcements by one car maker or another and leaves the impression that within the next few weeks or maybe months that the self-driving car will be here. A casual non-technical reader would assume from these news flashes that in we must be on the cusp of a true self-driving car.

We are still quite a distance from having a true self-driving car. A true self-driving car is akin to a moonshot. In the same manner that getting us to the moon was an incredible feat, likewise, is achieving a true self-driving car. Anybody that suggests or even brashly states that the true self-driving car is nearly here should be viewed with great skepticism. Indeed, you'll see that I often tend to use the word "hogwash" or "crock" when I assess much of the decidedly ***fake news*** about self-driving cars.

Indeed, I've been writing a popular blog post about self-driving cars and hitting hard on those that try to wave their hands and pretend that we are on the imminent verge of true self-driving cars. For many years, I've been known as the AI Insider. Besides writing about AI, I also develop AI software. I do what I describe. It also gives me insights into what others that are doing AI are really doing versus what it is said they are doing.

Many faithful readers had asked me to pull together my insightful short essays and put them into another book, which you are now holding.

For those of you that have been reading my essays over the years, this collection not only puts them together into one handy package, I also updated the essays and added new material. For those of you that are new to the topic of self-driving cars and AI, I hope you find these essays approachable and informative. I also tend to have a writing style with a bit of a voice, and so you'll see that I am times have a wry sense of humor and poke at conformity.

As a former professor and founder of an AI research lab, I for many years wrote in the formal language of academic writing. I published in referred journals and served as an editor for several AI journals. This writing here is not of the nature, and I have adopted a different and more informal style for these essays. That being said, I also do mention from time-to-time more rigorous material on AI and encourage you all to dig into those deeper and more formal materials if so interested.

For those of you that are reading this book and have a penchant for writing code, you might consider taking a look at the open-source code available for self-driving cars. This is a handy place to start learning how to develop AI for self-driving cars. There are also many new educational courses spring forth. There is a growing body of those wanting to learn about and develop self-driving cars, and a growing body of colleges, labs, and other avenues by which you can learn about self-driving cars.

This book will provide a foundation of aspects that I think will get you ready for those kinds of more advanced training opportunities. If you've already taken those classes, you'll likely find these essays especially interesting as they offer a perspective that I am betting few other instructors or faculty offered to you. These are challenging essays that ask you to think beyond the conventional about self-driving cars.

THE MOTHER OF ALL AI PROJECTS

In June 2017, Apple CEO Tim Cook came out and finally admitted that Apple has been working on a self-driving car. As you'll see in my essays, Apple was enmeshed in secrecy about their self-driving car efforts. We have only been able to read the tea leaves and guess at what Apple has been up to. The notion of an iCar has been floating for quite a while, and self-driving engineers and researchers have been signing tight-lipped Non-Disclosure Agreements (NDA's) to work on projects at Apple that were as shrouded in mystery as any military invasion plans might be.

Tim Cook said something that many others in the Artificial Intelligence (AI) field have been saying, namely, the creation of a self-driving car has got to be the mother of all AI projects. In other words, it is in fact a tremendous moonshot for AI. If a self-driving car can be crafted and the AI works as we hope, it means that we have made incredible strides with AI and that therefore it opens many other worlds of potential breakthrough accomplishments that AI can solve.

Is this hyperbole? Am I just trying to make AI seem like a miracle worker and so provide self-aggrandizing statements for those of us writing the AI software for self-driving cars? No, it is not hyperbole. Developing a true self-driving car is really, really, really hard to do. Let me take a moment to explain why. As a side note, I realize that the Apple CEO is known for at times uttering hyperbole, and he had previously said for example that the year 2012 was "the mother of all years," and he had said that the release of iOS 10 was "the mother of all releases" – all of which does suggest he likes to use the handy "mother of" expression. But, I assure you, in terms of true self-driving cars, he has hit the nail on the head. For sure.

When you think about a moonshot and how we got to the moon, there are some identifiable characteristics and those same aspects can be applied to creating a true self-driving car. You'll notice that I keep putting the word "true" in front of the self-driving car expression. I do so because as per my essay about the various levels of self-driving cars, there are some self-driving cars that are only somewhat of a self-driving car. The somewhat versions are ones that require a human driver to be ready to intervene. In my view, that's not a true self-driving car. A true self-driving car is one that requires no human driver intervention at all. It is a car that can entirely undertake via automation the driving task without any human driver needed. This is the essence of what is known as a Level 5 self-driving car. We are currently at the Level 2 and Level 3 mark, and not yet at Level 5.

Getting to the moon involved aspects such as having big stretch goals, incremental progress, experimentation, innovation, and so on. Let's review how this applied to the moonshot of the bygone era, and how it applies to the self-driving car moonshot of today.

Big Stretch Goal

Trying to take a human and deliver the human to the moon, and bring them back, safely, was an extremely large stretch goal at the time. No one knew whether it could be done. The technology wasn't available yet. The cost was huge. The determination would need to be fierce. Etc. To reach a Level 5 self-driving car is going to be the same. It is a big stretch goal. We can readily get to the Level 3, and we are able to see the Level 4 just up ahead, but a Level 5 is still an unknown as to if it is doable. It should eventually be doable and in the same way that we thought we'd eventually get to the moon, but when it will occur is a different story.

Incremental Progress

Getting to the moon did not happen overnight in one fell swoop. It took years and years of incremental progress to get there. Likewise, for self-driving cars. Google has famously been striving to get to the Level 5, and pretty much been willing to forgo dealing with the intervening levels, but most of the other self-driving car makers are doing the incremental route. Let's get a good Level 2 and a somewhat Level 3 going. Then, let's improve the Level 3 and get a somewhat Level 4 going. Then, let's improve the Level 4 and finally arrive at a Level 5. This seems to be the prevalent way that we are going to achieve the true self-driving car.

Experimentation

You likely know that there were various experiments involved in perfecting the approach and technology to get to the moon. As per making incremental progress, we first tried to see if we could get a rocket to go into space and safety return, then put a monkey in there, then with a human, then we went all the way to the moon but didn't land, and finally we arrived at the mission that actually landed on the moon.

Self-driving cars are the same way. We are doing simulations of self-driving cars. We do testing of self-driving cars on private land under controlled situations.

We do testing of self-driving cars on public roadways, often having to meet regulatory requirements including for example having an engineer or equivalent in the car to take over the controls if needed. And so on. Experiments big and small are needed to figure out what works and what doesn't.

Innovation

There are already some advances in AI that are allowing us to progress toward self-driving cars. We are going to need even more advances. Innovation in all aspects of technology are going to be required to achieve a true self-driving car. By no means do we already have everything in-hand that we need to get there. Expect new inventions and new approaches, new algorithms, etc.

Setbacks

Most of the pundits are avoiding talking about potential setbacks in the progress toward self-driving cars. Getting to the moon involved many setbacks, some of which you never have heard of and were buried at the time so as to not dampen enthusiasm and funding for getting to the moon. A recurring theme in many of my included essays is that there are going to be setbacks as we try to arrive at a true self-driving car. Take a deep breath and be ready. I just hope the setbacks don't completely stop progress. I am sure that it will cause progress to alter in a manner that we've not yet seen in the self-driving car field. I liken the self-driving car of today to the excitement everyone had for Uber when it first got going. Today, we have a different view of Uber and with each passing day there are more regulations to the ride sharing business and more concerns raised. The darling child only stays a darling until finally that child acts up. It will happen the same with self-driving cars.

SELF-DRIVING CARS CHALLENGES

But what exactly makes things so hard to have a true self-driving car, you might be asking. You have seen cruise control for years and years. You've lately seen cars that can do parallel parking. You've seen YouTube videos of Tesla drivers that put their hands out the window as their car zooms along the highway, and seen to therefore be in a self-driving car. Aren't we just needing to put a few more sensors onto a car and then we'll have in-hand a true self-driving car? Nope.

Consider for a moment the nature of the driving task. We don't just let anyone at any age drive a car. Worldwide, most countries won't license a driver until the age of 18, though many do allow a learner's permit at the age of 15 or 16. Some suggest that a younger age would be physically too small to reach the controls of the car. Though this might be the case, we could easily adjust the controls to allow for younger aged and thus smaller stature. It's not their physical size that matters. It's their cognitive development that matters.

To drive a car, you need to be able to reason about the car, what the car can and cannot do. You need to know how to operate the car. You need to know about how other cars on the road drive. You need to know what is allowed in driving such as speed limits and driving within marked lanes. You need to be able to react to situations and be able to avoid getting into accidents. You need to ascertain when to hit your brakes, when to steer clear of a pedestrian, and how to keep from ramming that motorcyclist that just cut you off.

Many of us had taken courses on driving. We studied about driving and took driver training. We had to take a test and pass it to be able to drive. The point being that though most adults take the driving task for granted, and we often "mindlessly" drive our cars, there is a significant amount of cognitive effort that goes into driving a car. After a while, it becomes second nature. You don't especially think about how you drive, you just do it. But, if you watch a novice driver, say a teenager learning to drive, you suddenly realize that there is a lot more complexity to it than we seem to realize.

Furthermore, driving is a very serious task. I recall when my daughter and son first learned to drive. They are both very conscientious people. They wanted to make sure that whatever they did, they did well, and that they did not harm anyone. Every day, when you get into a car, it is probably around 4,000 pounds of hefty metal and plastics (about two tons), and it is a lethal weapon. Think about it. You drive down the street in an object that weighs two tons and with the engine it can accelerate and ram into anything you want to hit. The damage a car can inflict is very scary. Both my children were surprised that they were being given the right to maneuver this monster of a beast that could cause tremendous harm entirely by merely letting go of the steering wheel for a moment or taking your eyes off the road.

In fact, in the United States alone there are about 40,000 deaths per year by auto accidents, which is more than 100 per day. Given that there are about 263 million cars in the United States, I am actually more amazed that the number of fatalities is not a lot higher.

During my morning commute, I look at all the thousands of cars on the freeway around me, and I think that if all of them decided to go zombie and drive in a crazy maniac way, there would be many people dead. Somehow, incredibly, each day, most people drive relatively safely. To me, that's a miracle right there. Getting millions and millions of people to be safe and sane when behind the wheel of a two-ton mobile object, it's a feat that we as a society should admire with pride.

So, hopefully you are in agreement that the driving task requires a great deal of cognition. You don't' need to be especially smart to drive a car, and we've done quite a bit to make car driving viable for even the average dolt. There isn't an IQ test that you need to take to drive a car. If you can read and write, and pass a test, you pretty much can legally drive a car. There are of course some that drive a car and are not legally permitted to do so, plus there are private areas such as farms where drivers are young, but for public roadways in the United States, you can be generally of average intelligence (or less) and be able to legally drive.

This though makes it seem like the cognitive effort must not be much. If the cognitive effort was truly hard, wouldn't we only have Einstein's that could drive a car? We have made sure to keep the driving task as simple as we can, by making the controls easy and relatively standardized, and by having roads that are relatively standardized, and so on. It is as though Disneyland has put their Autopia into the real-world, by us all as a society agreeing that roads will be a certain way, and we'll all abide by the various rules of driving.

A modest cognitive task by a human is still something that stymies AI. You certainly know that AI has been able to beat chess players and be good at other kinds of games. This type of narrow cognition is not what car driving is about. Car driving is much wider. It requires knowledge about the world, which a chess playing AI system does not need to know. The cognitive aspects of driving are on the one hand seemingly simple, but at the same time require layer upon layer of knowledge about cars, people, roads, rules, and a myriad of other "common sense" aspects. We don't have any AI systems today that have that same kind of breadth and depth of awareness and knowledge.

As revealed in my essays, the self-driving car of today is using trickery to do particular tasks. It is all very narrow in operation. Plus, it currently assumes that a human driver is ready to intervene. It is like a child that we have taught to stack blocks, but we are needed to be right there in case the child stacks them too high and they begin to fall over.

AI of today is brittle, it is narrow, and it does not approach the cognitive abilities of humans. This is why the true self-driving car is somewhere out in the future.

Another aspect to the driving task is that it is not solely a mind exercise. You do need to use your senses to drive. You use your eyes as vision sensors to see the road ahead. You vision capability is like a streaming video, which your brain needs to continually analyze as you drive. Where is the road? Is there a pedestrian in the way? Is there another car ahead of you? Your senses are relying a flood of info to your brain. Self-driving cars are trying to do the same, by using cameras, radar, ultrasound, and lasers. This is an attempt at mimicking how humans have senses and sensory apparatus.

Thus, the driving task is mental and physical. You use your senses, you use your arms and legs to manipulate the controls of the car, and you use your brain to assess the sensory info and direct your limbs to act upon the controls of the car. This all happens instantly. If you've ever perhaps gotten something in your eye and only had one eye available to drive with, you suddenly realize how dependent upon vision you are. If you have a broken foot with a cast, you suddenly realize how hard it is to control the brake pedal and the accelerator. If you've taken medication and your brain is maybe sluggish, you suddenly realize how much mental strain is required to drive a car.

An AI system that plays chess only needs to be focused on playing chess. The physical aspects aren't important because usually a human moves the chess pieces or the chessboard is shown on an electronic display. Using AI for a more life-and-death task such as analyzing MRI images of patients, this again does not require physical capabilities and instead is done by examining images of bits.

Driving a car is a true life-and-death task. It is a use of AI that can easily and at any moment produce death. For those colleagues of mine that are developing this AI, as am I, we need to keep in mind the somber aspects of this. We are producing software that will have in its virtual hands the lives of the occupants of the car, and the lives of those in other nearby cars, and the lives of nearby pedestrians, etc. Chess is not usually a life-or-death matter.

Driving is all around us. Cars are everywhere. Most of today's AI applications involve only a small number of people. Or, they are behind the scenes and we as humans have other recourse if the AI messes up. AI that is driving a car at 80 miles per hour on a highway had better not mess up. The consequences are grave.

Multiply this by the number of cars, if we could put magically self-driving into every car in the USA, we'd have AI running in the 263 million cars. That's a lot of AI spread around. This is AI on a massive scale that we are not doing today and that offers both promise and potential peril.

There are some that want AI for self-driving cars because they envision a world without any car accidents. They envision a world in which there is no car congestion and all cars cooperate with each other. These are wonderful utopian visions.

They are also very misleading. The adoption of self-driving cars is going to be incremental and not overnight. We cannot economically just junk all existing cars. Nor are we going to be able to affordably retrofit existing cars. It is more likely that self-driving cars will be built into new cars and that over many years of gradual replacement of existing cars that we'll see the mix of self-driving cars become substantial in the real-world.

In these essays, I have tried to offer technological insights without being overly technical in my description, and also blended the business, societal, and economic aspects too. Technologists need to consider the non-technological impacts of what they do. Non-technologists should be aware of what is being developed.

We all need to work together to collectively be prepared for the enormous disruption and transformative aspects of true self-driving cars.

WHAT THIS BOOK PROVIDES

What does this book provide to you? It introduces many of the key elements about self-driving cars and does so with an AI based perspective. I weave together technical and non-technical aspects, readily going from being concerned about the cognitive capabilities of the driving task and how the technology is embodying this into self-driving cars, and in the next breath I discuss the societal and economic aspects.

They are all intertwined because that's the way reality is. You cannot separate out the technology per se, and instead must consider it within the milieu of what is being invented and innovated, and do so with a mindset towards the contemporary mores and culture that shape what we are doing and what we hope to do.

WHY THIS BOOK

I wrote this book to try and bring to the public view many aspects about self-driving cars that nobody seems to be discussing.

For business leaders that are either involved in making self-driving cars or that are going to leverage self-driving cars, I hope that this book will enlighten you as to the risks involved and ways in which you should be strategizing about how to deal with those risks.

For entrepreneurs, startups and other businesses that want to enter into the self-driving car market that is emerging, I hope this book sparks your interest in doing so, and provides some sense of what might be prudent to pursue.

For researchers that study self-driving cars, I hope this book spurs your interest in the risks and safety issues of self-driving cars, and also nudges you toward conducting research on those aspects.

For students in computer science or related disciplines, I hope this book will provide you with interesting and new ideas and material, for which you might conduct research or provide some career direction insights for you.

For AI companies and high-tech companies pursuing self-driving cars, this book will hopefully broaden your view beyond just the mere coding and development needed to make self-driving cars.

For all readers, I hope that you will find the material in this book to be stimulating. Some of it will be repetitive of things you already know. But I am pretty sure that you'll also find various eureka moments whereby you'll discover a new technique or approach that you had not earlier thought of. I am also betting that there will be material that forces you to rethink some of your current practices.

I am not saying you will suddenly have an epiphany and change what you are doing. I do think though that you will reconsider or perhaps revisit what you are doing.

For anyone choosing to use this book for teaching purposes, please take a look at my suggestions for doing so, as described in the Appendix. I have found the material handy in courses that I have taught, and likewise other faculty have told me that they have found the material handy, in some cases as extended readings and in other instances as a core part of their course (depending on the nature of the class).

In my writing for this book, I have tried carefully to blend both the practitioner and the academic styles of writing.

It is not as abstract as is typical academic journal writing, but at the same time offers depth by going into the nuances and trade-offs of various practices.

The word "deep" is in vogue today, meaning getting deeply into a subject or topic, and so is the word "unpack" which means to tease out the underlying aspects of a subject or topic. I have sought to offer material that addresses an issue or topic by going relatively deeply into it and make sure that it is well unpacked.

In any book about AI, it is difficult to use our everyday words without having some of them be misinterpreted. Specifically, it is easy to anthropomorphize AI. When I say that an AI system "knows" something, I do not want you to construe that the AI system has sentience and "knows" in the same way that humans do. They aren't that way, as yet. I have tried to use quotes around such words from time-to-time to emphasize that the words I am using should not be misinterpreted to ascribe true human intelligence to the AI systems that we know of today. If I used quotes around all such words, the book would be very difficult to read, and so I am doing so judiciously. Please keep that in mind as you read the material, thanks.

Some of the material is time-based in terms of covering underway activities, and though some of it might decay, nonetheless I believe you'll find the material useful and informative.

COMPANION BOOKS BY DR. ELIOT

1. **"Introduction to Driverless Self-Driving Cars"** by Dr. Lance Eliot
2. **"Innovation and Thought Leadership on Self-Driving Driverless Cars"**
3. **"Advances in AI and Autonomous Vehicles: Cybernetic Self-Driving Cars"**
4. **"Self-Driving Cars: The Mother of All AI Projects"** by Dr. Lance Eliot
5. **"New Advances in AI Autonomous Driverless Self-Driving Cars"**
6. **"AV Driverless Self-Driving Cars & AI"** by Dr. Lance Eliot and Michael B. Eliot
7. **"Transformative Artificial Intelligence Driverless Self-Driving Cars"**
8. **"Disruptive Artificial Intelligence and Driverless Self-Driving Cars"**
9. **"State-of-the-Art AI Driverless Self-Driving Cars"** by Dr. Lance Eliot
10. **"Top Trends in AI Self-Driving Cars"** by Dr. Lance Eliot
11. **"AI Innovations and Self-Driving Cars"** by Dr. Lance Eliot
12. **"Crucial Advances for AI Driverless Cars"** by Dr. Lance Eliot
13. **"Sociotechnical Insights and AI Driverless Cars"** by Dr. Lance Eliot.
14. **"Pioneering Advances for AI Driverless Cars"** by Dr. Lance Eliot
15. **"Leading Edge Trends for AI Driverless Cars"** by Dr. Lance Eliot
16. **"The Cutting Edge of AI Autonomous Cars"** by Dr. Lance Eliot
17. **"The Next Wave of AI Self-Driving Cars"** by Dr. Lance Eliot
18. **"Revolutionary Innovations of AI Driverless Cars"** by Dr. Lance Eliot
19. **"AI Self-Driving Cars Breakthroughs"** by Dr. Lance Eliot
20. **"Trailblazing Trends for AI Self-Driving Cars"** by Dr. Lance Eliot
21. **"Ingenious Strides for AI Driverless Cars"** by Dr. Lance Eliot
22. **"AI Self-Driving Cars Inventiveness"** by Dr. Lance Eliot
23. **"Visionary Secrets of AI Driverless Cars"** by Dr. Lance Eliot
24. **"Spearheading AI Self-Driving Cars"** by Dr. Lance Eliot
25. **"Spurring AI Self-Driving Cars"** by Dr. Lance Eliot
26. **"Avant-Garde AI Driverless Cars"** by Dr. Lance Eliot
27. **"AI Self-Driving Cars Evolvement"** by Dr. Lance Eliot
28. **"AI Driverless Cars Chrysalis"** by Dr. Lance Eliot
29. **"Boosting AI Autonomous Cars"** by Dr. Lance Eliot
30. **"AI Self-Driving Cars Trendsetting"** by Dr. Lance Eliot
31. **"AI Autonomous Cars Forefront"** by Dr. Lance Eliot
32. **"AI Autonomous Cars Emergence"** by Dr. Lance Eliot
33. **"AI Autonomous Cars Progress"** by Dr. Lance Eliot
34. **"AI Self-Driving Cars Prognosis"** by Dr. Lance Eliot
35. **"AI Self-Driving Cars Momentum"** by Dr. Lance Eliot
36. **"AI Self-Driving Cars Headway"** by Dr. Lance Eliot
37. **"AI Self-Driving Cars Vicissitude"** by Dr. Lance Eliot
38. **"AI Self-Driving Cars Autonomy"** by Dr. Lance Eliot
39. **"AI Driverless Cars Transmutation"** by Dr. Lance Eliot
40. **"AI Driverless Cars Potentiality"** by Dr. Lance Eliot
41. **"AI Driverless Cars Realities"** by Dr. Lance Eliot
42. **"AI Self-Driving Cars Materiality"** by Dr. Lance Eliot
43. **"AI Self-Driving Cars Accordance"** by Dr. Lance Eliot
44. **"AI Self-Driving Cars Equanimity"** by Dr. Lance Eliot
45. **"AI Self-Driving Cars Divulgement"** by Dr. Lance Eliot
46. **"AI Self-Driving Cars Consonance"** by Dr. Lance Eliot
47. **"Revelatory AI Self-Driving Cars"** by Dr. Lance Eliot
48. **"Edifying AI Self-Driving Cars"** by Dr. Lance Eliot
49. **"Apprising AI Driverless Cars"** by Dr. Lance Eliot
50. **"Improving AI Self-Driving Cars"** by Dr. Lance Eliot
51. **"Progressing AI Driverless Cars"** by Dr. Lance Eliot
52. **"AI Self-Driving Cars Imminence"** by Dr. Lance Eliot

These books are available on Amazon and at other major global booksellers.

CHAPTER 1
ELIOT FRAMEWORK FOR AI SELF-DRIVING CARS

This chapter is a core foundational aspect for understanding AI self-driving cars and I have used this same chapter in several of my other books to introduce the reader to essential elements of this field. Once you've read this chapter, you'll be prepared to read the rest of the material since the foundational essence of the components of autonomous AI driverless self-driving cars will have been established for you.

When I give presentations about self-driving cars and teach classes on the topic, I have found it helpful to provide a framework around which the various key elements of self-driving cars can be understood and organized (see diagram at the end of this chapter). The framework needs to be simple enough to convey the overarching elements, but at the same time not so simple that it belies the true complexity of self-driving cars. As such, I am going to describe the framework here and try to offer in a thousand words (or more!) what the framework diagram itself intends to portray.

The core elements on the diagram are numbered for ease of reference. The numbering does not suggest any kind of prioritization of the elements. Each element is crucial. Each element has a purpose, and otherwise would not be included in the framework. For some self-driving cars, a particular element might be more important or somehow distinguished in comparison to other self-driving cars.

You could even use the framework to rate a particular self-driving car, doing so by gauging how well it performs in each of the elements of the framework. I will describe each of the elements, one at a time. After doing so, I'll discuss aspects that illustrate how the elements interact and perform during the overall effort of a self-driving car.

At the AI Self-Driving Car Institute, we use the framework to keep track of what we are working on, and how we are developing software that fills in what is needed to achieve Level 5 self-driving cars.

D-01: Sensor Capture

Let's start with the one element that often gets the most attention in the press about self-driving cars, namely, the sensory devices for a self-driving car.

On the framework, the box labeled as D-01 indicates "Sensor Capture" and refers to the processes of the self-driving car that involve collecting data from the myriad of sensors that are used for a self-driving car. The types of devices typically involved are listed, such as the use of mono cameras, stereo cameras, LIDAR devices, radar systems, ultrasonic devices, GPS, IMU, and so on.

These devices are tasked with obtaining data about the status of the self-driving car and the world around it. Some of the devices are continually providing updates, while others of the devices await an indication by the self-driving car that the device is supposed to collect data. The data might be first transformed in some fashion by the device itself, or it might instead be fed directly into the sensor capture as raw data. At that point, it might be up to the sensor capture processes to do transformations on the data. This all varies depending upon the nature of the devices being used and how the devices were designed and developed.

D-02: Sensor Fusion

Imagine that your eyeballs receive visual images, your nose receives odors, your ears receive sounds, and in essence each of your distinct sensory devices is getting some form of input. The input befits the nature of the device. Likewise, for a self-driving car, the cameras provide visual images, the radar returns radar reflections, and so on. Each device provides the data as befits what the device does.

At some point, using the analogy to humans, you need to merge together what your eyes see, what your nose smells, what your ears hear, and piece it all together into a larger sense of what the world is all about and what is happening around you. Sensor fusion is the action of taking the singular aspects from each of the devices and putting them together into a larger puzzle.

Sensor fusion is a tough task. There are some devices that might not be working at the time of the sensor capture. Or, there might some devices that are unable to report well what they have detected. Again, using a human analogy, suppose you are in a dark room and so your eyes cannot see much. At that point, you might need to rely more so on your ears and what you hear. The same is true for a self-driving car. If the cameras are obscured due to snow and sleet, it might be that the radar can provide a greater indication of what the external conditions consist of.

In the case of a self-driving car, there can be a plethora of such sensory devices. Each is reporting what it can. Each might have its difficulties. Each might have its limitations, such as how far ahead it can detect an object. All of these limitations need to be considered during the sensor fusion task.

D-03: Virtual World Model

For humans, we presumably keep in our minds a model of the world around us when we are driving a car. In your mind, you know that the car is going at say 60 miles per hour and that you are on a freeway.

You have a model in your mind that your car is surrounded by other cars, and that there are lanes to the freeway. Your model is not only based on what you can see, hear, etc., but also what you know about the nature of the world. You know that at any moment that car ahead of you can smash on its brakes, or the car behind you can ram into your car, or that the truck in the next lane might swerve into your lane.

The AI of the self-driving car needs to have a virtual world model, which it then keeps updated with whatever it is receiving from the sensor fusion, which received its input from the sensor capture.

D-04: System Action Plan

By having a virtual world model, the AI of the self-driving car is able to keep track of where the car is and what is happening around the car. In addition, the AI needs to determine what to do next. Should the self-driving car hit its brakes? Should the self-driving car stay in its lane or swerve into the lane to the left? Should the self-driving car accelerate or slow down?

A system action plan needs to be prepared by the AI of the self-driving car. The action plan specifies what actions should be taken. The actions need to pertain to the status of the virtual world model. Plus, the actions need to be realizable.

This realizability means that the AI cannot just assert that the self-driving car should suddenly sprout wings and fly. Instead, the AI must be bound by whatever the self-driving car can actually do, such as coming to a halt in a distance of X feet at a speed of Y miles per hour, rather than perhaps asserting that the self-driving car come to a halt in 0 feet as though it could instantaneously come to a stop while it is in motion.

D-05: Controls Activation

The system action plan is implemented by activating the controls of the car to act according to what the plan stipulates.

This might mean that the accelerator control is commanded to increase the speed of the car. Or, the steering control is commanded to turn the steering wheel 30 degrees to the left or right.

One question arises as to whether or not the controls respond as they are commanded to do. In other words, suppose the AI has commanded the accelerator to increase, but for some reason it does not do so. Or, maybe it tries to do so, but the speed of the car does not increase.

The controls activation feeds back into the virtual world model, and simultaneously the virtual world model is getting updated from the sensors, the sensor capture, and the sensor fusion. This allows the AI to ascertain what has taken place as a result of the controls being commanded to take some kind of action.

By the way, please keep in mind that though the diagram seems to have a linear progression to it, the reality is that these are all aspects of the self-driving car that are happening in parallel and simultaneously. The sensors are capturing data, meanwhile the sensor fusion is taking place, meanwhile the virtual model is being updated, meanwhile the system action plan is being formulated and reformulated, meanwhile the controls are being activated.

This is the same as a human being that is driving a car. They are eyeballing the road, meanwhile they are fusing in their mind the sights, sounds, etc., meanwhile their mind is updating their model of the world around them, meanwhile they are formulating an action plan of what to do, and meanwhile they are pushing their foot onto the pedals and steering the car. In the normal course of driving a car, you are doing all of these at once. I mention this so that when you look at the diagram, you will think of the boxes as processes that are all happening at the same time, and not as though only one happens and then the next.

They are shown diagrammatically in a simplistic manner to help comprehend what is taking place. You though should also realize that they are working in parallel and simultaneous with each other. This is a tough aspect in that the inter-element communications involve latency and other aspects that must be taken into account. There can be delays in one element updating and then sharing its latest status with other elements.

D-06: Automobile & CAN

Contemporary cars use various automotive electronics and a Controller Area Network (CAN) to serve as the components that underlie the driving aspects of a car.

There are Electronic Control Units (ECU's) which control subsystems of the car, such as the engine, the brakes, the doors, the windows, and so on.

The elements D-01, D-02, D-03, D-04, D-05 are layered on top of the D-06, and must be aware of the nature of what the D-06 is able to do and not do.

D-07: In-Car Commands

Humans are going to be occupants in self-driving cars. In a Level 5 self-driving car, there must be some form of communication that takes place between the humans and the self-driving car. For example, I go into a self-driving car and tell it that I want to be driven over to Disneyland, and along the way I want to stop at In-and-Out Burger. The self-driving car now parses what I've said and tries to then establish a means to carry out my wishes.

In-car commands can happen at any time during a driving journey. Though my example was about an in-car command when I first got into my self-driving car, it could be that while the self-driving car is carrying out the journey that I change my mind. Perhaps after getting stuck in traffic, I tell the self-driving car to forget about getting the burgers and just head straight over to the theme park. The self-driving car needs to be alert to in-car commands throughout the journey.

D-08: V2X Communications

We will ultimately have self-driving cars communicating with each other, doing so via V2V (Vehicle-to-Vehicle) communications. We will also have self-driving cars that communicate with the roadways and other aspects of the transportation infrastructure, doing so via V2I (Vehicle-to-Infrastructure).

The variety of ways in which a self-driving car will be communicating with other cars and infrastructure is being called V2X, whereby the letter X means whatever else we identify as something that a car should or would want to communicate with.

The V2X communications will be taking place simultaneous with everything else on the diagram, and those other elements will need to incorporate whatever it gleans from those V2X communications.

D-09: Deep Learning

The use of Deep Learning permeates all other aspects of the self-driving car. The AI of the self-driving car will be using deep learning to do a better job at the systems action plan, and at the control's activation, and at the sensor fusion, and so on.

Currently, the use of artificial neural networks is the most prevalent form of deep learning. Based on large swaths of data, the neural networks attempt to "learn" from the data and therefore direct the efforts of the self-driving car accordingly.

D-10: Tactical AI

Tactical AI is the element of dealing with the moment-to-moment driving of the self-driving car. Is the self-driving car staying in its lane of the freeway? Is the car responding appropriately to the controls commands? Are the sensory devices working?

For human drivers, the tactical equivalent can be seen when you watch a novice driver such as a teenager that is first driving. They are focused on the mechanics of the driving task, keeping their eye on the road while also trying to properly control the car.

D-11: Strategic AI

The Strategic AI aspects of a self-driving car are dealing with the larger picture of what the self-driving car is trying to do. If I had asked that the self-driving car take me to Disneyland, there is an overall journey map that needs to be kept and maintained.

There is an interaction between the Strategic AI and the Tactical AI. The Strategic AI is wanting to keep on the mission of the driving, while the Tactical AI is focused on the particulars underway in the driving effort.

If the Tactical AI seems to wander away from the overarching mission, the Strategic AI wants to see why and get things back on track. If the Tactical AI realizes that there is something amiss on the self-driving car, it needs to alert the Strategic AI accordingly and have an adjustment to the overarching mission that is underway.

D-12: Self-Aware AI

Very few of the self-driving cars being developed are including a Self-Aware AI element, which we at the Cybernetic Self-Driving Car Institute believe is crucial to Level 5 self-driving cars.

The Self-Aware AI element is intended to watch over itself, in the sense that the AI is making sure that the AI is working as intended. Suppose you had a human driving a car, and they were starting to drive erratically. Hopefully, their own self-awareness would make them realize they themselves are driving poorly, such as perhaps starting to fall asleep after having been driving for hours on end. If you had a passenger in the car, they might be able to alert the driver if the driver is starting to do something amiss.

This is exactly what the Self-Aware AI element tries to do, it becomes the overseer of the AI, and tries to detect when the AI has become faulty or confused, and then find ways to overcome the issue.

D-13: Economic

The economic aspects of a self-driving car are not per se a technology aspect of a self-driving car, but the economics do indeed impact the nature of a self-driving car. For example, the cost of outfitting a self-driving car with every kind of possible sensory device is prohibitive, and so choices need to be made about which devices are used. And, for those sensory devices chosen, whether they would have a full set of features or a more limited set of features.

We are going to have self-driving cars that are at the low-end of a consumer cost point, and others at the high-end of a consumer cost point. You cannot expect that the self-driving car at the low-end is going to be as robust as the one at the high-end.

I realize that many of the self-driving car pundits are acting as though all self-driving cars will be the same, but they won't be. Just like anything else, we are going to have self-driving cars that have a range of capabilities. Some will be better than others. Some will be safer than others. This is the way of the real-world, and so we need to be thinking about the economics aspects when considering the nature of self-driving cars.

D-14: Societal

This component encompasses the societal aspects of AI which also impacts the technology of self-driving cars. For example, the famous Trolley Problem involves what choices should a self-driving car make when faced with life-and-death matters. If the self-driving car is about to either hit a child standing in the roadway, or instead ram into a tree at the side of the road and possibly kill the humans in the self-driving car, which choice should be made?

We need to keep in mind the societal aspects will underlie the AI of the self-driving car. Whether we are aware of it explicitly or not, the AI will have embedded into it various societal assumptions.

D-15: Innovation

I included the notion of innovation into the framework because we can anticipate that whatever a self-driving car consists of, it will continue to be innovated over time. The self-driving cars coming out in the next several years will undoubtedly be different and less innovative than the versions that come out in ten years hence, etc.

Framework Overall

For those of you that want to learn about self-driving cars, you can potentially pick a particular element and become specialized in that aspect. Some engineers are focusing on the sensory devices. Some engineers focus on the controls activation. And so on. There are specialties in each of the elements.

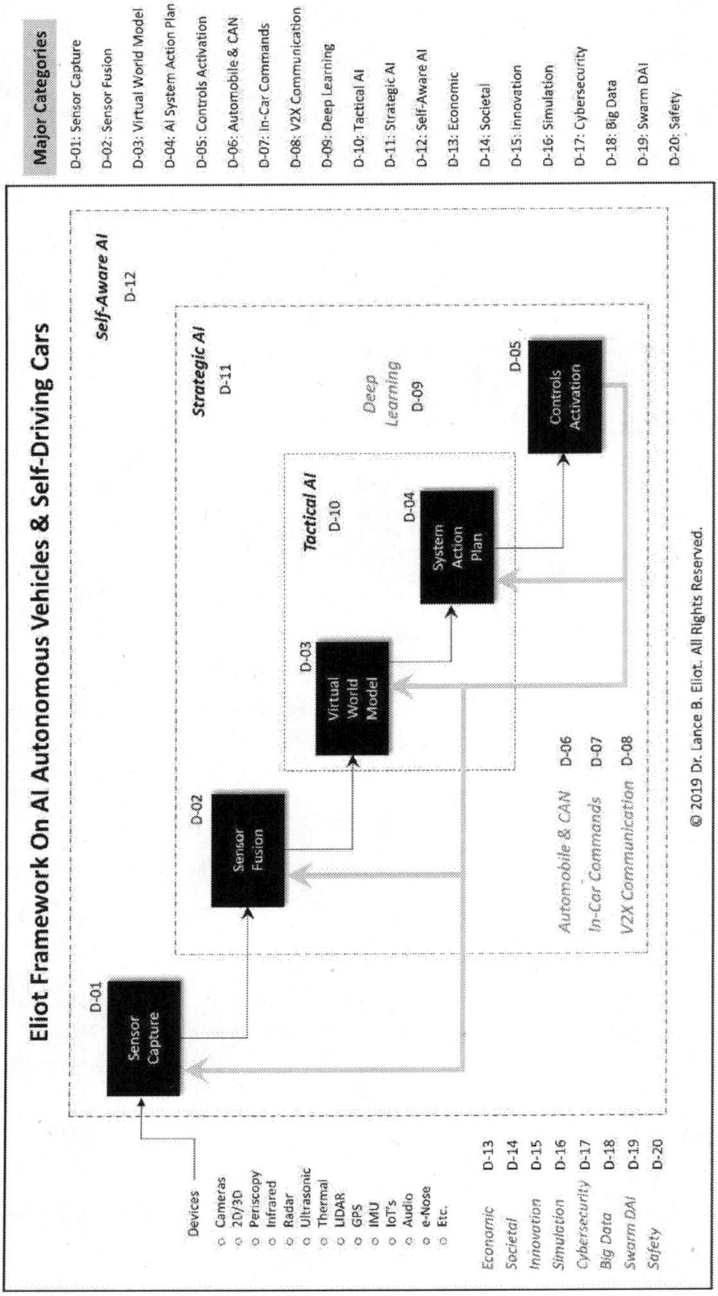
Eliot Framework On AI Autonomous Vehicles & Self-Driving Cars
Self-Aware AI
D-12
Strategic AI
D-11
Tactical AI
D-10
Deep Learning
D-09
Sensor Capture
D-01
Sensor Fusion
D-02
Virtual World Model
D-03
System Action Plan
D-04
Controls Activation
D-05
Automobile & CAN D-06
In-Car Commands D-07
V2X Communication D-08
Devices
Cameras
2D/3D
Periscopy
Infrared
Radar
Ultrasonic
Thermal
LIDAR
GPS
IMU
IoT's
Audio
e-Nose
Etc.
Economic D-13
Societal D-14
Innovation D-15
Simulation D-16
Cybersecurity D-17
Big Data D-18
Swarm DAI D-19
Safety D-20
© 2019 Dr. Lance B. Eliot. All Rights Reserved.
Major Categories
D-01: Sensor Capture
D-02: Sensor Fusion
D-03: Virtual World Model
D-04: AI System Action Plan
D-05: Controls Activation
D-06: Automobile & CAN
D-07: In-Car Commands
D-08: V2X Communication
D-09: Deep Learning
D-10: Tactical AI
D-11: Strategic AI
D-12: Self-Aware AI
D-13: Economic
D-14: Societal
D-15: Innovation
D-16: Simulation
D-17: Cybersecurity
D-18: Big Data
D-19: Swarm DAI
D-20: Safety

CHAPTER 2

STALKERWARE AND SELF-DRIVING CARS

Thankfully, there is a growing effort toward *AI For Good.*

This latest mantra entails ways to try and make sure that the advances in AI are being applied for the overall betterment of mankind. These are assuredly laudable endeavors and reassuringly crucial that the technology underlying AI is aimed and deployed in an appropriate and assuredly positive fashion.

Unfortunately, whether we like it or not, there is the ugly side of the coin too, namely the despicable *AI For Bad.*

Bad people will do bad things, even with the greatest advances in AI.

As an example of how some might attempt to twist goodness into badness, let's consider the use of self-driving cars for a disturbingly real possibility of carrying out a stalking pursuit.

What does that mean?

First, let's be clear that in today's world the overall notion of stalking is usually considered a form of criminal harassment or sometimes referred to as an act of criminal menace. The word "stalking" previously had a less sinister connotation, for example having been used in the relatively benign context of how to hunt for food and meant as a set of techniques for doing stealthy tracking of wild animals.

Modern times have seen not only the physical kind of evil intentions oriented tracking but has also introduced cyberstalking too. Using the Internet, you can eerily be tracked as to what web sites you visit, what purchases you make online, and otherwise, be surreptitiously followed across the web via the use of various nefarious hacking methods.

One future possibility of stalking could be undertaken via the advent of self-driving cars, utilizing AI-based or Autonomous Vehicle (AV) capabilities to conduct a stalking pursuit. If this arises, perhaps it will be coined as "autonomous stalking" or simply stated as self-driving car stalking.

Before we get into the details, some might argue that no one should discuss these matters as it will merely give horrible people some terrible ideas of what types of appalling things to do with this newest AI-enabled innovation. Please realize that this is a classic dilemma that confronts the computer field (and other realms) all the time. For example, in the cybersecurity realm, some try to suggest that research about cracking computer systems should not be published and nor discussed at conferences. Keep it all under tight wraps, they say.

But the proverbial head-in-the-sand approach is essentially fatally flawed in that the evildoers will one way or another discover or find out how to achieve *AI For Bad* and then we will all be caught flatfooted by not having properly prepared for such an eventuality. All told, within reasonable limits, it tends to make sense to bring these topics into the open and thus increase awareness overall, aiming to effectively handle adverse or outright criminal behavior.

With that in mind, we can gingerly explore how a self-driving car might be used for stalking and then examine the offsetting means to mitigate or prevent such a nightmarish activity.

Here's then the intriguing question to contemplate: *Will the advent of AI-based true self-driving cars potentially open the door toward using the AI-powered vehicles to perform stalking and if so what can be done about it?*

Let's unpack the matter and see.

Understanding The Levels Of Self-Driving Cars

As a clarification, true self-driving cars are ones that the AI drives the car entirely on its own and there isn't any human assistance during the driving task.

These driverless vehicles are considered a Level 4 and Level 5, while a car that requires a human driver to co-share the driving effort is usually considered at a Level 2 or Level 3. The cars that co-share the driving task are described as being semi-autonomous, and typically contain a variety of automated add-on's that are referred to as ADAS (Advanced Driver-Assistance Systems).

There is not yet a true self-driving car at Level 5, which we don't yet even know if this will be possible to achieve, and nor how long it will take to get there.

Meanwhile, the Level 4 efforts are gradually trying to get some traction by undergoing very narrow and selective public roadway trials, though there is controversy over whether this testing should be allowed per se (we are all life-or-death guinea pigs in an experiment taking place on our highways and byways, some contend).

Since semi-autonomous cars require a human driver, the adoption of those types of cars won't be markedly different than driving conventional vehicles, so there's not much new per se to cover about them on this topic (though, as you'll see in a moment, the points next made are generally applicable).

For semi-autonomous cars, it is important that the public needs to be forewarned about a disturbing aspect that's been arising lately, namely that despite those human drivers that keep posting videos of themselves falling asleep at the wheel of a Level 2 or Level 3 car, we all need to avoid being misled into believing that the driver can take away their attention from the driving task while driving a semi-autonomous car.

You are the responsible party for the driving actions of the vehicle, regardless of how much automation might be tossed into a Level 2 or Level 3.

Self-Driving Cars And Stalking

For Level 4 and Level 5 true self-driving vehicles, there won't be a human driver involved in the driving task.

All occupants will be passengers.

The AI is doing the driving.

By-and-large, AI-powered self-driving cars will be used to take someone or something from point A to point B. You get into a self-driving car, indicate the desired destination, and the AI driving system does the driving for you. Many are hoping that by having the AI as the driver, we'll be able to avert the 40,000 annual fatalities and 2.3 million estimated injuries that arise due to car crashes in the United States alone.

The AI won't drink-and-drive and will otherwise avoid the numerous human driving foibles that regrettably lead to the prevailing number of deaths and injuries in a human driving world.

One aspect about self-driving cars that is a marvel and eye-catching is the notion that there does not need to be a human driver at the wheel of the car. In fact, the steering wheel and the driving controls are likely to no longer be included since there is no need for them to be available to humans. The AI uses under-the-hood means to drive the vehicle. You've undoubtedly seen conventional cars that are hooked-up for AI driving and therefore the steering wheel and pedals are still present, but the future will undoubtedly have redesigned cars that will open up the interior for passenger luxury purposes.

In any case, a self-driving car does not necessarily need to have any passengers at all. A self-driving car might be transporting something such as perhaps delivering groceries from a grocery store to someone at home. Or a self-driving car might be roaming to be available whenever a ride request occurs. In short, we will eventually get used to the idea that there will be self-driving cars all around us, driving on our streets and byways, and be seemingly utterly empty. This will be entirely acceptable and actually become commonplace.

Hard to imagine, but undeniably inevitable.

Okay, overall, this is all part of the decidedly *AI For Good* pledged promise or a hoped-for heartwarming result of creating self-driving cars, namely that they will drive us around, there will be much fewer car crashes, and we can use the self-driving cars to even haul our stuff from place to place. But, as mentioned earlier herein, the tools of mankind can seemingly always be used to the detriment of humanity, or so it seems, given the long history of technologies that were started with the best of intentions and then later turned into mechanisms of undesirable ends.

Let's shift gears and ponder how self-driving cars can be used in objectionable ways, including for stalking. As another prime example of the *AI For Bad* and self-driving cars, there is the shameless use of self-driving cars as a drug mule for the illicit drug trade.

Envision that an evildoer decides they want to try and follow someone and opts to use a self-driving car in that malevolent plot.

The person to be followed is already known by the stalker to be residing at 1234 Main Street and so the stalker instructs a self-driving car to go nearby, perhaps parking across the street at 1235 Main Street. This would be relatively easy to do, simply request that a self-driving car is needed to pick up someone at the 1235 Main Street location and that once it arrives there it should park and patiently wait for a presumed rider to get into the vehicle.

Meanwhile, once parked at the location, the sensors of the self-driving car are kept active and the engine is kept running. The various sensors on a self-driving car tend to include video cameras, radar, LIDAR, thermal imaging, ultrasonic, and so on. These devices are the eyes and ears, as it were, providing the AI with data about whatever is outside of the self-driving car. This is used to do scene analysis and figure out where the road is, where other cars are, and so on.

We already know and generally, accept the aspect that video cameras can be used for facial recognition.

Increasingly, companies and governments are using facial recognition as a means of biometric identification, such as allowing entry into a restricted building due to a facial recognition scan or perhaps gaining access to your banking funds at an ATM.

I bring up this point because one facet of self-driving cars that I've repeatedly exhorted in my columns is the incredible and yet also disturbing capacity of self-driving cars to be a seemingly omnipresent roving eye (that's the phrase I've used to describe the matter). Wherever a self-driving car goes, it presumably can record whatever it senses, and thus have a complete video recording (and the other sensory elements too) of having gone down a city street during the day, been on a neighborhood street at night, etc.

This data can be pushed up into the cloud of the automaker or self-driving tech firm or fleet owner of the self-driving car, using OTA (Over-The-Air) electronic communications to do so. Imagine all the video of a self-driving car that has been roaming all around town for an entire day, and an entire week, and an entire month, all of which captures the daily comings and goings of us all. This data could readily be examined using computer-based algorithms to try and find patterns.

For example, suppose that self-driving cars go past your office building each day. By inspecting the data, it would be possible to detect that you seem to go into your office building in the mornings, come out around lunchtime, go back into the office just after lunch, and leave the office in the evening at about 5:30 p.m. All of this was captured via the video cameras of the self-driving cars that were moving along the street upon which your office building borders.

That's an alarmingly intrusive and privacy-invading use of that data.

There are those that point out the same data can be used for more above-board intentions. For example, suppose a realtor wants to be able to showcase a house that you might be interested in buying. Right now, there are usually one-time pictures that the realtor might take of the property, and perhaps you might look online via a search engine and see a picture that was taken several months ago.

Via the treasure trove of data being collected daily by self-driving cars, you could get an up-to-date video of how that property looks today, maybe even right now.

In addition, you could see what else happens on that same street. Maybe kids routinely play in the front yard across the street from the house you are considering buying. The house next door is meanwhile getting an add-on and the construction work has been taking weeks, all of which you could watch on the video that was recorded by those self-driving cars passing by or roaming around.

You probably get the gist of where this is leading in terms of how the roving eye relates to the seedy act of stalking.

The self-driving car parked on Main Street is asked to be on the watch for the person that the stalker wants to follow. Via the onboard AI-enabled facial recognition, the AI driving system is scanning the scene and watching for the targeted individual. When the person comes out of their house across the street, the AI driving system lets the stalker know (likely conveying as such to the smartphone of the stalker).

At this juncture, the stalker could remotely command the AI to follow the person such as if the individual goes for a jog or a long walk. Or, if the person gets into a conventional car and drives away, the self-driving car could be put into the pursuit of that vehicle. And so on.

You might assume that certainly the person being followed would be suspicious of a self-driving car that has no one in it and seems to be nearby to them. As mentioned, we are going to eventually get used to seeing self-driving cars all around us, empty of anyone, and routinely driving along or parked. We are unlikely to take notice and will not give these ubiquitous self-driving cars any undue attention.

For reasons of cautious discretion, I won't go into any further details about how the stalking could be conducted, other than to point out some other augmented tools that could be used too.

There are efforts underway to pair drones with self-driving cars, allowing a self-driving car to survey a scene in a bird's eye view, sending the drone aloft from the roof of the car, or letting a drone land on the car. Some fast-food eateries are even considering delivering a bag of hamburgers and fries to an in-motion self-driving car that perchance is on the freeway, which is the fastest of fast-food delivery.

Another facet of self-driving cars is their likely facility to electronically communicate with each other, using V2V (vehicle-to-vehicle) electronic communications. Normally, this might be used by a self-driving car that detects debris on the roadway and opts to forewarn other nearby self-driving cars.

In theory, this same kind of capability and via the drones too could be used for self-driving cars to coordinate with each other, including doing a tag team effort of following someone and having each self-driving car insidiously inform the others.

Whoa, some might exclaim, this is like one of those wild conspiracy theory notions, for which a lot of oddball and unlikely elements would need to line-up for this to become real.

Before you become overly concerned or frantic about this self-driving car-enabled stalking, numerous system-based barriers make this a lot harder to pull-off than might seem at initial glance.

The odds are that self-driving cars will be maintained and operated in a manner that would make the stalking scenario incredibly difficult to undertake by the everyday person.

This includes strident system-imposed limits on being able to get the AI driving system to scan for someone, plus strict limits or prohibition on being able to follow someone, etc. Assuming that the proper kinds of system controls are going to be put in place, which is expected and might equally be mandated by regulations, the chances of doing this type of stalking are very slim.

That being said, the possibility does exist that this same approach could be utilized by a government that was in cahoots with the company running the self-driving cars involved in such an effort.

Speaking of government activities, you might vaguely be aware that in 1994 the Driver's Privacy Protection Act (DPPA) was federally passed in the U.S. and put into law the aspect that your driver's info as stored or used by a Department of Motor Vehicles (DMV) must abide by mandated privacy guidelines and protocols.

This helped in putting the kibosh on attempts to potentially stalk or track someone online in terms of at least getting their driving record. Imagine that if somehow self-driving car stalking does emerge, despite the odds against it happening, one would undoubtedly expect federal regulations would be enacted to aid in counteracting such machinations.

Conclusion

The good news is that we are only in the infancy of self-driving cars and so far it would appear that trying to use them for this type of guise is relatively infeasible.

Breathe a hefty sigh of relief. Nonetheless, we would be unwise to let our guard down. We ought to be considering how those wrongdoers bent on *AI For Bad* might try to distort the benefits of AI-based true self-driving cars for vile deeds.

If you perchance spot a self-driving car following you down the street, know that the odds are it is not actually following you and merely happenstance that it seems to be doing so.

Well, unless of course it actually is.

CHAPTER 3

LOOKING LIKE A SELF-DRIVING CAR

Quickly, tell me what you think a self-driving car looks like.

Most people have not seen a self-driving car in the flesh, so to speak, having only seen self-driving cars indirectly and as shown in online videos, automotive advertisements, and glossy pictures posted on social media or used in daily news reports.

For those people that perchance live in an area wherein self-driving cars are being tested out on public roadways, they tend to see self-driving cars quite often.

The first reaction to seeing a self-driving car with your own eyes is that it is an amazing sight to see. This is the future, right before your very eyes. One day, presumably, self-driving cars will be everywhere, and they will be a common sight. We won't take notice of self-driving cars at that juncture, treating them as rather mundane, ordinary, and all-out ho-hum.

Right now, they are a marvel to behold.

Imagine if you had been around when horses were used as the mainstay for transportation around town. You kept hearing stories about a contraption that became known as a car, and you were puzzled, intrigued, and unsure of what the thing might exactly do or look like. If you suddenly found yourself walking along and happened upon a car coming down the road, undoubtedly your mouth would gape open and you would stare in utter amazement and disbelief.

That is somewhat the reaction for those that are living and driving in areas that have self-driving cars puttering around on their local streets and highways.

After a while, though, the excitement and allure wear off.

Sure, there is still some residual thrill when you see a self-driving car, but that initial surge of adrenaline has worn off and you begin to envisage that the self-driving car is, well, a car. What that portends is that if you are driving your car, and a self-driving car comes into your lane, you don't especially care that it is a self-driving car. You treat it like any other car and merely want to get around it or are irked when it goes too slowly for your driving journey and you are traffic-wise stuck behind it.

When I asked you to indicate what a self-driving car looks like, it was somewhat of a trick question, or maybe a tricky question per se.

The essence of the question amounts to whether you would even realize that a self-driving car is coming down your street or that it has pulled in front of you on that multi-lane highway that you are zipping along on. There is a strong possibility that a self-driving car could be right next to you, and potentially you didn't even know it was there.

You might be thinking, gosh, that just doesn't seem possible, since you would quite obviously know a self-driving car if you happened upon one.

Why is that?

The easiest answer is that there would presumably be an entire rack of electronic gear and spiffy looking gadgets all over the rooftop of the self-driving car. We've all seen and gotten used to the idea that a self-driving car has an entire suite of specialized sensors, consisting of video cameras galore, radar, LIDAR, ultrasonic units, thermal imaging, and so on. Surely, this is a dead giveaway that a self-driving car is a self-driving car.

Today's question then is this: *How can you visually discern or recognize a self-driving car versus other conventional cars that are ostensibly not self-driving?*

Before I address that fascinating point, let's take a moment to make sure we are all discussing the topic of self-driving cars in the same manner. I mention this facet because there is an abundance of confusion about what it means when you refer to a self-driving car.

Let's unpack that definition and then return to contemplating whether or not you can recognize a self-driving car if the time comes to do so.

Understanding The Levels Of Self-Driving Cars

As a clarification, true self-driving cars are ones that the AI drives the car entirely on its own and there isn't any human assistance during the driving task.

These driverless vehicles are considered a Level 4 and Level 5, while a car that requires a human driver to co-share the driving effort is usually considered at a Level 2 or Level 3. The cars that co-share the driving task are described as being semi-autonomous, and typically contain a variety of automated add-on's that are referred to as ADAS (Advanced Driver-Assistance Systems).

There is not yet a true self-driving car at Level 5, which we don't yet even know if this will be possible to achieve, and nor how long it will take to get there.

Meanwhile, the Level 4 efforts are gradually trying to get some traction by undergoing very narrow and selective public roadway trials, though there is controversy over whether this testing should be allowed per se (we are all life-or-death guinea pigs in an experiment taking place on our highways and byways, some contend).

Since semi-autonomous cars require a human driver, the adoption of those types of cars won't be markedly different than driving conventional vehicles, so there's not much new per se to cover about them on this topic (though, as you'll see in a moment, the points next made are generally applicable).

For semi-autonomous cars, it is important that the public needs to be forewarned about a disturbing aspect that's been arising lately, namely that despite those human drivers that keep posting videos of themselves falling asleep at the wheel of a Level 2 or Level 3 car, we all need to avoid being misled into believing that the driver can take away their attention from the driving task while driving a semi-autonomous car.

You are the responsible party for the driving actions of the vehicle, regardless of how much automation might be tossed into a Level 2 or Level 3.

Self-Driving Cars And Spotting Them In The Wild

For Level 4 and Level 5 true self-driving vehicles, there won't be a human driver involved in the driving task.

All occupants will be passengers.

The AI is doing the driving.

Returning to the mainstay of this discussion, consider whether you would recognize that a car is a self-driving car, doing so by simple visual inspection and not particularly by digging under-the-hood or having someone hand you a testimonial that you are indeed looking at a bona fide self-driving car (we'll consider a self-driving car as one that is now or is trying sincerely to achieve or attain a Level 4 or a Level 5 capability).

Okay, as mentioned earlier, perhaps you would know via the rack of sensory devices that are protruding from the top of the car that the vehicle you are observing must be a self-driving car. In localities that have a slew of self-driving cars that are crisscrossing a town or city, such as in Silicon Valley, there are so many of these self-driving cars that the racks appear plentiful, as though every car was handed a rack of handy dandy electronic gizmos.

As an aside, a funny anecdote might suffice here.

The humorous twist is that during the winter months (obviously, Silicon Valley doesn't get the harsh winters seen on the other coast, but the residents can drive an hour or two and get to mountains with snowy conditions), many people put ski racks on their conventional car rooftops. When you are driving on a busy street in the Silicon Valley area, you might see cars all around you with rooftop paraphernalia.

All of them have at a quick glance the same bulkiness of objects piled onto the top of the car and thus some might be hosting a state-of-the-art sensor suite, while others have winter camping gear and maybe skis. All in all, it is a veritable sea of cars that have contraptions on their rooftops.

The humor being that suddenly all cars look alike (by rooftop clutter alone), implying they are all self-driving cars, or perhaps they are all ordinary cars that perchance have a smattering of wintery odds-and-ends on them.

Of course, turns out there are only a few that are self-driving cars, while the rest are conventional cars.

At least that's the prevalence right now.

But let's put to the side the potential confusion or confounding of one type or rooftop rack versus another. Other than the possibility of being momentarily fooled into thinking that a car is a self-driving car by some other type of mundane rooftop rack, can you be one hundred percent certain that a rooftop rack that appears to consist of electronics is thusly mounted onto a (there you have it!) self-driving car?

Well, maybe.

There are two problems with this kind of identification scheme.

First, as self-driving cars are becoming more advanced, you might have noticed that the racks have generally gotten slimmer, more streamlined, and less obtrusive.

The early days consisted of seemingly wantonly mounted gear that seemed to look like someone just stuck a bunch of wires and oddball equipment onto the roof of a car. It was garish and immediately obvious to the eye.

No mistaking a self-driving car since it was the vehicle with the dome top and spinning or flashing lights and contrivances.

Gradually, much of that gear is being fitted into the overall shape of the car. Also, the electronics have gotten smaller and have a dramatically lessened footprint. There are also ways to essentially disguise the devices, making them seem as though they belong rightfully on the vehicle, rather than looking like a Frankenstein that has weird parts in jutting or overhanging places.

Secondly, conventional cars that are progressively getting more advanced ADAS are also being outfitted with many of the same sensory devices as those on a true self-driving car. In that manner, a modern conventional car is going to look a lot like a self-driving car.

The initial self-driving cars were dramatic looking and had that elephant in the room splendor about them. They could not be missed. They could not be mistaken. Nowadays, the elephant has been transformed into the herd of bison, and even regular bison are starting to morph toward the same look as the transformed elephants.

They say you can tell a zebra by its stripes, but suppose you tone down the stripes and also are adding stripes to the preponderance of donkeys or everyday mules that cart us around on our byways and streets.

Sorry to say that a rooftop rack of gaudy electronics is not going to be a surefire sign of a self-driving car.

I'm guessing that some of you might already have been yelling out that instead of looking at the rooftop there is another obvious place that you ought to be looking at, namely the driver's seat.

If there is a human in the driver's seat, the car is presumably conventional. If there is no one sitting in the driver's seat, and the car is in motion, the car must be a self-driving car.

Case closed.

Well, you are onto something there, but this spying technique has its downsides.

Let's see why.

To try and expediently pursue self-driving cars, most of the automakers and self-driving tech firms have chosen to use conventional cars and retrofit them with the self-driving tech stuff.

In the future, we might instead have specially designed self-driving cars. For example, there won't be a need for a steering wheel and nor any pedals, since the AI driving system will be working on the inside of the vehicle and not need those human usable driving controls. Some vehemently insist that we must get rid of the human driving controls, otherwise, there will be people that are going to be tempted to drive a car that ought to be driven solely by the AI driving system.

Part of the logic is that there are about 40,000 annual fatalities due to car crashes in the United States alone, and around 2.5 million injuries. These are to a great extent considered attributable to human drivers that are driving while intoxicated, driving while distracted, and so on. The hope is that by using self-driving cars and reducing the number of human drivers or the volume of human driving, we won't have those same human driving foibles and consequential deaths or injuries.

Thus, remove the driving controls from self-driving cars.

Period.

We don't know yet that this is going to be entirely acceptable, at least in the following way. If the removal of driving controls from self-driving cars is going to somehow lead to no longer allowing conventional cars to exist, and ergo denying people the opportunity to drive cars, some are quite upset about that outcome. It is said that people are stating they will never give up their driving until you pry their cold dead hands from the steering wheel.

If there aren't any steering wheels, at all, seemingly there is no prying off needed.

Anyway, shifting our attention back to the driver's seat, the assumption would be that if there is not a human seated in the driver's seat, and the vehicle is underway, it must be a self-driving car.

The thing is, as mentioned, many of the self-driving cars that are currently being tested are conventional cars and there is a driver's seat and there is a steering wheel. In theory, a human could try to sit in the driver's seat. In that case, the assumption that a self-driving car is a self-driving due to the absence of someone in the driver's seat is no longer always a truism (i.e., it is a self-driving car, and yet there is, in fact, a person sitting in the driver's seat).

By-and-large, these self-driving cars have locked-out the use of the driving controls, or upon an attempt to use a driving control by someone inside the car, the AI driving system emits an alert and will take some action such as bringing the vehicle to a safe halt. Therefore, we can properly consider the car to be a self-driving car, albeit it might *appear* to be a conventional car because a human has manhandled their way into the driver's seat and yet is not at all driving the vehicle.

The point is though that a person could be seated in the driver's seat and yet not driving the car.

A quick glance at the car would only showcase that a person is sitting in the driver's seat, and you would not necessarily realize they aren't actively operating the driving controls.

Furthermore, with many of the ADAS, such as even the simplest form of cruise control, someone might be sitting in the driver's seat, and they are considered fully responsible for the driving, but they do not have their hands on the steering wheel (depending upon the type of monitoring or setup devised by the ADAS maker).

Here's another variation.

Envision a self-driving car that looks like a conventional car, doing so because it is based on a conventional car that has been retrofitted to be a self-driving car. Suppose that the driving controls have been entirely removed (there are legal ramifications regarding this, which is why you don't see this particular happening as yet).

A human is seated in the seat that was once the driver's seat. There aren't any driving controls, but that's fine in the sense that the AI driving system is going to be doing the driving. This person is really a passenger now and no longer a driver. They are a passenger that just so happens to be seated in the seat that we customarily associate with a driver's seat.

You glance over at this self-driving car as it passes you on the highway. From your perspective, there is a person seated in the driver's seat. It is nearly impossible to gauge whether or not they are a driver, since maybe they are using cruise control or otherwise are somehow driving but maybe doing a lousy job of the driving task.

Once again, we have a circumstance of a self-driving car that has a person seemingly "at the wheel" in the manner of a human sitting in the driver's seat.

I know what you are thinking, which is that there isn't a steering wheel and therefore this is an entirely noticeable indicator that despite a human in the driver's seat, this must be a self-driving car.

Really?

It seems a bit of a stretch that we are now basing the difference between a self-driving car and a conventional car on the appearance or lack of appearance of a steering wheel.

On a related topic, we cannot include the pedals since that is an absurdity of distinction, whereby from outside of a car, the odds of being able to readily see whether a car has a gas pedal, and a brake pedal is on the borderline of ridiculousness. You would have to (somewhat literally) place your face against the glass window and look straight into the vehicle to readily figure out whether there are any pedals included.

We'll stick with the steering wheel as a telltale clue.

If you are driving in clogged traffic, do you really believe that you can glance around and peer sufficiently into other cars to detect whether they have a steering wheel or not?

You might be able to marginally do so, though it would take a concerted effort to make sure that what you were seeing is what you were seeing. In other words, your mind might convince you there is a steering wheel when there isn't one, plus your mind might trick you into thinking there isn't a steering wheel when there is one there. Realize we are discussing a circumstance whereby you are driving in your car, which is underway at some speed such as 40 miles per hour, and you are glancing at a swarm of cars around you, all of which are also moving at a similar speed.

We can add to this conundrum that many cars have tinted windows or otherwise are rather hard to peer into.

The bottom-line to all of this discussion is that you might not be able to readily discern that a self-driving car is a self-driving car. Everything else being equal, a self-driving car is going to potentially look a lot like conventional cars, and conventional cars are going to look a lot like self-driving cars. Unless you take a microscopic kind of inspection, it will be hard to tell one from the other by any scant glance.

You might remember from various war movies that during World War II there were silhouette checklists or charts that were used to try and figure out what kind of enemy ship you might see while at sea. From afar, you might see a naval ship and not be sure whether it was friend or foe. Also, it was important to know what kind of a ship it was, whether it might be an aircraft carrier versus a destroyer.

In terms of self-driving cars, just a few years ago, a silhouette chart would easily allow you to look at a self-driving car and instantly know that it was a self-driving car and who the maker was. Not so much anymore, and likely increasingly lessening.

Conclusion

Now that we've covered that ground, the other question that has likely popped into your head is whether it makes a difference whether you can discern a self-driving car from a conventional car at a glance.

I'd argue that yes, it does indeed make a difference.

For the automakers and self-driving tech firms, it makes a difference in that they want you to know that they are making a self-driving car and you ought to recognize as such that their car going down your street is their self-driving car.

Not just any self-driving car, but their specific brand.

That's important to them as brand recognition.

There is an intense race toward who will get self-driving cars first. Also, if someone else's self-driving car messes up, you certainly don't want the general public and nor regulators to think it was your brand, and instead realize straightforwardly that it was a competing brand.

Beyond the desires of those that make or operate self-driving cars, are there other reasons to be able to distinguish a self-driving car from a conventional car?

One viewpoint is that human drivers need to know which cars around them are human-driven versus which ones are being driven by AI. Human drivers have a right to know, one would assert.

On the other hand, a counterargument is that if the self-driving cars are operating properly and lawfully, it ought to not make one bit of difference whether you are aware that the car is self-driving. You should treat all cars as equals, regardless of human-driven ones or AI-driven ones.

Is this a molehill being made into a mountain?

While you ponder the matter, it is a pretty good bet that the automakers and self-driving car firms are going to want to ensure that you know that a self-driving car, their self-driving car brand, is the car that is driving next to you on the roadway.

Similar to how Uber and Lyft want to make sure that you know you are riding in one of "their" requested ridesharing cars, the same will be true for those vaunted self-driving cars.

You've likely already noticed that self-driving cars are being painted with specific color schemes by the various makers and also brandish the company name or nickname.

I suppose there is another way to readily know that a self-driving car is a self-driving car. This is maybe the easiest way and doesn't require any fancy rooftop rack, nor a specialized spectacular paint job, or any other visually standout indications or accouterments.

Just ask about the car.

If it's a true self-driving car, hopefully, the AI is good enough to tell you so.

CHAPTER 4
GHOST TAKES A SELF-DRIVING CAR

Hey, dude, where's my car?

That was the question on my mind when I walked out to the parking lot to get into my car and it was not there.

This particular parking lot was quite expansive and there wasn't any numbering system associated with the parking spots. Thus, I had to remember where my car was supposed to be as based entirely on my own mental "global positioning" brain ware, and absent of having any tangible and more reliable form of tracing.

Relying on my noggin alone was not a sure bet.

I was pretty sure that the parking spot of my car was next to a lamppost and about midway down a row of cars that was visually aligned with a sandwich shop outside of the fenced perimeter of the parking lot. That seems byzantine, I realize. Hey, at least it was a means to pin down generally where my car *had* to be.

But my car was not where it was supposed to be. Indeed, it wasn't anywhere near to where it was supposed to be. I stood in the presumed parking spot and looked all around me, stretching on my tippy toes and scanned the horizon like a sailor desperately trying to spy land ahoy.

You might be thinking that I ought to remember what other cars were parked next to my car and thus I could just look for that pattern of say a red pickup truck and a yellow sportscar that were next to me.

Unfortunately, this gambit wasn't going to work out. I had parked my car very early in the morning that day, and it was now quite late in the evening. Most of the cars in this particular lot had turned over and a newer crop of cars had gradually entered into and parked here and there.

The initial reaction to not immediately being able to find my car was somewhat muted since I assumed that my mind was playing tricks on me. I routinely parked in this specific lot and had to jockey each day to discover an available empty space. As a result, each day my car was parked in some semi-randomly chosen spot such that I never knew beforehand where an open spot might exist. This all meant that I could readily be thinking about where I parked *yesterday*, rather than accurately remembering where I parked today.

I decided that the brute force method of searching was required in this instance.

I stridently walked up-and-down every row of the parking lot. This was done slowly and cautiously, wanting to make sure that I did not go hastily and inadvertently miss seeing my car. I assumed that by methodically searching, I would certainly find my car and the whole affair would be laughed off as a quirky moment of existence. If I were to sprint around in a panic, I figured it would only make me more panicky and I would be unlikely to detect my car, therefore end-up not finding it and shamefully enter into a mind-bending berserk mode accordingly.

Well, the thoughtfully crafted brute force approach failed to unearth my car, which ostensibly meant that it was indeed missing. I was now begrudgingly convinced that my car was no longer in this parking lot.

I knew absolutely that I had parked there. I knew absolutely that I was not somehow in the wrong parking lot. I knew for sure that I had not gotten a lift that morning or otherwise gotten to work by a method other than driving my car. Yes, the car was supposed to be here and it wasn't, that was unnervingly the plain and agonizing truth.

What did the heck happen to my car (I say that, minus the dude part, respectively)?

I have already now covered the possibility that I had "misplaced" my car in terms of having thought it was in one spot and yet perhaps it was sitting quietly in another spot. So, misplacement was no longer on the list of possibilities.

If my car wasn't there, it must have been moved.

I realize that seems blatantly obvious. Sorry, but that's what goes through your mind when the shock of having a missing car strikes you to the bone. I liked my car. It was my favorite car of all the cars I've owned to date. Even if I didn't somehow favor the car, nonetheless it was my car and it ought to be ready and waiting for me.

Well, how could my car have been moved?

One possibility that came to mind was that my car had been towed. Maybe my car was illegally parked while it was sitting in the parking lot. I have no idea how that could be, though perhaps some obscure parking rule had gotten my vehicle in trouble. Or perhaps my car had done something wrong, such as the horn suddenly squawking and nobody could stand the blaring sounds, so the parking lot management had my vehicle towed out of there.

I summarily rejected the notion that aliens from another planet had beamed-up my car. That kind of thinking is fun when making a movie script or playing wild what-if games, but when your prized car is really gone, the practical ways of how it came to be missing are more valued and prudent to consider.

There wasn't an attendant in the parking lot. Near the exit gate, there was a payment kiosk and it had a red button to remotely make contact with someone associated with the parking aspects. I used the red button. Speaking to a human voice that emitted from a rather balky speaker, we determined that the parking establishment had not towed my car.

Of course, someone else could have come into the parking lot and towed it, like one of the bounty hunter episodes. That fleeting thought was instantly rejected as being nearly equal to the alien invasion from Mars.

Okay, it was now down to the remaining possibility that someone drove my car off the lot.

I was the only person with a key to my car. If I had loaned out my spare key to someone else, they would immediately be a suspect in this budding crime scene. Those comedic shows where they pull a gag on someone can at times involve enlisting a friend of the unsuspecting dupe that then helps to drive off with their car, or subtly move it, sparking the person to be baffled at how their car was in a different spot than expected. This was inapplicable in my case.

Anyway, it now seemed apparent that someone unknown to me had spirited away with my car. They must have devilishly gotten into my car and used one of those insidious under-the-dashboard sneaks to start my car and drive it away. Sadness ensued.

I reported the matter to the police.

They informed me that the odds were that my car was long gone by the time I had reported it missing. Having grown up watching TV shows that involve an all-points bulletin of citywide searches for a missing whatever, I was disappointed to discover that not only was such a street-by-street search not going to be undertaken, but there were also lots of other cars stolen on that day. In that sense, my stolen car was one of many and now was a statistic rather than something that had seemed very personal and personable to me.

Shifting gears, the future of cars involves the emergence of self-driving cars.

Here is today's interesting question: *Is it possible for an AI-based true self-driving car to go missing, and if so, what happens next?*

Let's unpack the matter and see.

Understanding The Levels Of Self-Driving Cars

As a clarification, true self-driving cars are ones that the AI drives the car entirely on its own and there isn't any human assistance during the driving task.

These driverless vehicles are considered Level 4 and Level 5, while a car that requires a human driver to co-share the driving effort is usually considered at Level 2 or Level 3. The cars that co-share the driving task are described as being semi-autonomous, and typically contain a variety of automated add-on's that are referred to as ADAS (Advanced Driver-Assistance Systems).

There is not yet a true self-driving car at Level 5, which we don't yet even know if this will be possible to achieve, and nor how long it will take to get there.

Meanwhile, the Level 4 efforts are gradually trying to get some traction by undergoing very narrow and selective public roadway trials, though there is controversy over whether this testing should be allowed per se (we are all life-or-death guinea pigs in an experiment taking place on our highways and byways, some contend).

Since semi-autonomous cars require a human driver, the adoption of those types of cars won't be markedly different than driving conventional vehicles, so there's not much new per se to cover about them on this topic (though, as you'll see in a moment, the points next made are generally applicable).

For semi-autonomous cars, it is important that the public needs to be forewarned about a disturbing aspect that's been arising lately, namely that despite those human drivers that keep posting videos of themselves falling asleep at the wheel of a Level 2 or Level 3 car, we all need to avoid being misled into believing that the driver can take away their attention from the driving task while driving a semi-autonomous car.

You are the responsible party for the driving actions of the vehicle, regardless of how much automation might be tossed into a Level 2 or Level 3.

Self-Driving Cars And When They Go Missing

For Level 4 and Level 5 true self-driving vehicles, there won't be a human driver involved in the driving task.

All occupants will be passengers.

The AI is doing the driving.

First, let's dispense with the idea that the AI is somehow sentient. It is not. The AI of today is programmed and involves the same everyday kind of computers as found in your smartphone or laptop. To clarify, yes there are specialized computer processors that are built to aid in self-driving activities, such as chips that can process Machine Learning and Deep Learning algorithms rapidly, but those are still in the realm of conventional computing.

I bring this up due to the interest in addressing the question about what happens if a self-driving car goes missing.

We can reject outright the possibility that the AI of its own accord might drive the vehicle away from a particular place or parking spot. If the AI driving system drives the vehicle, it is because there is some everyday world reason for it. Thus, this does not include the AI as a sentient being that somehow decides today is the day it will go for a drive and showcase its freedom from the bonds of mankind.

Let's consider the reasonable possibilities for why a self-driving car might go missing.

When my conventional car was missing, I initially assumed that I had "misplaced" my car. This meant that I was potentially confused about where I had last left my car.

Perhaps I had parked it in place X and my mind was trying to convince me that I had parked it in place Y. The car was still sitting in place X and therefore was right where it was to start with. The alleged movement was only in my mind.

Is it feasible for a self-driving car to get "misplaced" in the same manner as a conventional car?

A fair answer to that question is that yes, it is conceivable.

Suppose you owned a self-driving car and you parked it in the same parking lot as to where I work. You could readily do the same thing I did, namely coming back out later on and not be able to immediately find the self-driving car. In my case, it really was gone, but it was seemingly equally likely that I could have failed to remember accurately where it was parked.

The beauty of a self-driving car is likely to be that it can be remotely activated and retrieved.

A conventional car won't drive itself to you. The best that most conventional cars can do is wink their headlights and toot their horn when you try to access them remotely. A true self-driving car would be able to properly and safely pull out of a parking spot and drive to wherever you might be standing and waiting for it to arrive (doing so entirely autonomously, and no human hand or guidance involved).

In that sense, it is going to be very hard to misplace your self-driving car per se. No matter where your self-driving car was originally parked, it doesn't especially matter, since it can find its way to you, assuming that it can be accessed remotely.

I emphasize this remote access facet due to the off-chance that the electronic communications to your self-driving car are unable to function, perhaps being in a remote area or having some other form of communications networking issues. In that case, you would presumably have no means of alerting the self-driving car that it is needed and that it ought to startup and come to you.

Likewise, if the self-driving car is out of battery charge and does not have the needed electrical energy to function, this also implies that you would not be able to remotely communicate with the vehicle. The proverbial dead battery is apt to make the self-driving car into a multi-ton paperweight, which of course could be said of any conventional car too.

The point overall is that you could "misplace" a self-driving car, though finding it is altogether going to be relatively easy since you won't search for it, and instead it will search for you (or, more likely, come to you).

There is an added twist to this misplacement aspect.

Since the self-driving car can drive itself, there is a chance that it might have opted to move from the parking spot that it was originally left in. With a conventional car, there is no chance that the car will opt to move (a human might do so, but not by the acts of the car alone). This suggests that if you did decide to walk out to find your self-driving car, it readily might not be in the original parked spot.

The AI could have chosen to move the vehicle.

Why would the AI do such a thing?

Again, it is not as a result of sentience. Put aside any anthropomorphizing of today's AI. The rational and easily explainable reason could be that the AI might have been programmed to detect adverse conditions while being parked. For example, suppose another car was backing into a spot that was head-to-head with the parked self-driving car. If the AI driving system was active, it might detect this danger, and start the car to move it away from getting dinged by the other car. The AI might then seek a different parking spot.

In theory, the AI driving system would then send out an electronic message to indicate it had moved. The fleet operator or perhaps the owner would hopefully get dutifully notified. In any case, regardless of whether a notification was to occur, the notion is that the AI driving system can move the car, doing so for some programmatic reason.

Indeed, it could be that the fleet operator opted to remotely activate the self-driving car, sending it to a local carwash. Unbeknownst to you, the AI driving system left the parking lot, drove to a carwash, went through the carwash, perhaps refueled, and came back to the parking lot. All of that might take place without your awareness. That being said, this is somewhat farfetched in that if you owned the self-driving car, the odds are that the fleet operator would likely inform you of such actions.

As an aside, some pundits reject wholescale the idea that individuals will own self-driving cars. The logic is that self-driving cars will only be owned in large fleets and by sizable companies, such as major automakers, major ridesharing firms, and the like. I am known for my contrarian stance that argues there will be individual ownership of self-driving cars.

I bring up this particular point because some would insist that you will never have a self-driving car and therefore never be able to "lose" a self-driving car (obviously, if you don't have one, you can't somehow lose it or misplace it). The future will consist of people always riding in self-driving cars on a ridesharing basis. A self-driving car will pick you up and take you to your destination. At no juncture will you care about where the self-driving car is parked. All that you know is that it appears when you need it, and it goes away when you don't need it.

For the moment, go with me on the perspective that people will be able to individually own a self-driving car. If you are agreeable to giving that notion some airtime, it means that we can continue the discussion about what happens when a self-driving car goes missing (which, as an aside, can be said to even apply when owned by a fleet, since the fleet owner could have similar concerns arise).

Here's where we are on this matter.

A self-driving car that is parked can readily move from the parking spot.

In contrast, a conventional car cannot readily be moved. It can be towed, of course. It can be driven by a human too. Each of those actions is somewhat harder to pull off than the same act of moving a self-driving car. With a self-driving car, there is an AI driving system in the car and ready to go, and for which can act somewhat on its own (perhaps pre-programmed to leave the parking lot at a particular time of day) or by remote activation.

Could a self-driving car be towed?

Yes, absolutely.

We all need to realize that self-driving cars are in fact going to be towed from time to time. A self-driving car is still a car. Cars have various mechanical failures and breakdowns. An AI driving system cannot drive a car that is broken, any more than a human could drive such a vehicle. As such, you should not be surprised to witness self-driving cars getting towed to repair shops.

Could a human steal a self-driving car by breaking into the vehicle and driving it off?

For a conventional car, a criminal can potentially break into a car, start the car, and drive it away. A quite natural question arises as to whether a human could do the same to a self-driving car.

Well, eventually, the idea is that true self-driving cars won't have any human-accessible driving controls. The thinking is that it will be best to prevent humans from driving cars since otherwise, they will continue to drive while drunk and drive while distracted. The hope is that by making self-driving cars only drivable by an AI driving system, we can reduce dramatically the number of car crashes and car-related fatalities and injuries. If that comes to pass, which not everyone agrees will necessarily happen, there won't be any direct means for a car thief to drive away with a stolen car. They might be able to break into the self-driving car. They won't have access to the driving controls.

The odds are that self-driving cars will employ some form of Natural Language Processing (NLP) system for human riders to be able to tell the AI driving system where the person wants to go. In that case, presumably, the thief that has broken into a self-driving car could try to verbally instruct the AI driving system to spirit away with the car.

This seems an unlikely scenario in that the odds are that NLP for AI driving systems will potentially use various security measures to make sure that the instructions being given are coming from the appropriate source. All told, the breaking into the vehicle is most certainly going to be detected by the AI driving system and that alone would setoff various alarms and alerts. A crook that then frantically tries to command the AI to drive away is bound to get nowhere.

And, some predict that we will rarely have self-driving cars stolen at all.

The sensors of the self-driving car will capture on video the car thief. The electronic communications of the self-driving car can instantly send out a message to the police and other authorities. Without any readily accessible driving controls, the thief cannot just hotwire the vehicle and drive away.

Stealing a self-driving car also doesn't make much sense for other various important reasons. For example, most self-driving cars will automatically be in touch with the fleet operator to indicate where the car is, what its status consists of, where it is going, etc. This is a vital form of traceability and monitoring by the fleet operator. A car thief would be tracked and generally unable to sneak away with the self-driving car (unless they could use some form of cybersecurity hacks to subvert or avoid the tracing, see my columns covering that looming prospect).

Conclusion

The good news is that stealing a self-driving car is going to be a tough crime to successfully commit.

Even if a thief decided to steal a self-driving car via the act of towing (rather than driving off with the vehicle), the odds are that the towing action would readily be detected by the AI driving system and would emit automatically an electronic tipoff to the fleet operator that something has gone amiss.

The somewhat unsettling news is that wherever you believe that you parked your self-driving car, there are lots of valid reasons why it might not be there anymore. At the same time, it won't especially matter to you. You can park your car and forget where you parked it, doing so to your heart's content.

Almost akin to a beloved dog like Lassie, the AI driving system can come and find you when the time arises for you to need a ride. To clarify, the AI won't be showering you with love and affection, and don't expect those cherished canine slobbering kisses, since the self-driving car will only be doing what it was programmed to do.

Perhaps someday we will have sentient AI, in which case the AI might be happy to see you, though the downside is that the AI might arbitrarily decide that it doesn't want to give you a ride and will refuse to come and pick you up.

We might need special *Blade Runner*-style bounty hunters that can wrangle those ornery AI driving systems that have decided purposely to go missing

CHAPTER 5

HUMOR USED IN AI DRIVING SYSTEMS

Humor can be quite useful.

Let's see how.

Suppose you are having a bad day (I realize this seems a bit dour and gloomy, but the venerated gallantry of well-placed humor will turn this around, wait and see).

While on the way home from work, you opt to use a ridesharing or ride-hailing service. After settling into the car and getting ready to have a quiet and solemnly introspective ride home, the driver suddenly speaks up and tells you an entertaining joke that causes you to laugh out loud. The merriment of the humorous anecdote sparks you to get out of your dismally sour mood. It was one of the best jokes you have ever heard, a knee-slapping and side-splitting piece of humor.

Things are looking up, and when you arrive home, your perspective and attitude about the world have shifted into one of peacefulness and content.

All due to letting some humor enter into your day.

Admittedly, that is the smiley face version of humor. There is also the other side of the coin, namely humor that is off-target, bleak, and at times insulting and entirely offensive.

You might have gotten into that ridesharing vehicle and the joke told by the driver could have inadvertently made your day even worse. How dare the driver tell such a joke? It was disgusting and abundantly inappropriate.

The thing is, the situation or contextual setting under which humor is encountered can make a big difference in both how the humor is received and what you can do about the presented humor. For example, when watching a TV or cable show that is spewing forth foul humor, you can presumably switch channels or turn off the offending drivel. If you are at work and your boss tells you a mildly improper joke, you need to weigh the potential consequences of telling them that the humor was misplaced versus simply doing a weak smile and letting the matter slide past you.

In short, your ability to react to humor can be mitigated by the circumstances under which the humor is being employed.

Return to the use case of being a passenger inside a car. When the driver tells an altogether untoward joke, it might seem obvious that you should right away correct the driver and tell them they have transgressed. On the other hand, you must also weigh the fact that the driver is the driver. This means that the fate of you and the vehicle is in the hands of that driver. Any immediate and debate sparking response to the driver about a bad joke that they have just told could rattle them and the next thing you know the car is veering or being driven recklessly. One supposes that you are inclined to laugh at any humorous utterances of the driver that are within bounds, merely to placate them and try to keep attention to the act of driving versus a prolonged and driver-distracting discussion about the appropriateness of joke-telling.

Okay, so we've established that there can be adverse consequences when foul humor is used, including rancorous consequences for the person telling the joke and for the person receiving the humor. Meanwhile, by luck of the draw, humor that turns out to be well-received can be an upside for both parties, though this has to be weighed against the potential downsides that can also be incurred.

There is a tradeoff involved in leveraging humor, that's for sure.

Should someone try to use humor and aim for the aspirational goal of providing humor that brightens the day, or avoid humor due to the potential for getting into the muck and ruining things for all involved?

A ridesharing driver might believe that telling jokes is a great way to bond with passengers and ostensibly get a better rating or earn a heightened tip for doing the driving. Of course, not everyone is made of the right stuff to be a comedian. The joke teller might provide a joke that falls flat and seems to be entirely bereft of anything funny at all. The attempt at comedy could go beyond simply being flat, and venture into the zone of being offensive.

Most ridesharing services seek customer feedback from riders. A joke-telling driver that routinely gushes out lousy humor that rankles passengers is likely to end up with low ratings and risks losing their privileges of being a ridesharing driver. In that manner, some passengers might decide to quietly or silently ding the joke-telling driver via scoring them in an app, rather than confronting the driver directly during the driving journey.

Another possibility of letting the driver know that the humor was humorless and distasteful would be to wait until the ride is over. After exiting from the vehicle, you can now relatively safely unleash your tongue and provide the driver with a bit of some lesson-gleaning insights about how to not tell jokes. Some drivers will get the drift, while others will shrug off the feedback and figure that they'll continue to use their humor on other riders and write off your reaction as an outlier reaction.

Scholars that have studied humor tend to divide humorous utterances into one of four types, labeled as affiliative, self-enhancing, aggressive, and self-defeating.

Not everyone necessarily agrees that those are the complete and exhaustive list of humor types, and there is even disagreement about the scope and slippage amongst the claimed four types. As they say, your mileage may vary (wait for a second, was that a kind-of joke or humorous anecdote about the nature of humor?).

We can go ahead and address each of the four types and then think about the ramifications thereof.

Affiliative. The affiliative type of humor is used by the joke teller to try and bond with others and create an affiliation, giving rise to a social relationship with the receiver.

Consider this in a driving and rider context.

The driver of a ridesharing vehicle doesn't know you and you don't know them. A handy ice breaker or opener to the conversation could be a well-timed and well-shaped piece of humor. That might start the ball rolling in terms of chatting throughout the traversal. Notably, it could also stomp down on any chance of conversation and be so off-putting that only stony silence remains the rest of the ride.

Self-enhancing. Self-enhancing humor tends to involve telling jokes that will enhance the image or semblance of the teller, doing so in the eyes and perspective of the receiver.

In a driving journey context, a driver might make a joke as an attempt to demonstrate that they are more than simply *somebody* driving a car. The rider suddenly realizes that the driver is a human being, a regular person, and not some unfeeling form of automata that perchance is at the wheel of the vehicle. Humor in this context is intended to showcase something about the joke teller. It might cause the receiver to think of the teller as being clever, witty, smart, etc.

The backlash can be that the receiver perceives the joke teller as unrefined, rude, outlandish, out-of-touch, or suffers from other similar societally undesirable traits.

Aggressive. The aggressive type of humor seeks to enhance the person telling the joke and yet do so at the expense of the person receiving the joke. That's a dicey line to hoe. Perhaps you've seen the antics of a Don Rickles or akin type of comedian.

For a driver, imagine that they opt to make a joke about what the rider is wearing, such as a hat or coat, or shoes. The receiver of the humor is being made fun of. This can right away go awry. Perhaps the worn apparel is beloved. Any jokes about the clothing could be instantaneously rebuffed.

There is a chance that the humor might work. Maybe the rider has always thought that their hat was a bit silly and pretentious. The driver pointing out this facet might prod the rider into a fit of laughter. Good luck on trying those potential landmines.

Self-defeating. The self-defeating type of humor is the now-classic and widely utilized self-deprecating or self-disparaging approach in our daily narrative, laced with something funny mixed into the concoction.

Envision a driver that tells you something humorous about themselves that is actually self-disparaging. I used to be a medical doctor, the driver might say, but I decided that there wasn't enough stress in saving people's lives in the operating room and ergo chose instead to relish an even more stressful life by driving in the congested traffic of this great city.

Maybe you find that funny, maybe not, but the point is that the humor aims to undercut the teller and as being told by the teller. The receiver is often leaned toward sympathizing with the joke teller due to the self-deprecating aspect of the humor. It seems as though the teller is proffering a sense of humility, though we also know these days that people on online social media try to use this approach as a form of honor brag.

When AI Becomes Humorous

This discussion has brought to the surface and highlighted that humor is a dual-edged sword.

Humans sometimes get things right and tell a good joke at the right time to the right receiver. Presumably, that's how professional comedians make their money, somehow knowing how to strike that chord.

The problem with a dual-edge sword is that you can get pretty banged up and harmed by the other edge of that slicing and dicing. Thus, humans sometimes get things wrong and tell a bad joke at the wrong time and to the wrong receiver.

Once the joke has been told, the chances of unwinding it are relatively slim. You can try to backtrack and assert that you didn't mean it. You can try to tell another joke that tries to cover up the offensiveness of the already uttered joke. The problem is that once the bell has been rung, unringing the bell is a huge challenge.

Let's slightly shift gears and go beyond the realm of human joke-telling.

What about Artificial Intelligence (AI) as a joke teller?

Believe it or not, some believe we ought to have AI systems that can utilize humor.

You can plainly see the logic by considering what the overarching aim of AI espouses to be. The viewpoint is that AI is an attempt to devise machines that can exhibit intelligent behavior. By and large, this aspiration is shaped around making computer systems that seem to act smartly or intelligently, akin to what humans do or are supposed to do.

Upon giving some reflective thought about human behavior, we can likely all agree that humor seems to be a component of human behavior. Going further, some would argue vehemently that humor is a vital or integral element of human behavior. In brief, perhaps the notion of intelligence is also wrapped into the inoculation of humor. The assertion is that humor is either a needed aspect for giving rise to intelligence, or it is at least an integral byproduct that emerges from intelligence.

You might not buy into that theory.

The counterargument is that there is very little to do between intelligence and humor per se. We can have perfectly fine intelligence and have absolutely no humor somehow infused at all. Humor is a completely separable characteristic. In fact, by daring to contend that humor is somehow essential to intelligence, you are going to distract the strident pursuit of crafting machine-based intelligence and divert attention into something that has little or no substantive bearing on the genuine matter at hand.

I'll let you mull over that philosophical conundrum.

Meanwhile, there is not much doubt that today's AI systems could potentially make use of humor and indeed this is already happening. Whether this gets us any closer to the far reaches of attaining AI is a separate, interesting, and discernable question, but not one to be solved at this moment.

You might have interacted with an AI system that purportedly is using humor. These are usually pre-canned humorous statements that the programmers planted into the system and are nothing more than the recital of text. The AI is not sentient. It has no "understanding" about the humor. The jokes being told are even less than a monkey-see-monkey-do since the odds are that a monkey would potentially have a grasp of the meaning of humor (there is interesting research about the use of humor by animals, and you might find it worthwhile to take a look at such works).

The use of humor in an AI system could be classified as being flat or of a recital nature and essentially be entirely prescribed beforehand by the AI system designers and developers. That is about the least or lowest level of using humor in an AI system.

A step up from there entails AI that has been crafted to try and create humor on the fly. This is a lot trickier. Further up the ladder would be AI that is both able to emit humor and receive the humor, doing so in an interactive mode.

Where would AI that can emit humor be used?

The answer might seem smarmy but there is an opportunity to use humor in AI wherever the AI is being used that otherwise, a human might have opted to use humor.

That might seem confusing.

To clarify, suppose you go to see your primary physician about a sore shoulder. You raise your arm and explain to the medical doctor that it hurts when you do that. The physician looks at you and in a straight-faced voice declares, well, don't do that (bada-bing bada-boom!). This rather worn-torn joke showcases that humor can be used in the medical field. As repeatedly emphasized earlier, leveraging humor can be a stress reducer and be tremendously helpful or it can be poorly pitched and be abysmal. The same applies to using humor in medicine.

There is another realm that AI and humor can be considered for use. All this talk about ridesharing and what a driver might say is a handy segue into the topic of AI and self-driving cars.

The question to consider is this: *Should AI-based true self-driving cars make use of humor?*

Time to unpack the matter and see.

Understanding The Levels Of Self-Driving Cars

As a clarification, true self-driving cars are ones that the AI drives the car entirely on its own and there isn't any human assistance during the driving task.

These driverless vehicles are considered Level 4 and Level 5, while a car that requires a human driver to co-share the driving effort is usually considered at Level 2 or Level 3. The cars that co-share the driving task are described as being semi-autonomous, and typically contain a variety of automated add-on's that are referred to as ADAS (Advanced Driver-Assistance Systems).

There is not yet a true self-driving car at Level 5, which we don't yet even know if this will be possible to achieve, and nor how long it will take to get there.

Meanwhile, the Level 4 efforts are gradually trying to get some traction by undergoing very narrow and selective public roadway trials, though there is controversy over whether this testing should be allowed per se (we are all life-or-death guinea pigs in an experiment taking place on our highways and byways, some contend).

Since semi-autonomous cars require a human driver, the adoption of those types of cars won't be markedly different than driving conventional vehicles, so there's not much new per se to cover about them on this topic (though, as you'll see in a moment, the points next made are generally applicable).

For semi-autonomous cars, it is important that the public needs to be forewarned about a disturbing aspect that's been arising lately, namely that despite those human drivers that keep posting videos of themselves falling asleep at the wheel of a Level 2 or Level 3 car, we all need to avoid being misled into believing that the driver can take away their attention from the driving task while driving a semi-autonomous car.

You are the responsible party for the driving actions of the vehicle, regardless of how much automation might be tossed into a Level 2 or Level 3.

Self-Driving Cars And Using Humor

For Level 4 and Level 5 true self-driving vehicles, there won't be a human driver involved in the driving task.

All occupants will be passengers.

The AI is doing the driving.

One aspect to immediately discuss entails the fact that the AI involved in today's AI driving systems is not sentient. In other words, the AI is altogether a collective of computer-based programming and algorithms, and most assuredly not able to reason in the same manner that humans can.

Why this added emphasis about the AI not being sentient?

Because I want to underscore that when discussing the role of the AI driving system, I am not ascribing human qualities to the AI. Please be aware that there is an ongoing and dangerous tendency these days to anthropomorphize AI. In essence, people are assigning human-like sentience to today's AI, despite the undeniable and inarguable fact that no such AI exists as yet.

With that clarification, you can envision that the AI driving system won't natively somehow "know" about humor and the use of humor. Any use of humor and whatever it entails will need to be programmed as part of the hardware and software of the self-driving car.

Let's dive into the myriad of aspects that come to play on this topic.

You get into a self-driving car and the AI driving system greets you with a joke.

Is that a good thing to do or a bad thing to do?

Well, if you are stressed out about potentially using a self-driving car, the use of humor could put you at ease. You might relax and feel like you are simply going on a ride, as though a human was driving the vehicle.

On the other hand, you might interpret this use of humor as horribly misplaced. You want an AI driving system that takes the act of driving as a quite serious matter. Maybe the AI doesn't care much about the troubles of driving and instead the focus is on joke-telling. When your life is about to be placed into the hands of the AI, you'd rather that it was attentive to the roadway.

There's that double-edge sword again.

Most of the self-driving car tryouts are likely to eschew using humor for now. Keep things simpler and cleaner, for the moment, and maybe add some touches of humor later on.

A complaint that is likely to get lodged about AI using humor in the case of driving a self-driving car is that it could mislead passengers into believing that the AI is in fact sentient. This takes us back to the discussion about navigating away from portraying AI as though it is on par with humans (we ought to avoid going the anthropomorphic route).

An alternative way to sneak humor into this realm would be to have the humor delivered by humans. You get into a self-driving car and a screen inside the car begins to show you a short video. The video shows a spokesperson that explains the greatness of this self-driving car and the aspect that you are riding in it is quite astute on your part. The recorded video then provides some humor to get you relaxed about your ride.

Notice that this keeps the humor separated from the AI. The joke-telling arose via the human spokesperson and not due to the AI system.

Here's another twist for you.

Suppose the AI driving system does have some kind of humor-emitting component. This brings up a technical concern. If the AI driving system is using its computer processors to do joke-telling, doesn't that imply that those same processing cycles are not being used toward the driving task? And, if so, wouldn't it be more prudent to use any and all processing capacity to try and maximize the safest possible driving journey, rather than expending such effort on humor?

You could make that argument.

The retort or counterargument could be that the processing of the AI-based humor emission is coming from a separate onboard computer that is used for other facets such as in-car entertainment. You wouldn't presumably be arguing that the radio or in-car TV is somehow usurping the processing for the AI driving system, so why should it be of concern to do so when telling jokes?

The AI joke-telling could be entirely distinct from the AI driving system. This might be an add-on or some other augmented feature that the self-driving car can download and use. Again, think of this as a form of in-car entertainment.

During the driving journey, the AI joke-telling might be tapping into the AI driving system to keep track of how the driving is coming along. Suppose the AI driving system takes a turn that is particularly sharp and maybe slightly jostles the passenger inside the self-driving car.

The AI joke-telling system might be on alert for such situations and blurt out that it was quite a fancy turn, making light of the driving action.

Good idea or bad idea?

It might ease the tension and the rider would realize that the AI realizes that the turn was a bit tight.

Or it might heighten the tension if the rider didn't notice the sharp turning action and now, all of a sudden, become leery of what the AI driving system is doing.

One seemingly irrefutable advantage of the AI-based humor telling would be that the AI won't get ruffled or upset if you decide the joke wasn't funny.

You could presumably berate the AI to your heart's content, and not worry that the AI is going to change how it is driving such that it suddenly gets emotional and drives oddly.

Unlike a human driver, the AI won't have such reactive qualities (though, just to clarify, this is based on the assumption that the AI would be programmed to not do so, and that it would be just as easy to have the programmed AI to indeed become erratic or respond poorly if that's what seemed like a desirable outcome as devised by the programmers).

Conclusion

The automakers and self-driving tech firms have their hands full right now as they try to get self-driving cars to simply drive from any given point A to point B.

Thoughts about adding humor are at best a lowly ranked edge or corner case, meaning that it sits on a list of things to do and resides at a very low priority. That being said, it would be relatively easy to plug in an AI-based humor component if all that you wanted to do was have some kind of AI-related humor telling capacity.

Furthermore, most self-driving cars will have inward-facing cameras and audio microphones, allowing this kind of AI to try and detect what reactions passengers have to the emitted humor.

A real-time AI-based humor component of sophistication would be able to do an immediate analysis of the passengers using facial recognition and other Machine Learning pattern matching to try and discern how someone is responding to the humor. This is somewhat akin to how any joke teller tries to read the crowd, as it were.

Perhaps the next time that you feel a strident need to enjoy some peppy standup comedy, you'll beckon a self-driving car and go for a ride. That reminds me, have you ever heard the one about the self-driving car and the self-driving truck that walk into a bar?

It is quite a hilarious knee slapper.

CHAPTER 6
MASS TAKEOVER OF SELF-DRIVING CARS

There are a lot of movies and TV shows that depict a mass control takeover of self-driving cars.

This seems to be on our minds.

For quite good reasons.

If a malicious evildoer was somehow able to take command of Autonomous Vehicles (AVs) such as self-driving cars, the outcome could be disastrous. This almost goes without saying. The usual portrayal in films is that the villain opts to have cars crash into each other. Well, that's just for starters. The self-driving cars are rammed into anything that isn't nailed down, and by gosh also steer into and collide with objects that are ostensibly nailed down too.

Humans riding inside self-driving cars are harmed. Humans in nearby conventional cars are harmed. Pedestrians are harmed. The gist is that self-driving cars under the command of a baddie will become a frightening and seemingly unstoppable destructive force.

How would you avoid becoming prey?

The key would seem to be staying off the roadways.

By keeping yourself indoors, it is highly unlikely that a devilishly directed self-driving car could reach you. Sure, one supposes that the autonomous vehicle could be instructed to try and ram your house.

We already know that this happens today from time to time when a human driver loses control of the wheel and swerves into a domicile (thus, it occurs at the direct hands of the human driver). Perhaps if several self-driving cars were directed to this malevolent task, it might become endangering. The odds are though that being indoors would be sufficiently protective.

We would need to abundantly curtail our travel activities.

Anyone on a bicycle becomes a potential target. Driving a conventional car is also going to be a target. Armored trucks would be a target, plus if they were self-driving capable, they could be added to the arsenal of the wrongdoer.

Pedestrians could potentially sprint from spot to spot, going through narrow passages that a self-driving car could not traverse. That won't be much satisfaction for trying to go from any given point A to point B on any long-distance basis. We would be essentially trapped in our nearest domains and be unable to do any extensive traveling.

When you see these kinds of portrayals, one question that some ask entails the matter of the vehicles running out of gas. Wouldn't self-driving cars eventually run out of gas? And if so, they would become useless paperweights. Without the fuel needed to be underway, any such self-driving car that is empty would no longer be much of a threat to anyone.

This might seem like a means of overcoming the feared invasion of the overlord-snatched AI-based self-driving cars, but regrettably, there is a catch. You see, there are plans afoot of trying to make refueling for self-driving cars an unmanned chore. A self-driving car pulls up to a gas pump or charging station, and an automated robotic arm makes sure that the hose connects with the vehicle.

You would certainly want this if we had a lot of everyday self-driving cars on our roadways.

Suppose you owned a self-driving car. Rather than having to take it over to the gas station or charging station to keep refueling the darned thing, you would just send it there on its own. In fact, assuming that you are likely using the self-driving car as ridesharing or ride-hailing vehicle, making you some extra dough, you would merely indicate to the AI driving system that whenever there is idle time and nothing else to do, route over to the nearest fueling station and get stocked up.

I realize this seems to be a disappointment for those hoping that it was the Achilles heel of self-driving cars that are surreptitiously overtaken by awful people.

You might say that another angle on how to stop this incursion would be that those self-driving cars are bound to eventually have something go awry since they are still cars when it comes down to it. A tire might blow out. The engine might conk out. Some kind of mechanical failure or breakage has got to ultimately arise.

There is some goods news and bad news on that front.

First, the bad news is that it is generally presumed that self-driving cars are going to be kept in a rather pristine shape. Those that own and run their self-driving cars are going to want to keep the maintenance at tiptop condition. The logic is somewhat obvious. If you are using your self-driving car to make money by providing rides, the time spent in a repair facility is lost income. To avoid extended stays in a repair shop, you'd better keep the vehicle in the best possible order.

This implies that upon the takeover of self-driving cars, the vehicles will most likely be in great shape and able to go quite a while before things start to fall apart. That's the bad news about pinning your hopes on the breakage vulnerability.

The good news somewhat is that eventually wear-and-tear would occur, and assuming that nobody will be willing to then fix up a self-driving car, we'll have those vehicles sloppily stuck and completely out of sorts. They will come to a grinding halt of their own accord, gradually and inevitably. Of course, we would be living in fear and uncertainty until that day arrived.

Here's yet another believed way to deal with those wayward self-driving cars.

You sneak up to a self-driving car. In your hands, you have a USB memory stick or equivalent. Upon getting into the vehicle, you plug in the device. It contains some form of programming that can undercut the existing programming. This will allow you to get the AI driving system to no longer be under the command or spell of the mastermind.

Aha, humanity and goodness will triumph once again.

Hold on for a second, there are problems with that proposed solution.

Sneaking up on a self-driving car could be a challenging affair.

Most self-driving cars are chockful of handy sensors such as video cameras, radar, LIDAR, ultrasonic units, thermal imaging, and the like. We can most likely assume that the takeover of the self-driving car has kept those sensory devices intact and underway. Without the use of those sensors, the AI driving system can't do much in terms of ascertaining where to drive the car (as a side note, the use of maps could be resorted upon, though this could be undermined in various ways by those trying to prevent the now-blinded self-driving cars from getting around readily).

The evildoer would presumably have the AI driving system be on constant alert for anyone approaching the vehicle, and then have the self-driving car skirt away (or try to drive at the person).

The idea of trying to secretly get into a self-driving car in this takeover scenario is rather outstretched. I'm not saying that it cannot be done and simply emphasizing that it would be difficult to successfully achieve.

Even if you did get into the vehicle, the other problem is that your effort to reprogram the AI driving system might not be feasible.

Think of it this way.

If self-driving cars could easily be reprogrammed by merely getting into the vehicle and installing a memory stick or other programming tool, this would be a huge and dangerous exposure for all self-driving cars. It would imply that anybody riding in a self-driving car can pretty much willy-nilly change the AI driving system.

It is hoped and generally anticipated that there will be rigorous cybersecurity protections included in self-driving cars. This is intended to avert the odds of someone doing the very thing that we are now suggesting is wanted. Most of the time, we won't want someone to be able to take such an act. In the rare and so far fictional notion of a mass takeover, we might regret that we built such impenetrable protections, but meanwhile, it makes indubitable sense to have them.

For those of you that perchance know something about cybersecurity, you know that it is an ongoing cat and mouse game. As such, even if self-driving cars are well-protected from such an attack, there is still the chance of finding a way around the fortress of barriers and blockages. One guesses that if a mass takeover occurred, and upon virtually bringing together the most notable of cybersecurity experts and potential good-oriented hackers, perhaps a means could be figured out to make this USB memory stick containing an AI driving system reprogramming become a reality.

Remember though that getting into the car would be a challenge unto itself.

Plus, imagine that you were trying to go to every self-driving car and do this corrective action. We don't know how many self-driving cars we might eventually have on our roadways, so the number is still unknown. On the other hand, there are about 250 million conventional cars in the United States alone. Some predict that by and large, we will gradually wean ourselves away from conventional cars. If that happens, we might end up with the same number of self-driving cars, namely on the order of 250 million or so.

There are arguments about the number of self-driving cars that we will need.

Since most conventional cars are only used about 5% or less of their available time (sitting parked about 95% or more of the time), we might not need the same number of self-driving cars due to the built-in AI driving system and that they can operate 24x7. Some believe we can have a lot fewer self-driving cars to make up for the eventual junking of all those conventional cars.

Other experts suggest that our demand to use self-driving cars will skyrocket as we realize how convenient they are. This suggests we all might go for journeys in cars more so than we do today. Ergo, it is conceivable that we might need just as many self-driving cars as the number of today's conventional cars, or perhaps even more self-driving cars will be desired.

The key point is that trying to go to each and every self-driving car to insert the antidote, as it were, would be laborious and seemingly impractical.

That doesn't end the case for trying to do the AI driving system reprogramming. There is another potential avenue.

Self-driving cars will be making use of OTA (Over-The-Air) electronic communication capabilities. This is akin to what happens when you get your laptop or smartphone updated. It is expected that self-driving cars will connect to the cloud of the fleet owner or operator, doing so to get updates to the onboard software.

In addition, the self-driving car can upload data to the cloud. This might include the status of the vehicle, along with the sensory data collected during a driving journey.

I think you know where I am heading.

Rather than having to physically get into each self-driving car, perhaps we could exploit the OTA to try and change the AI driving system. All we would need to do is get the OTA to willingly download some patches that we had put together. This might either turn the AI driving system back into what it was supposed to be doing or maybe we have it be blanked out entirely. The approach of blanking out the AI driving system would seem the more assured approach to stop the evildoer takeover, though this also means that the vehicle becomes a doorstop.

Turns out that there are lots of twists and turns now that we've introduced the OTA aspects into this scenario.

Before jumping further into the details, I'd like to clarify what is meant when referring to AI-based true self-driving cars.

Understanding The Levels Of Self-Driving Cars

As a clarification, true self-driving cars are ones that the AI drives the car entirely on its own and there isn't any human assistance during the driving task.

These driverless vehicles are considered Level 4 and Level 5, while a car that requires a human driver to co-share the driving effort is usually considered at Level 2 or Level 3. The cars that co-share the driving task are described as being semi-autonomous, and typically contain a variety of automated add-on's that are referred to as ADAS (Advanced Driver-Assistance Systems).

There is not yet a true self-driving car at Level 5, which we don't yet even know if this will be possible to achieve, and nor how long it will take to get there.

Meanwhile, the Level 4 efforts are gradually trying to get some traction by undergoing very narrow and selective public roadway trials, though there is controversy over whether this testing should be allowed per se (we are all life-or-death guinea pigs in an experiment taking place on our highways and byways, some contend).

Since semi-autonomous cars require a human driver, the adoption of those types of cars won't be markedly different than driving conventional vehicles, so there's not much new per se to cover about them on this topic (though, as you'll see in a moment, the points next made are generally applicable).

For semi-autonomous cars, it is important that the public needs to be forewarned about a disturbing aspect that's been arising lately, namely that despite those human drivers that keep posting videos of themselves falling asleep at the wheel of a Level 2 or Level 3 car, we all need to avoid being misled into believing that the driver can take away their attention from the driving task while driving a semi-autonomous car.

You are the responsible party for the driving actions of the vehicle, regardless of how much automation might be tossed into a Level 2 or Level 3.

Self-Driving Cars And Malicious Mass Takeover

For Level 4 and Level 5 true self-driving vehicles, there won't be a human driver involved in the driving task.

All occupants will be passengers.

The AI is doing the driving.

One aspect to immediately discuss entails the fact that the AI involved in today's AI driving systems is not sentient. In other words, the AI is altogether a collective of computer-based programming and algorithms, and most assuredly not able to reason in the same manner that humans can.

Why this added emphasis about the AI not being sentient?

Because I want to underscore that when discussing the role of the AI driving system, I am not ascribing human qualities to the AI. Please be aware that there is an ongoing and dangerous tendency these days to anthropomorphize AI. In essence, people are assigning human-like sentience to today's AI, despite the undeniable and inarguable fact that no such AI exists as yet.

With that clarification, you can envision that the AI driving system won't natively somehow "know" about the facets of driving. Driving and all that it entails will need to be programmed as part of the hardware and software of the self-driving car.

Let's dive into more of the myriad of aspects that come to play on this topic.

We were earlier discussing the use of OTA as a means to try and infuse a devised cure or antidote that might curtail the malicious mass takeover of self-driving cars. The beauty of using OTA is that we could presumably do so massively across the gamut of self-driving cars that have been villainously overtaken. Rather than trying to physically go to each self-driving car by hand, we can on a widespread basis electronically communicate the presumed remedy that we've hurriedly crafted.

Sounds good, and a relief that the matter is seemingly settled.

Not so fast.

There are plenty of gotchas and holes in that corrective scheme.

One aspect that we've not yet discussed is how in the heck did the takeover happen to begin with? In other words, we took at face value that somehow the maniac mastermind has been able to take over self-driving cars. Let's explore that overthrow and then return to considering how to undo or overtake the overtaking.

As already suggested, one approach would be to physically get into a self-driving car and use some immediate means to try and reprogram the AI driving system, doing so for evildoer purposes rather than to correct whatever an evildoer has already done. There are a variety of ways that this in-car invasion could be approached. One would hope that the cybersecurity of the AI driving system has been mindfully constructed and will not be especially readily breached. That's not to say it cannot necessarily be flouted, only that it will be hard to do.

Of course, the laborious chore of going from self-driving car to self-driving car would seem not very expedient if the fiend is aiming to perform a mass takeover. The alternative would be to use the OTA. Yes, the same OTA that is purposely included by the automaker or self-driving tech firm for aiding in making desired updates could be sneakily used for wicked intent.

The OTA provides an opportunity for badness. If a crook can somehow plant something into the cloud of the self-driving car fleet, there is a chance of getting that distributed out and into the self-driving cars via the OTA. This might occur by hiding the untoward element inside an otherwise accepted and everyday update going down to the autonomous vehicles. Or it could consist of a special update package that convinces the OTA mechanism that everything is okay and the element should be sent out.

As might be evident, the OTA is a dual-edged sword.

Then again, maybe it is a tri-edged sword.

Here's why.

The OTA is normally used to send approved updates that are downloaded and installed into the AI driving system. There is the chance that a malicious code leverages the OTA and gets downloaded and installed. And there is the possibility of using the OTA to correct or delete the malicious code. Perhaps that's at least three sides of the sword, though we could continue this line of thought indefinitely and continue the cat and mouse game indefinitely.

Since the OTA is the drawbridge that connects the fortress to the rest of the world, there needs to be a lot of protection about allowing the drawbridge to be used. For those automakers and self-driving tech firms, they do not want the drawbridge to be used by those devilish intruders.

Meanwhile, the devilish intruder would likely not only realize that their best shot would be to exploit the OTA drawbridge, but they also might decide to try and cut off the drawbridge after successfully making an invasion. Either burn the drawbridge to the ground and stop any further OTA or try to alter the drawbridge so that only they can continue to make use of it.

We need to also bring up another crucial factor.

Not all self-driving cars will be the same.

A particular automaker might choose to develop or select a self-driving stack of code that befits their specific brands and makes of self-driving cars. When you see a self-driving car that is made by company X, the odds are that the software and systems running onboard are quite different from the self-driving cars made by company Y. The same can be generally said about the OTA being used.

The reason this is notable in the case of a mass takeover of self-driving cars is that it is going to be somewhat harder to intrude across all variants of self-driving cars. An evildoer might focus on a particular set of self-driving cars made by company X. Whether they can do the same against the self-driving cars of company Y is not necessarily assured.

What this means is that it might not be a mass per se, and only a subset of self-driving cars that the maniacal takeover occurs. Suppose that we had a city with hundreds of self-driving cars made by company X, and other hundreds of self-driving cars made by company Y. It could be that only the company X self-driving cars are part of the takeover, while an attempt to overrun the company Y was rebuffed or not even tried at all.

This might not be of much solace if there are millions upon millions of those company X self-driving cars out on our public roadways. You could say that only those company X self-driving cars are being conquered, but that still is a potentially large number of autonomous vehicles and ostensibly dangerous to have in the takeover column.

Conclusion

Much more can be examined in this doom-and-gloom scenario.

When or if such a mass takeover were to occur, one key question is whether the self-driving cars would now have wholly contained whatever their foul mission is to be, or would they rely upon the OTA or some other form of electronic communication to get instructions during their adverse takeover journeys.

In essence, one approach involves infusing the AI driving system with whatever bad acts it is supposed to undertake, and then try to break off any further electronic communications. Another approach involves seeking to communicate on a mass basis to direct the self-driving cars while they are in this deranged takeover mode. This allowance for communicating though becomes a point of potential weakness in the takeover plot since it can possibly be used to disrupt or ultimately nullify the malevolent scheme.

Makes your head spin at all of the trickery involved.

Not wanting to further be glum, but there is a similar chance of doing the same kind of mass takeover for cars that are not self-driving cars. Those vehicles that are at Level 2 and Level 3 are bound to eventually have OTA. Everything we've just discussed applies to Level 2 and Level 3 and has an added variation. Since Level 2 and Level 3 presume that a human driver is available at the wheel, this means that the programmed takeover could end up becoming a struggle between the human driver and the automation.

You might be thinking that the solution to nearly all of this would be to have a big red button or an on-off switch inside all cars that could be used to turn off the automation. Some pundits are pushing for this arguable solution.

Okay, so where does this leave us?

For those that are devising self-driving cars (and pretty much any automotive vehicles containing advanced automation), the importance of establishing rigorous cybersecurity protections is paramount.

That is a tall order. There is a myriad of ways to undercut the computer system security of an automobile. Lots and lots of possible attack vectors and vulnerable paths exist.

Discussing the notion of a mass takeover seems like a crying wolf to some. Those skeptics ought to also take into account the role of nation-states as it pertains to self-driving cars.

The purpose herein was not to suggest that a mass takeover will of necessity happen. The intent is to awaken the awareness of what all automakers and self-driving tech firms need to be doing, namely devoting a tremendous amount of energy, expertise, and devoted attention to securing their automation from cyberattacks.

In the rush to try and deploy self-driving cars onto the roadways, seeking to have those vehicles safely proceed from point A to point B, it can be easy to lose sight of the cybersecurity considerations.

Those leading the existent self-driving car efforts are at times preoccupied with the point A to point B tryouts (naturally so), and not equally garnering focus on the cybersecurity elements. Sadly, some even have that "we'll worry about it later" perspective, figuring they have plenty of time to one day get the cybersecurity in place for their AI driving systems.

Let's not allow the strident pursuit of self-driving cars to become a vulnerability by undervaluing or being distracted from the concerns and dangers that are looming from those evildoers that would seek to do malicious cyberhacking on a mass sized basis.

The veritable hand wringing on this topic is well worth the stress and abject worry, mark my words.

CHAPTER 7
DUMP FROM OVERPASS AND SELF-DRIVING CARS

Asphalt is all around us, that's for sure.

Our highways are typically made of asphalt. Streets are made from asphalt. Parking lots. Airport runways. Even tennis courts and the very rooftops on our homes are oftentimes reinforced or entirely composed of some quite handy dandy asphalt.

Asphalt that is used to construct these various everyday elements is usually trucked to the location that needs the asphalt for building purposes.

During transit, the asphalt is normally kept at around 300 degrees Fahrenheit. This ensures that the potent mixture remains fluid-like and can be readily poured into place. To further enhance the liquidity of the material there is an added ingredient of either kerosene or diesel oil. And, you might be surprised to know that some dump trucks are outfitted to purposely feed their heated engine exhaust into the body of the asphalt pile, providing an extra means of keeping the asphalt pliable while being transported.

You've undoubtedly seen dump trucks carrying asphalt and witnessed them from time to time as they crisscrossed your city streets on their way to a nearby construction site.

I'm betting that you've even been on a freeway and had the distinctly unfavorable honor of driving directly behind a truck loaded with some of that roasting asphalt. You can usually smell the stinky distinctive odor emanating from the loaded-up vehicle.

Furthermore, when the truck is full and carrying a heavy load of the material, there is a high chance that the bulky vehicle will be moving along relatively slowly in comparison to the rest of the traffic.

Your angst suffers a double whammy. There is that foul odor and you are crawling along at a snail's pace.

Be forewarned that the fumes of the steaming asphalt can be dangerous to your health. The odds though of getting harmed by a few whiffs of the stuff as it is being carted along seems ostensibly remote. Another potential danger consists of getting hot asphalt onto your skin. That can be horrendous and besides the burning aspects, there are also the chances of the material being absorbed into your skin.

A word to the wise, do not let small children go play with freshly deposited asphalt. Adults are at times tempted to let kids go ahead and mess around with a newly laid piece of street or parking lot asphalt. Do not do this.

Enough said.

Returning to the notion of at times finding yourself driving behind a truck that is loaded up with fresh asphalt, one consideration that might pop into your noggin is the oddball chance that the asphalt might somehow be bumped out of the truck and onto the roadway in front of you. Perhaps the truck strikes a big piece of debris causing the truck to take a bit of a jump, and the next thing that you know there is a slushing of this liquefied asphalt plopping onto the freeway or highway.

Yikes!

What would you do?

I suppose it depends upon how close you were to the inadvertently slushed material and how much of it was dumped out.

The hope would be that you could just continue straight ahead and straddle the material so that your car harmlessly passed over the yucky stuff. With luck, your tires wouldn't get mired in the foul mixture.

For a brief instant, you would have likely been immensely startled and dreading the worst of outcomes. Upon zooming over the toxic mess, you would glance in your rearview mirror and be thankful that by your lucky stars the potential hazard was evaded.

Suppose though that the volume of the inadvertently dumped asphalt was much larger. In that case, you might try to veer into another lane and avoid the scary mound of noxious slush. The act of sharply switching lanes might have its own dangers. If there are cars in those lanes you then risk the chance of colliding with those vehicles.

Which would you prefer, potentially striking other nearby moving vehicles or plowing into a large pile of heated asphalt?

Doing so at freeway speeds such as 60 miles per hour.

None of us ever wants to face that kind of worst-of-two-evils choices.

It is the proverbial classic case of being between a rock and a hard place.

You might be right now thinking that the odds of being behind a dump truck that has a full load of heated asphalt and having any of the material falls onto the roadway in front of you is just about nil. In other words, sure, there is some wildly bizarre chance that this could someday happen, but it seems as unlikely as having space aliens beam you up into a visiting spacecraft from outer space.

Well, I guess you ought to start looking skyward.

Why so?

A dump truck carrying a fresh load of asphalt was on an overpass above a freeway and the driver accidentally collided with the side railings. In doing so, the dump truck pitched to its side and the asphalt summarily poured onto the traffic below.

Take a moment to let that scene soak into your mind (sorry, bad pun).

Maybe the phrasing of saying that it poured out is not an entirely apt way to describe the ghastly act. The asphalt gushed out. It flowed at what seems like the speed of light (not really, but you know what I mean). One second the asphalt was wholly contained in the dump truck, and merely a minuscule couple of seconds later it was all drenching down onto the freeway below.

In the earlier discussion, the scenario envisioned was that a dump truck in *front of you* might inadvertently unleash some asphalt. That would be bad, but at least you would undoubtedly see it happen. Your eyes are normally riveted on the traffic ahead of you.

How often do you look upward for potential dangers to your car?

Not very often.

We tend to assume that it is unlikely to have something plummet from above and strike our vehicles.

Indeed, I was driving past a golf course one day and got caught unawares by a loud smack of something that whacked into my front windshield, cracking it quite a bit. Yes, this was an errant golf ball. Some golfer had a really bad swing and managed to send a golf ball out of the golf course and into traffic. And into my car.

Just my luck.

I admit that I didn't see it coming. Please be aware that the wayward golf ball had gotten over a tall netting that was surrounding the golf course. I mention this aspect because some friends were at first surprised that I was somehow so clueless to not see the golf ball before it struck my car. They made me out to be a lousy driver that I didn't see this tiny speck that just so happened to archway above my normal gaze and plummet at bullet-like speeds down into my windshield.

Give me a break.

Anyway, imagine that you are driving along on a freeway, minding your own business. You are attentive to the traffic around you. You are watching the traffic ahead of you. Let's assume you aren't watching cat videos and nor trying to text on your smartphone while driving. You are exclusively in the mental zone of being a courteous and mindful driver.

A torrent of steaming asphalt suddenly appears out of nowhere, flowing in front of you as though a raging river of asphalt was unleashed. Keep in mind that the asphalt was coming down from the overhead overpass. It is akin to a waterfall, though consisting of dangerous, toxic, stinky, burning, slimy, mushy, and altogether a frightening tsunami of hot asphalt.

That's when you know that fate is not being kind to you.

There is a viral video on social media that captures the whole scene (the event occurred in Shanghai, China). A stunning aspect is how quickly the event happened. Within two or three seconds of the dump truck hitting the railing, it gets pitched to its side and the asphalt rains out.

Wham. Slush. Bam.

There isn't some lengthy time involved about the asphalt slowly oozing over the railings. Nope. In nearly the time that it takes to snap your fingers, the asphalt goes from the bed of the dump truck and immediately and without any hesitation down onto the traffic below.

By a miracle of sorts, only four cars got caught in the mess and just two people got injured (according to news reports).

Things could have been a lot worse.

One thing to ponder is whether you might have been able to notice the dump truck going across the overpass, which certainly seemed visible from the freeway below. Maybe you would have realized what destiny was aiming to unleash.

We all drive on highways and freeways that go underneath overpasses. This is common.

Do you routinely look up at overpasses?

Maybe somewhat yes, maybe somewhat no.

The odds are that you visually see the overpass but do not give it any undue mental focus. Without any direct noodling, your mind is presumably subconsciously looking for anything only out of the ordinary.

For example, if a person is standing up there on the overpass and facing the freeway below, this might catch your eye. There have been reported cases of miscreants that opted to toss rocks or bricks onto passing cars (a decidedly criminal act). Knowing that this can happen, you would certainly be observant of someone suspiciously standing still on an overpass and facing the traffic.

Thankfully, those outlandish happenings are a rarity.

All told, probably 99% of the time, you do not give any explicit attention to overpasses. Unless the overpass is crumbling from old age, or maybe there is a parade of specially decorated cars going across it, the roadway above you is stridently out of mind and not of particular concern. There is enough other stuff to concentrate on, such as the vehicles in front of you and to your sides.

I would further submit that even if you perchance noticed a dump truck going across the overpass, that too would not cause you any mental stir. Trucks and big vehicles are constantly using overpasses. If you continuously took your attention away from the hectic freeway and kept staring at whatever was crossing the overpass, you probably would be getting into numerous roadway accidents down below.

Okay, you are probably thinking, it might seem unlikely to notice the dump truck when it was properly and without noticeability going across the overpass. But what about once it struck the railing, certainly you would notice it then. At that point, your concern would rise like that of a startled cat that gets poised for action.

Being a catlike driver, you would then be eyeing the dump truck and waiting to see what happens next.

Maybe the whole darned truck is going to fall onto the freeway. Perhaps broken-off parts of the truck and bits of railing will come down. And so on.

Would you really though be thinking that hazardous asphalt is going to massively drench down upon the freeway?

Seems nearly unimaginable.

It is also doubtful that you would realize that the dump truck was hauling asphalt. You would need to be very observant to not only spy the dump truck, see that it is hitting the railing, watch as the truck pivots, and also keenly observe that it so happens to be carrying asphalt. That's a lot of unbelievably astute observations. Pat yourself on the back.

The thing is, the entire incident took place in just a few split seconds. Entirely out of the blue. You weren't expecting it to happen. I'll therefore ask the question again, doing so in the context that you are caught entirely flatfooted, not necessarily paying attention to the overpass, and are primarily and sensibly worrying about the fast-flowing traffic surrounding your car on an everyday freeway.

Would you anticipate that asphalt is going to flow down upon the freeway?

Realistically, the answer is no.

Shifting gears, the future of cars consists of AI-based true self-driving cars.

Allow me a moment to elaborate.

There isn't a human driver involved in a true self-driving car. Keep in mind that true self-driving cars are driven via an AI driving system. There isn't a need for a human driver at the wheel, and nor is there a provision for a human to drive the vehicle.

Here's an intriguing question that is worth pondering: *How would an AI-based true self-driving car do in the extraordinary circumstance of the dump truck that has spilled hot asphalt from an overpass onto an active freeway?*

Quite an interesting puzzler.

Before jumping into the details of what would likely happen, I'd like to further clarify what is meant when I refer to true self-driving cars.

Understanding The Levels Of Self-Driving Cars

As a clarification, true self-driving cars are ones that the AI drives the car entirely on its own and there isn't any human assistance during the driving task.

These driverless vehicles are considered Level 4 and Level 5, while a car that requires a human driver to co-share the driving effort is usually considered at Level 2 or Level 3. The cars that co-share the driving task are described as being semi-autonomous, and typically contain a variety of automated add-on's that are referred to as ADAS (Advanced Driver-Assistance Systems).

There is not yet a true self-driving car at Level 5, which we don't yet even know if this will be possible to achieve, and nor how long it will take to get there.

Meanwhile, the Level 4 efforts are gradually trying to get some traction by undergoing very narrow and selective public roadway trials, though there is controversy over whether this testing should be allowed per se (we are all life-or-death guinea pigs in an experiment taking place on our highways and byways, some contend).

Since semi-autonomous cars require a human driver, the adoption of those types of cars won't be markedly different than driving conventional vehicles, so there's not much new per se to cover about them on this topic (though, as you'll see in a moment, the points next made are generally applicable).

For semi-autonomous cars, it is important that the public needs to be forewarned about a disturbing aspect that's been arising lately, namely that despite those human drivers that keep posting videos of themselves falling asleep at the wheel of a Level 2 or Level 3 car, we all need to avoid being misled into believing that the driver can take away their attention from the driving task while driving a semi-autonomous car.

You are the responsible party for the driving actions of the vehicle, regardless of how much automation might be tossed into a Level 2 or Level 3.

Self-Driving Cars And Falling Flying Asphalt

For Level 4 and Level 5 true self-driving vehicles, there won't be a human driver involved in the driving task.

All occupants will be passengers.

The AI is doing the driving.

One aspect to immediately discuss entails the fact that the AI involved in today's AI driving systems is not sentient. In other words, the AI is altogether a collective of computer-based programming and algorithms, and most assuredly not able to reason in the same manner that humans can.

Why this added emphasis about the AI not being sentient?

Because I want to underscore that when discussing the role of the AI driving system, I am not ascribing human qualities to the AI. Please be aware that there is an ongoing and dangerous tendency these days to anthropomorphize AI. In essence, people are assigning human-like sentience to today's AI, despite the undeniable and inarguable fact that no such AI exists as yet.

With that clarification, you can envision that the AI driving system won't natively somehow "know" about the facets of driving. Driving and all that it entails will need to be programmed as part of the hardware and software of the self-driving car.

Let's dive into the myriad of aspects that come to play on this topic.

The first consideration in this dump truck scenario entails the potential detection of the showering asphalt.

As earlier pointed out, we would not have expected that human drivers would necessarily be intently observing the overpass when everything appeared to be normal and hunky-dory. Only if something suspiciously stood out would a human driver take notice of the traffic above them on the overpass.

Once the dump truck struck the railing, this unseemly act would be undoubtedly sufficient to arouse a semblance of attention by human drivers on the freeway. Likewise, as the dump truck pivoted and the fluid-like asphalt poured out, you can bet that this would be overtly noticed.

Of course, upon the asphalt cascading onto the freeway itself, there is no longer much debate that this would absolutely be seen by the human drivers (it is nearly inconceivable otherwise, as per the famous quip in *The Princess Bride*).

Consider the various stages of observable steps in the dump truck dumping event: A normal passage of a truck on an overpass, followed by the railing crash, then the rapid pivoting of the truck and spewing of the asphalt, finished by gobs of asphalt raining in the air and thudding onto the freeway.

What would take place if an AI self-driving car was on that freeway and in the midst of approaching the eventual asphalt apocalypse?

Detection is vital to all of this.

A self-driving car is typically equipped with a sensor suite to try and identify the driving scene. The sensors might include video cameras, radar, LIDAR, ultrasonic units, thermal imagining, and other such sensory devices. Those devices are mounted on the self-driving car. During a driving journey, the sensors are switched on and avidly collecting data. The data is being fed into the AI driving system.

The AI driving system is usually composed of Machine Learning (ML) and Deep Learning (DL) algorithms that computationally are doing pattern matching. This pattern matching is trying to analyze the data to discern what kinds of objects exist nearby and what those objects are. Along with assessing the nature of the objects, there is also a mathematical effort taking place by the computers to figure out the speed of those objects and their respective direction or headings.

We can reasonably assume that a well-equipped self-driving car would be ascertaining the traffic on the freeway that was in front of the autonomous vehicle, along with traffic adjacent to and also that is directly behind the self-driving car. The video camera would be streaming in the visual scene. The radar would be pinging off the objects that are nearby. Etc.

The AI driving system ought to have been programmed to detect the overpass if nothing else to gauge the allowed height underneath.

Any kind of bridge or structure that extends over the freeway is deserving of computational analysis to try and ensure that the self-driving car will be able to pass underneath it safely.

Imagine that a bridge had collapsed onto the freeway or at least was bulging downward, thus narrowing the gap between the freeway and the ceiling level of the structure. We would certainly expect a human driver to notice that there is insufficient clearance and therefore would stop before striking the low-hanging elements. A well-designed and properly programmed AI-based self-driving car should be doing the same.

When I mention this caveat that the self-driving car ought to be doing that kind of analysis, I am trying to purposely indicate that you don't know for sure that an AI driving system has been programmed with that kind of capability. It could easily be the case that an AI driving system does not have that feature and the presumed thinking by the AI developers is that it is a so-called edge or corner case.

An edge or corner case is considered any aspect that seemingly is outside the core of the primary task at hand. If some automaker or self-driving tech firm decides that low-hanging bridges are an edge or corner case, they would put this consideration on a list of low priorities. At some future time, they would come back to that item and opt to program it into the AI driving system.

You would naturally assume that something as fundamental as discerning whether there is sufficient clearance for the self-driving car would axiomatically be included in all AI driving systems. Generally, you might be right, but there is no ironclad basis to stake a claim that this is for sure something as yet programmed. By and large, most of the AI driving systems have this, though some might not (or, they have a crude version and for which numerous exceptions would be missed or unaccounted for).

To simplify this discussion, let's assume that we are envisioning an AI driving system that is especially robust and has all of today's presumed everyday capabilities.

Start the clock in terms of the unfolding event.

The dump truck enters onto the overpass, driving along perfectly fine so far.

The self-driving car on the freeway would computationally examine the streaming video of the driving scene and presumably detect the overpass. The odds are that the floor-to-ceiling gap would be estimated. This estimate would indicate that the self-driving car can easily pass underneath the overpass. The overpass does not present any issues in the sense that there aren't any other objects protruding or anything else that makes the overpass especially notable.

Our vaunted self-driving car continues to proceed forward and the AI driving system anticipates passing underneath the overpass, easy-peasy.

The clock ticks.

Ill-fated dump truck rams into the railing.

AI driving system detects the crash. The chances are that the programming of the AI driving system would not consider the matter of any alert. This is due to the notion that nothing is protruding or extending downward that could impede or strike the self-driving car.

Clock ticks again.

The dump truck pivots to its side, asphalt begins to pour out.

The motion of the asphalt might be detected. Since the impending mass seems to be heading downward, there is an off-chance that this might be calculated as a potential future issue.

The prediction component in the planning portion of the AI driving software calculates the distance of the self-driving car to the overpass, the speed of the self-driving car, the speed of the falling asphalt.

A potential intersection of the two is calculated.

It is highly unlikely that the AI driving system computational pattern matching is able to identify what the falling mass consists of. Humans would likely recognize it as asphalt, due to the color, shape, movement, etc., and by logically deducing that it is material coming directly from the bed of a dump truck.

That is pretty much a form of common-sense reasoning for a human being.

Humans know about the world around them. They can figure out things by tapping into their semblance of common sense. AI systems do not yet have any kind of common sense. The development of common sense for AI is an unsolved problem that has continued to stubbornly defy numerous Herculean efforts to devise.

In short, unless the AI developers had somehow envisioned that someday the AI driving system needed to do pattern matching on fluid-like asphalt (put that into the no-chance bucket), the mass of falling stuff is classified by the AI as an unknown.

Whatever this falling stuff is, it could be dangerous. On the other hand, it could be soft ash and fall to the freeway with no significant weighty impact (though perhaps obstructing vision, which is bad in its own right). The AI driving system would mark this as undetermined.

Make another click of the clock.

Wham, the asphalt lands onto the freeway.

This is now totally within the usual purview of the AI driving system. The self-driving car sensors are tuned to find obstructions and debris that sit straight ahead of the autonomous vehicle. That's pretty much a given.

What should the AI self-driving car do at this juncture?

The odds are that the AI driving system will attempt to stop the autonomous vehicle before it strikes the mysterious material. Though the self-driving car might also be programmed to consider changing lanes, given the narrow time window of this event as it unraveled, the odds are that a lane change was summarily dismissed as an immediately viable option, if calculated at all.

Conclusion

Anyone taking bets on what today's self-driving cars might do in this harrowing circumstance would have to go with the notion that the detection would occur primarily once the material landed or was somewhat mid-air but directly in front of the autonomous vehicle. The resulting AI programming would likely go with the seemingly default response of halting the vehicle.

It would be surprising to envision that any of today's AI driving systems would do much more than that.

That is not to suggest that future iterations and more advanced versions would similarly be limited in what they detected and what options were calculated and computationally assessed. Ongoing efforts to further expand the capabilities are stridently occurring.

There is a bit of the nefarious Trolley Problem that sits at the ugly underbelly of this dump truck scenario.

The Trolley Problem entails having to make difficult choices, contextually herein in the nature of driving decisions, and is often offhand dismissed by some as a misleading folly in the self-driving realm. In contrast and as a stout contrarian on the matter, I instead argue ardently that the Trolley Problem is a useful tool and applies to the real-world and practical use of self-driving cars.

Overall, a claimed advantage for self-driving cars will be that if an AI driving system encounters an extraordinary event, this can then be used by the AI developers as a learning insight that can be programmed into subsequent versions of an AI driving system.

Go ahead and thusly add this: *Dump truck on overpass dumps a load of noxious asphalt onto freeway traffic below.*

Hopefully, we can add that to the school-of-hard-knocks catalog of lessons learned.

CHAPTER 8
BLIND CURVES AND SELF-DRIVING CARS

Think about the last time that you found yourself driving a particularly treacherous blind curve.

Pretty darned scary, I'd bet.

Indeed, I realize that even the mere act of thinking about such an alarming encounter can be traumatic, so no need to reflectively linger on that reenactment in your mind. Go ahead and change your thought patterns to something less stressful such as mulling over the latest online cat videos or perhaps that delicious scoop of ice cream you recently consumed.

Meanwhile, let's have a heart-to-heart serious talk about blind curves.

When first learning to drive, few newbies are specifically instructed about blind curves. Sure, there might be discussions about what to do when reaching an especially sharp curve, but the whole conundrum of dealing with a sharp *and* blind curve is not necessarily resolutely covered.

You see, a blind curve denotes that you cannot readily see what is up ahead on the roadway. In contrast, a sharp curve could potentially be completely visible and you can discern what lies on the other side of the driving maneuver. The trickiness about blind curves is that you never know what you are going to get, just like that proverbial and infamous box of chocolates.

It could be that another vehicle is coming around that curve toward you, though you don't know that this potential calamity is taking place. Well, not at least until the last possible moment (and then some!). As you enter into the curve, a seemingly hidden vehicle suddenly appears as it rounds the curve going in the opposite direction. This can be startling.

Not only can it startle you, but the other question that immediately pops into your noggin is whether or not that vehicle is going to make the traversal properly. I'm sure that you've seen many instances wherein the car in the opposite direction decides to try and somehow navigate the blind curve in a manner that brings that vehicle partially into your lane.

If that happens, you have just split seconds to decide what to do.

Do you try to veer away from that rabbit-out-of-a-hat appearance? But if you veer then it is conceivable that you might go flying off the edge of a cliff or ram into the wall that borders the blind curve. So, you stay your course. The thing is, that guided missile could strike your car and force you off the roadway or otherwise smash up you and your vehicle.

You hope upon hopes that the transgressing driver will opt to get back into their lane. Or if you are lucky the intrusion into your lane is minimal and there is a no-harm no-foul result. There is a good chance that afterward, assuming nothing untoward has transpired, you will have to take a short respite and let your heart get back to a normal pace. The odds too are that you'll be bone-shaking for a while and need to change your undergarments due to the overwhelming anxiety.

Those other ditzy drivers can readily misjudge a blind curve.

Dolts!

Sheepishly, let's admit that any of us can do the same.

You might be that driver (at times).

As you come into a blind curve, you leisurely assume that you have the full width of your lane. Unfortunately, you are going just a tad fast. A feeling of gravity pulling at you like being on an amusement park roller coaster ride is starting to emerge. Anyone that is a seasoned driver knows that this could be a precursor to losing direct control of the vehicle.

I hope you've never had this happen.

As you take a blind curve overly confident, the car begins to lose traction on the roadway. If this continues, the vehicle can begin to skid. Once a skidding action grabs hold of the car, you might not have many options about how to keep the vehicle from moving rather uncontrollably. Panic can take over your mind and body.

In the midst of panic or by being purely reactionary, you try to oversteer. Or maybe you try to understeer. Flailing at the driving controls is not good. Some drivers believe they can accelerate out of the mess. Sadly, in some circumstances, doing so adds fuel to the fire, as it were. Other drivers assume they can hit the brakes to get out of the skidding effect. This can also backfire and make matters worse.

It all depends upon a variety of factors, such as the nature of the blind curve, the roadway surface, the weather conditions such as being dry or rainy, the speed of the car, the weight of the car, the status of the tires, and so on. Not only aren't newbies usually prepared for these situations, but seasoned drivers are also frequently ill-prepared too.

We can up the ante on the terrifying nature of blind curves.

Suppose you are nearing a blind curve but fail to realize that you are doing so. It could be that you are rocketing along at maximum speeds, not a care in the world. I know that it would seem nearly impossible that somebody would not detect that a blind curve is up ahead. They would have to be nutty to not discern this, so it would seem.

Two words: *Distracted drivers.*

A driver might be watching a funny chipmunk video on their in-car display and not paying attention to the roadway. Maybe the driver is texting on their smartphone. Heck, the driver might be engaged in a quarrel with a passenger about how many licks are needed to consume a tootsie pop and therefore their eyes and mind (and tastebuds) are inadvertently diverted away from the highway ahead.

We can toss into the mix a slew of human foibles when it comes to being behind the wheel of a car. Drowsy drivers are dull-witted and sleepy while at the driving controls. Drunk drivers are another consideration. You can count a zillion reasons why a driver might not be cognizant that a blind curve awaits them.

The good news is that usually there is a posted traffic sign that forewarns about blind curves being up ahead of you.

The bad news is that not a lot of people seem to notice those signs, or they give the notification a rather gruff and careless response. I've seen drivers that laughed at those posted signs. In their mind, those are signs for idiots that don't know how to drive. Certainly, someone as accomplished as they do not need some silly posted signs.

Anyway, if you see such a traffic sign or at least are aware that a blind curve is getting close, you can presumably slow down as needed.

That's a key to navigating blind curves, namely going slow enough as warranted for the nature of the curve and the circumstances at the moment of traversing the curve. Of course, trying to take a blind curve slowly can be a tough stance to take. Cars behind you might not like your act of slowing down. They will honk at you. Some drivers might tailgate you and aim to intimidate you into going faster.

This form of intimidation is not usually especially successful if it is a one-time instance of a blind curve. You can just keep going as you see fit. Let them be displeased, those malcontents, but at least everyone will live through the experience, hopefully.

Turns out though that oftentimes you come upon blind curves as an entire family of them. You have one blind curve that dumps you right away into another blind curve. These S-curves can be taking place again and again. Anyone behind you that believes that know better than you will probably go ballistic if you aren't moving at the speed of light through those successive curves.

Besides attempting to slow down and take a blind curve at an appropriate speed, you can also try to exploit the width of your given lane.

For example, in some cases, it makes sense to hug the line as you enter into the blind curve and then allow your car to naturally shift in the lane toward the other line boundary. This can help to reduce the angular momentum involved in navigating the curve. Some drivers don't know about this technique. Some do know about it but fail to use it. Others know about it and yet falter in making it work.

Another downside consideration concerning the leveraging of your lane width is that it can appear to any opposing traffic that maybe you are potentially losing control of your vehicle. In that case, the other opposing cars might make wanton moves under the assumption that you are potentially coming at them. All in all, though you weren't doing anything wrong, those other drivers can initiate a potential catastrophe simply by misinterpreting your actions.

I'm guessing that you've had instruction during your initial driver training courses that suggested it might be handy to use your horn when on a blind curve. This generally seems sensible. The sound of the horn will help to alert drivers around the bend that you are coming. One would assume that the other drivers will then prepare accordingly.

The horn honking works in some places, but not particularly well in others.

If there is a local custom or practice of honking a horn on a particular set of blind curves, the other drivers will know what is going on. The problem is that many places do not embrace that kind of practice. A car that is honking its horn has an entirely different connotation.

The opposing drivers might believe that you are honking because you have lost control of your car.

Maybe a deer is in the middle of the blind curve.

Perhaps outer space aliens from another planet are landing their UFO onto the roadway (I'd like to see that, so do let me know if that happens, thanks!).

More worrisome is that the honking might imply that you have opted to move into their lane and are now on their side of the highway. What should they do in response? Once again, this can create great difficulties due to a misunderstanding or misinterpretation.

Could be a darned if you do, darned if you don't, kind of situation.

Let's add up all of the proper steps or actions that can be potentially employed for coping with blind curves.

Look for posted signs that forewarn about a blind curve. Upon spying on such a sign, give the sign due to consideration and don't just shrug it off.

Reduce your speed to a sufficient speed that can safely traverse the blind curve. Any speed reduction should be done cautiously so that vehicles behind you are not caught off-guard and potentially rear-end your vehicle.

Use the lane wisely. If suitable, you can vary within your lane, though do so with caution and try not to spook the other traffic.

Stay within your lane. The moment you veer outside of your lane, troubles are bound to arise.

Watch for opposing traffic that might misjudge the blind curve. This includes that the opposing traffic can suddenly and shockingly enter your lane. Be anticipating this sour action and have your own contingencies planned and ready to enact.

Keep your mind on the driving. Keep your arms and legs actively on the driving controls. Utterly put aside those distractions and realize that a few seconds of devoted attention can be the difference between life and death.

I hadn't emphasized earlier the life-or-death aspects. I didn't want to make things seem overly glum. The point though is worth bringing up. In the handful of seconds that it usually takes to properly round a blind curve, you are staring not just at a dicey roadway situation, you are looking squarely in the eye at the Grim Reaper. The slightest slip-up as the driver can turn the blind curve into a killer curve.

Killer curves are blind curves that are, well, killers.

It seems perhaps dramatic to make such a proclamation, but I hope it will stick in your mind whenever your next perchance come upon a blind curve. Please take things mindfully and safely while driving a car.

Speaking of cars, the future of cars consists of AI-based true self-driving cars.

There isn't a human driver involved in a true self-driving car. Keep in mind that true self-driving cars are driven via an AI driving system. There isn't a need for a human driver at the wheel, and nor is there a provision for a human to drive the vehicle.

Here's an intriguing question that is worth pondering: *How will AI-based true self-driving cars handle blind curves, and what reactions will passengers potentially have?*

Before jumping into the details, I'd like to further clarify what is meant when I refer to true self-driving cars.

Understanding The Levels Of Self-Driving Cars

As a clarification, true self-driving cars are ones that the AI drives the car entirely on its own and there isn't any human assistance during the driving task.

These driverless vehicles are considered Level 4 and Level 5, while a car that requires a human driver to co-share the driving effort is usually considered at Level 2 or Level 3. The cars that co-share the driving task are described as being semi-autonomous, and typically contain a variety of automated add-on's that are referred to as ADAS (Advanced Driver-Assistance Systems).

There is not yet a true self-driving car at Level 5, which we don't yet even know if this will be possible to achieve, and nor how long it will take to get there.

Meanwhile, the Level 4 efforts are gradually trying to get some traction by undergoing very narrow and selective public roadway trials, though there is controversy over whether this testing should be allowed per se (we are all life-or-death guinea pigs in an experiment taking place on our highways and byways, some contend).

Since semi-autonomous cars require a human driver, the adoption of those types of cars won't be markedly different than driving conventional vehicles, so there's not much new per se to cover about them on this topic (though, as you'll see in a moment, the points next made are generally applicable).

For semi-autonomous cars, it is important that the public needs to be forewarned about a disturbing aspect that's been arising lately, namely that despite those human drivers that keep posting videos of themselves falling asleep at the wheel of a Level 2 or Level 3 car, we all need to avoid being misled into believing that the driver can take away their attention from the driving task while driving a semi-autonomous car.

You are the responsible party for the driving actions of the vehicle, regardless of how much automation might be tossed into a Level 2 or Level 3.

Self-Driving Cars And Blind Curves

For Level 4 and Level 5 true self-driving vehicles, there won't be a human driver involved in the driving task.

All occupants will be passengers.

The AI is doing the driving.

One aspect to immediately discuss entails the fact that the AI involved in today's AI driving systems is not sentient. In other words, the AI is altogether a collective of computer-based programming and algorithms, and most assuredly not able to reason in the same manner that humans can.

Why this added emphasis about the AI not being sentient?

Because I want to underscore that when discussing the role of the AI driving system, I am not ascribing human qualities to the AI. Please be aware that there is an ongoing and dangerous tendency these days to anthropomorphize AI. In essence, people are assigning human-like sentience to today's AI, despite the undeniable and inarguable fact that no such AI exists as yet.

With that clarification, you can envision that the AI driving system won't natively somehow "know" about the facets of driving. Driving and all that it entails will need to be programmed as part of the hardware and software of the self-driving car.

Let's dive into the myriad of aspects that come to play on this topic.

We have a rather definitive question that needs to be asked.

Will AI self-driving cars be able to properly cope with blind curves?

The answer, unfortunately, is somewhat mushy.

It all depends upon the programming and design of the AI driving system. Some automakers or self-driving tech firms will potentially devote more attention to the matter of blind curves than will others.

For example, a particular AI development team might believe that the overarching capability of driving any kind of curved roadways is sufficiently proficient to fully handle the specifics associated with blind curves. Therefore, they will not devise any elements that are honed to the nature of blind curves and instead rely on the generic curve handling features of their AI driving system.

In that case, the aspects of blind curves might be listed on an edge or corner cases listing, meaning that the AI developers acknowledge the potential need for something specific to blind curves, but they are busy with other matters and are opting to get around to blind curve programming at a later date. Of course, some might not even list blind curves as anything special to eventually be dealt with and altogether assume that their generic provisions for curved roadway handling will do.

This is partially why I politely suggest that the blind curve capabilities of AI self-driving cars could be a knuckle-gripping and panic-inducing affair.

You won't know for sure what the programming is able to handle. This is akin to having a human driver that you aren't sure can necessarily contend with blind curves. In the case of a human driver, you would usually try to size up the driver by observing them as they drive the car in everyday traffic. Even there, you still do not know exactly how they will deal with a blind curve.

One key difference about today's self-driving cars that might help feel you less queasy about their traversing of blind curves is that by and large, the odds are that the blind curve you are about to reach while riding inside a self-driving car is one that the AI driving system already is familiar with.

Here's why.

Most of today's AI self-driving cars are making use of specially devised maps. These maps tend to go far beyond what your normal maps consist of. The automaker or self-driving tech firm will typically pre-map an entire area that is going to be considered the geofenced realm of the self-driving car. These maps can also be purchased from a third party that has done the mapping work already.

Thus, the AI driving system will already be "informed" that a blind curve exists, along with having detailed specs about the nature of the blind curve. This can include roadway markings, roadway surface contours, and the like.

Human drivers are apt to drive in areas that they've never driven before. Ergo, coming upon a blind curve could catch a human driver unawares. For most self-driving cars, geofencing is done to try and ensure that the autonomous vehicle stays only within the bounds of areas that are pre-mapped (especially so for Level 4). This boundary constriction reduces surprises, though keep in mind that the maps might be outdated, plus the maps don't show what the conditions are at the moment of traversal (such as if rain is falling at the time of encountering the blind curve).

Another facet of today's self-driving cars is that usually there are a series of driving journeys taken in the geofenced area to try and traverse as many roadways and streets as feasible. This then augments the maps. Those trial runs of the self-driving car are oftentimes undertaken with a human backup or safety driver sitting at the wheel. This driver is trained to be watching the AI driving system efforts, and possibly disengage if trouble is brewing.

Okay, the bottom line is that presumably, an AI self-driving car will have already encountered a blind curve that you might someday witness as a passenger inside the self-driving car (realizing that this is usually only the case if using the same brand or software involved). Because the AI driving system has hopefully been prepared to deal with the blind curve instance, this does somewhat reduce your anxiety.

The thing is, none of that encompasses the *dynamics* of the blind curve in the real-time moments of traversal.

Imagine that the AI driving system begins to slow down as it approaches a blind curve. This slowing is likely induced by the pre-mapping and the prior trial runs. All's good so far. In a smiley face version of this traversal, the AI driving system successfully maneuvers through the blind curve. Case closed.

We can redo the scenario and make things more dynamic, as in dicier.

A human-driven car is coming in the opposite direction and heading into our blind curve.

Meanwhile, the self-driving car is outfitted with video cameras, radar, LIDAR, ultrasonic units, and other sensors. Assume that in this scenario that none of those sensors can detect what is beyond the blind curve. The self-driving car is obligingly staying in its lane and taking the blind curve as though there isn't any other traffic involved.

All of sudden, the human-driven car rounds the bend and now can be detected by the self-driving car.

What does the human driver do?

What does the AI driving system do?

In the case of the AI driving system, we might reasonably assume that the AI driving system will not do anything extraordinary and will simply continue its already underway driving effort.

No need to slow down since the AI has presumably already reduced speed to cope with the anticipated blind curve.

The human driver might continue along and not give any special attention to the car in the opposite lane of traffic. Thus, the human-driven car and the self-driving car pass each other, like two clouds passing in the night, none of them concerned about the other.

Or it could be that the human driver freaks out that this is a self-driving car. The human driver is worried that the self-driving car might not make the blind curve properly. So the human driver veers somewhat radically to get away from the self-driving car.

The AI driving system is bound to detect this sudden movement by the other car. Now the question arises as to what the AI driving system is going to do. Will it react in some fashion or ignore the movement and continued unabated?

A delicate and potentially life ascertaining ballet dance is now underway.

The human driver does not know what the AI driving system is possibly going to do. The AI driving system is computationally trying to mathematically predict what the human driver is going to do. Regrettably, this could spiral towards a worsening situation as they both try to anticipate and react to the other.

Sad face.

Conclusion

There are numerous additional twists and turns (sorry about the pun).

Suppose the human driver is using the technique of hugging the line and swinging over to the other line as the blind curve navigation takes place. The AI driving system could interpret this as a possibility that the other car is veering dangerously toward the self-driving car.

As such, the AI driving system might try to invoke some rapid emergency driving procedures, despite there not being a necessity per se to do so. I'll make things even tenser.

Assume that a boulder has fallen from a cliff that borders the blind curve. This oversized rock fell just a few minutes earlier. None of the maps that the AI driving system has would showcase that a dangerous obstruction is sitting in the middle of the roadway. This will be presumably detected in real-time.

How will the AI driving system handle the blind curve in this circumstance of the fallen rock?

Add to this driving scene that a car is coming in the opposite direction and honking its horn, doing so because the driver has noticed there is a boulder ominously laying in the lanes of traffic. Would the self-driving car hear the horn? Would the horn honking be incorporated into whatever actions the AI driving system is doing or planning to do? The variability of what can happen while driving a car is quite extensive.

Humans are usually able to adjust in real-time to unusual encounters. Whether the AI driving system has that kind of resilient or flexible programming is an open question. You can readily argue that the AI driving system won't get drunk, won't get drowsy, and won't get distracted, but a much harder case to be made is that the AI driving system will be adaptable to rapidly evolving roadway conditions that haven't been pre-programmed or prior simulated.

Passengers inside a self-driving car that is approaching a blind curve will find themselves perhaps second-guessing the AI driving system capabilities. You might want to practice your knuckle-gripping beforehand so you'll be ready for those moments when you sit in silence and get immersed into a blind curve traversal. Here's hoping that all goes well.

Keep your spirits up and we'll assume that those blind curves will be eyes-wide-open negotiated by the AI.

CHAPTER 9
NIGHT ONLY AND SELF-DRIVING CARS

Driving a car when it is very late at night or abundantly early in the morning can be refreshing, plus a bit eerie too.

The roads are usually relatively empty of traffic. Sure, there are those occasional instances where a cluster of cars get bunched up together, but this is not a particularly frequent occurrence and furthermore, the momentary snarls are quickly sorted out. You can usually drive along and not worry about being stuck behind that annoying driver that is going as slow as a tortoise. All you need to do is scoot around them. The traffic signals are typically green for any main roadways and you are able to proceed without those ill-timed red lights that during the day cause the traffic to become hindered.

You would also likely not be delayed by those pesky pedestrians that love to jaywalk or take their sweet time when lawfully crossing the street. There aren't many pedestrians at these oddball hours.

That seemingly stark visual cue does bring the eeriness factor into play. Without many people on the sidewalks, and with so few vehicles on the roadways, it almost can seem as though you have stepped into one of those sci-fi apocalyptic events and the rest of humanity has been somehow mysteriously wiped out.

Perhaps your mind at times wanders to that kind of scenario. There you are, driving on the empty streets, and it is you alone that has escaped the ghoulish fate of your fellow mankind. You are lucky to be alive. As you cruise the vacant streets and barren highways, the question arises as to whether you will ever see fellow humans again.

Of course, your daydreaming during this nighttime driving is bound to get disrupted by those nefarious and altogether life-threatening drunk drivers. Once the bars close, the odds are that there will be drivers that opt to get behind the wheel, despite being as drunk as a skunk. They endanger themselves and everyone else that perchance is out and about. The one thing you for sure need to do is to be on the watch for cars being driven erratically and try to remain as clear away from those drivers as feasible.

You might encounter a lot of trucks when driving during these wee hours.

Many trucking companies encourage their drivers to use city streets for deliveries or pick-ups at those late nights and extremely early morning times to avoid getting snagged in regular traffic. It is tough being a truck driver for a living. The moment you and your truck get embroiled in everyday traffic during daylight hours, you are likely falling behind on your schedule and will be losing money for each minute wasted by exasperating delays.

Since we're now discussing the business aspects of these unusual hours, there is a commonly accepted name given to this phenomenon. The hours that consist of roughly midnight to sunrise are often referred to in the workaday world as the *graveyard shift.*

You've undoubtedly heard that reference before. Some prefer to use wording that is less ghastly, such as calling it the third shift, the lobster shift, the sunrise watch, etc.

There is an ongoing debate about how the catchphrase of being on a graveyard shift came about. Some contend that the origins have to do with people that were inadvertently buried alive in coffins at graveyards. This was something that conceivably could and did happen from time to time. Medical science was not like it is today. There was a chance that a person in a coma or other deathlike state might be confined to a coffin and buried, yet they were ostensibly still alive.

The story goes that there were instances of coffins later exhumed and found to have clawing or scratch marks on the wood inside the inescapable confinement. This lent credence to the idea that perhaps people were at times being buried alive.

To deal with such a sordid predicament, some coffins were outfitted with a bell or a string connected to a bell. Presumably, a person falsely confined would at some point awaken and then realize they could ring the bell to alert others that they were still breathing and wanted to get out of the wooden box.

But ringing a bell would not do any good if there wasn't anyone around to hear it. You might find this reminiscent of the old line about whether a tree falling in the forest will make a sound if there isn't anyone around to hear it.

In any case, during the daytime, presumably, there might be people in a cemetery that was there to visit various graves of loved ones, and they would hear the bell and seek to rescue someone that was inappropriately buried alive. You would not though expect people to casually be milling around in a graveyard during the strange hours of late-night and before sunrise. Thus, a business or governmental agency responsible for the cemetery would hire someone to walk around the graveyard during those hours, protecting the graves from grave robbers and also listening for any ringing bells.

That is the prevailing saga about how the graveyard shift got its name, which some also say is known as the graveyard watch. Be aware that this is a somewhat fanciful accounting for the origins of the graveyard shift moniker and some believe it does not hold water, as it were.

Back to the focus about driving your car during these oddball and somewhat spooky hours.

You can usually go a tad faster than the speed limit due to the lack of prevailing traffic that might slow you down.

On the other hand, you might be at a heightened risk of getting nabbed for speeding because you are readily detected by the mere fact that so few other cars are around. You stand out like a sore thumb. A police car that is crisscrossing town looking for any overall criminal activity might by luck of the draw spot your car as it is exceeding the posted speed limit. That's a circumstance of being readily detectable that is not so lucky for you.

Another factor is the lack of bicycle riders.

You would not likely see many bike riders during the graveyard shift hours. During the day, bike riders can be all over the place. When driving a car, you need to continually be on the watch for bicyclists that seem to think they own the roadway. Which, I might quickly add before any bike riders yell at me about that remark, I'll also readily state that many car drivers are oblivious to bike riders or, worse still, treat bike riders with complete disdain.

One supposes that part of the reason there are so few bike riders at those hours is partially due to the fact that many bike riders are children, and hopefully, most children are nestled in bed at these sleeping time hours. On a pedestrian basis, it is also handy that kids aren't meandering around. If you've ever driven in areas where there are lots of kids going to or from school, you know how maddening it can be when the children opt to interrupt traffic and wander into the middle of the street. That being said, always be mindful to watch out for kids, keeping in mind that they are young and don't necessarily understand the dangers of entering into a street that has vehicular traffic.

Well, that covers some of the highlights and potential lowlights of driving during the so-called third shift or graveyard hours. I next have a bit of surprise for you that is quite an eye-opening idea about driving during those hours.

Consider that the future of cars consists of AI-based true self-driving cars.

There isn't a human driver involved in a true self-driving car. Keep in mind that true self-driving cars are driven via an AI driving system. There isn't a need for a human driver at the wheel, and nor is there a provision for a human to drive the vehicle.

Here's an intriguing question that is worth pondering: *Is it conceivable that AI-based true self-driving cars might be regulated by law to only operate from late at night to early morning, and if so, why would that be potentially a sensible restriction?*

I'd like to first further clarify what is meant when I refer to true self-driving cars.

Understanding The Levels Of Self-Driving Cars

As a clarification, true self-driving cars are ones that the AI drives the car entirely on its own and there isn't any human assistance during the driving task.

These driverless vehicles are considered Level 4 and Level 5, while a car that requires a human driver to co-share the driving effort is usually considered at Level 2 or Level 3. The cars that co-share the driving task are described as being semi-autonomous, and typically contain a variety of automated add-on's that are referred to as ADAS (Advanced Driver-Assistance Systems).

There is not yet a true self-driving car at Level 5, which we don't yet even know if this will be possible to achieve, and nor how long it will take to get there.

Meanwhile, the Level 4 efforts are gradually trying to get some traction by undergoing very narrow and selective public roadway trials, though there is controversy over whether this testing should be allowed per se (we are all life-or-death guinea pigs in an experiment taking place on our highways and byways, some contend).

Since semi-autonomous cars require a human driver, the adoption of those types of cars won't be markedly different than driving conventional vehicles, so there's not much new per se to cover about them on this topic (though, as you'll see in a moment, the points next made are generally applicable).

For semi-autonomous cars, it is important that the public needs to be forewarned about a disturbing aspect that's been arising lately, namely that despite those human drivers that keep posting videos of themselves falling asleep at the wheel of a Level 2 or Level 3 car, we all need to avoid being misled into believing that the driver can take away their attention from the driving task while driving a semi-autonomous car.

You are the responsible party for the driving actions of the vehicle, regardless of how much automation might be tossed into a Level 2 or Level 3.

Self-Driving Cars And The Graveyard Shift

For Level 4 and Level 5 true self-driving vehicles, there won't be a human driver involved in the driving task.

All occupants will be passengers.

The AI is doing the driving.

One aspect to immediately discuss entails the fact that the AI involved in today's AI driving systems is not sentient. In other words, the AI is altogether a collective of computer-based programming and algorithms, and most assuredly not able to reason in the same manner that humans can.

Why is this added emphasis about the AI not being sentient?

Because I want to underscore that when discussing the role of the AI driving system, I am not ascribing human qualities to the AI. Please be aware that there is an ongoing and dangerous tendency these days to anthropomorphize AI.

In essence, people are assigning human-like sentience to today's AI, despite the undeniable and inarguable fact that no such AI exists as yet.

With that clarification, you can envision that the AI driving system won't natively somehow "know" about the facets of driving. Driving and all that it entails will need to be programmed as part of the hardware and software of the self-driving car.

Let's dive into the myriad of aspects that come to play on this topic.

The general expectation is that self-driving cars will be operating alongside the use of conventional human-driven cars. When you go for a drive to the grocery store in your conventional car, there will be other human-driven cars among you and there will also be self-driving cars around you too. This will be a normal everyday occurrence.

Some pundits have postulated that we ought to have only self-driving cars on our roadways. This would presumably entail banning the use of human-driven cars. As you might imagine, getting the general public to give up their effort of driving cars would be quite a controversial lift. There are already stated proclamations by those anticipating such a ban on human driving that you will only take away their driving when you've pried their dead cold hands from the steering wheel.

Why would there even be a desire to make our roadways the exclusive province of self-driving cars?

One perspective is that self-driving cars will not drive while drunk, they will not drive drowsy, they will not drive while distracted, and otherwise will avoid committing the typical human foibles that lead to car crashes. In the United States, there are about 6.7 million car crashes annually, producing about 2.7 million injuries and approximately 40,000 deaths.

The hope and expectation are that the use of self-driving cars will demonstratively reduce the number of car crashes and ergo reduce the number of resultant injuries and related fatalities. This stands to reason and serves as a strong basis to push forward on the advent of self-driving cars. In short, the sooner that self-driving cars are prevalent, the sooner there will presumably be fewer vehicular-related calamities.

If you could somehow wave a magic wand and get rid of all human driving, being replaced by the use of self-driving cars, you would then eliminate whatever remaining aspects there are associated with human driving car crashes. This conjures up a visionary image of a society that has completely outlawed human driving. Our streets, highways, and byways would only have self-driving cars riding around.

The thing is, even if self-driving cars are able to be sufficiently devised as a considered replacement for the use of human driving, the pace of adoption is not going to occur overnight. There are about 250 million conventional cars in the United States alone. Those are not going to be summarily scrapped or forbidden for use.

I've stated repeatedly that it will be decades of a gradual transition from the use of human-driven cars toward the use of self-driving cars. At first, there will be very few self-driving cars on the roadways. Over time, the proportion of self-driving cars will grow and become sizable. Eventually, the tide will turn when we end up with more self-driving cars than human-driven cars. There is an open question as to the squeezing out of human driving altogether and whether this will happen by choice or by fiat.

An alternative approach entails allowing human-driven cars to be used in some situations and requires that self-driving cars be used in other settings.

For example, an oft proposed notion would be that downtown cities would proclaim that only self-driving cars will be allowed to operate in the downtown areas. No human-driven cars will be allowed. Those that wish to use human-driven cars can do so outside the boundaries of the downtown area.

But once they reach downtown, they have to park their human-driven car and if they wish to use a car, it would have to be a self-driving car.

Thus, one means of trying to enforce the use of self-driving cars would be to establish geographical boundaries for when self-driving cars versus the use of human-driven cars would be permitted. In theory, there would be places that allow only self-driving cars, and then all else would allow any mixture of both human-driven cars and self-driving cars. This would seem to placate those that insist on being able to partake in human driving, and yet glean the benefits of trying to use solely self-driving cars in particular settings.

Here's the rub.

The ongoing efforts to develop self-driving cars are continuing to be somewhat stymied or shall we say challenged by the dynamics of the driving environment. As I've explained in my columns, there are essentially too many dynamic objects in the driving scene and this can somewhat confound or at least stretch the existing limits of what AI driving systems can achieve.

Furthermore, outsized expectations are being floated at this time which will be nearly impossible for self-driving cars to somehow attain. One such false narrative is the claim that self-driving cars will be *uncrashable*, which is pure nonsense and regrettably is setting up society for a huge disappointment.

This takes us to a complicated conundrum.

On the one hand, we all presumably want self-driving cars to succeed, if nothing else due to the expected reduction in the number of car crashes. But self-driving cars are not yet advanced enough to provide some mythical notion of entirely and always avoiding any car crashes.

Suppose we could minimize the number of self-driving car crashes that might occur on our public roadways, keeping this to as small a number as feasible. Meanwhile, we would encourage self-driving cars to actively be put into use on our public roadways, doing so to further advance the capabilities and aim to make them less likely to get into car crashes.

This might provide breathing room for self-driving cars to be used on our roadways and simultaneously be ascertaining how to work out the kinks. Too, the hope would be to avoid any massive public relations nightmare that could arise if self-driving cars are used in an everyday fashion which might lead to headline-grabbing car crash mania exhortations.

Here's the clever or perhaps head-turning suggestion that some have proffered.

Establish that self-driving cars would operate *only* at the third shift or the late-night to sunrise time frame. This would be their designated time of usage. During the day, self-driving cars would be generally *not* allowed for use, other than for specified stated exceptions.

We already earlier covered the facet that there are few human-driven cars on the roads during the late-night and early morning hours. There are also very few pedestrians. There aren't many kids riding bikes and running around. All in all, the driving environment during those hours is a lot simpler than during daylight hours.

This creates for self-driving cars a driving environment that is less taxing on the AI driving systems. And it does so without causing a presumed uproar over the impact that it has on the everyday lives of humans. Depending upon how far you want to take this scenario, some would argue that there would be a restriction on human-driven cars during those hours, such that any human-driven car and the driver would get a hefty ticket for driving when the self-driving car driving period occurs.

Think too of other advantages for self-driving cars.

There is little to almost no traffic during those hours, even if the human-driven cars are still allowed at those times. This lessened amount of traffic makes things easier for the AI driving system. Fewer moving objects to deal with. Fewer chances of ramming into another car. Fewer chances of another car ramming into the self-driving car.

In addition, self-driving cars could potentially go slower than the prevailing speed limits.

A slower speed is typically easier for an AI driving system to handle in terms of computationally assessing the driving scene. For self-driving cars that are currently doing short hops to deliver goods to people's homes, those are oftentimes capped at a speed of about 20 miles per hour. The problem though with this slowed speed is that human drivers can go berserk when trapped behind such a delivering self-driving car. No worries at the late-night and early morning hours about going at a turtle's pace. There are either a scant few human drivers that will get inconvenienced or none at all. The roadway will primarily have just self-driving cars.

This brings up another useful aspect about self-driving cars, referred to as V2V (vehicle-to-vehicle) electronic communications.

Self-driving cars are going to be making use of V2V to send electronic messages to each other. Imagine that a self-driving car comes across debris on the roadway. The AI driving system can send out an electronic message to other nearby self-driving cars, letting those AI driving systems be informed about the debris. Those AI driving systems then would potentially route to a different path, or at least be computationally prepared to cope with the debris.

If self-driving cars were the predominant vehicles on the roadways during the late-night shift, which we'll also include self-driving trucks, they all could convey messages to each other via V2V. This could help in coordinating their movements and sharing useful tidbits about the roadway status.

This aspect of restricting self-driving cars to being deployed only during the third shift would not necessarily be a permanent fixture per se. At some point, the self-driving cars would seemingly have reached a capability that would make the restriction no longer applicable and would be removed.

Self-driving cars would thereafter operate at any time of the day, including still the nighttime and also during the usual daytime traffic.

Conclusion

There are a whole bunch of twists and turns to this proposal (can't cover them all herein, so here's a further taste).

Some automakers and self-driving tech firms are bound to vehemently oppose such restrictions. They would argue that it denies their AI driving systems the "experience" of daytime traffic activities. In that sense, you are ironically making things harder in terms of trying to progress the advent of self-driving cars.

Another concern is the somewhat sci-fi dystopian appearance that this might garner. Pretend that you go outside at nighttime and all that you see is this silent army of self-driving cars, going throughout your neighborhood and your local streets.

Yikes!

The machines seem to be taking over.

One for sure complaint would be that self-driving cars aren't going to be helping the needs of people that wish to travel. The nighttime treks are unlikely to involve people. By and large, the third shift activity for self-driving cars is going to be entail delivering goods.

That's unfortunate because a notable hope for the use of self-driving cars is that we will enter into an era of mobility-for-all. This is an anticipated era in which people can use cars and do so without today's usual accessibility barriers. The desire is those people that are today mobility disadvantaged will be able to readily use self-driving cars as a viable and affordable means of vehicular travel.

None of that seems to be in the cards for this nighttime self-driving car usage. Unless of course magically people started to travel around at those hours. This would seem unlikely as most of society is closed up during those periods.

Are you ready for a twist and turn on the twist?

Some suggest that if self-driving cars were readily available at nighttime and into the early morning, the availability would *induce* people to become livelier during those hours (this is akin to the concept of induced demand, see my coverage on the topic). Surprisingly, society might adjust to this newfound form of transit and become more active at the otherwise closed-up hours. Businesses would become more active at those hours.

Society might be spurred into a transformation that makes life 24-hours in duration, similar to how they say that some places like Las Vegas never sleeps.

I realize this seems farfetched and nearly unimaginable.

Okay, at least try this alternative on for size.

Some suggest that people could use self-driving cars during those hours as a means of going outstretched distances, sleeping inside the self-driving cars during the driving journey. Thus, you decide you want to visit relatives that are about a ten-hour drive away, and you simply get into a self-driving car in the evening, fall asleep since you don't have to be doing the driving, and awaken once you arrive at the house of your relatives.

That seems more within the realm of reasonable possibilities.

One last comment for now. You might have noticed that while discussing the aspects of self-driving cars, I tried to avoid referring to the late-night and early morning time frame as a *graveyard shift*. This was done purposely as an avoidance.

Here's why.

Those in the realm of the self-driving car industry have raised their eyebrows and displayed abject disgust that some might try to associate self-driving cars with driving only during a graveyard shift time frame. Their logic is impeccable as to why this would be a bad, bad thing.

Society might begin to associate self-driving cars with "graveyards" as a continual reminder that those shiny new self-driving cars are only being allowed to run around during the graveyard shift. This bodes for foul imagery of self-driving cars seemingly connected with graves and graveyards.

Not a pretty picture.

Maybe we could start a movement toward rebranding the graveyard shift. We could try to get people to expunge the graveyard shift moniker from their vocabulary. Instead, from then on, those hours are known as the self-driving car *shift*.

Yes, we would get society to believe that self-driving cars are working (tirelessly) the nighttime and early morning hours on our behalf. That's quite a grand gesture of those self-driving cars. Someday, they might get rewarded by being included in the everyday daylight shift. But only once they've earned the privilege to do so.

It makes you want to ring the bell.

CHAPTER 10
OFFRAMP SPEEDS AND SELF-DRIVING CARS

You may not know this word, but you most certainly know its meaning.

Velocitation.

What's that, you might be wondering?

It is the somewhat curious and altogether menacing phenomenon of misperceiving your speed, particularly encountered when driving a car and doing so at relatively high speeds.

Here's the deal.

You are minding your own business and driving across town via the everyday freeway system. Luckily, there isn't much traffic. You are zipping along at the allowed posted speed of 65 miles per hour, and admittedly juicing things a bit by going perhaps five to ten miles per hour faster. All in all, you are merely keeping up with the prevailing traffic.

In fact, to your credit, there are occasional cars that pass you, which means those drivers are going maybe 80 to 85 miles per hour. That seems excessive. Of course, it is downright illegal too. In any case, you watch them as they quickly come up from behind you and then zoom past you.

It is almost as though you are standing still or perhaps moving at a turtle's pace.

When you are in midst of traffic which is cruising along at your speed and on occasion somewhat faster, the whole ballgame is about relative speeds. You forget that *all of you* are moving at a high rate of speed. There is a semblance of relative speed versus thinking about the absolute speed that comes to the fore on this matter.

In those situations of everyone moving fast, your focus tends to be preoccupied with the relative differences in speeds.

To get a sense of this difference, imagine that you were standing on the side of the freeway and watching the traffic go by. A person standing still would perceive the cars as going monstrously fast. Each car would seemingly move like the wind and gush right past the unmoving observer. Those cars are all racing at breakneck speeds, so it seems.

On the other hand, when sitting in the driver's seat, and if you are moving at the same speed on the freeway as nearby cars, you don't get a visceral sense of going fast. You are all moving at the same general pace. Thus, when a car going maybe ten to twenty miles an hour goes past you, it almost seems as though you are standing still. The reality is a lot different and you are indeed proceeding at a breathtaking clip.

If you were to stay on the freeway for any substantive amount of time, you would gradually and ostensibly inexorably get used to the prevailing speed. This perception can be rudely altered or disrupted by for example getting stuck in crawling traffic that might cause you to dramatically reduce your speeds. Those bumper-to-bumper moments are bound to force you into a series of slow and fast measures, alternating as the traffic situation allows.

That knocks you out of the zoned mindless sense of a constantly high speed.

But when the speeds are steady, unbreaking, and proceeding at a top-notch pace, your mind begins to get settled into the rhythm of the speed. It is almost as though you undergo a subtle and subconscious mental calibration resetting your norms to the fast tempo. You are in the zone, as it were.

To some degree, you might not even be fully cognizant of how fast you are going.

Have you ever glanced down at your speedometer and been somewhat surprised at your speed?

That can readily happen when you are in the mental state of becoming numb to your existent pace. You were going at 55 miles per hour. Then, over a few minutes gradually increased to 65 mph. And then, you find yourself now going 75 mph. If this was done smoothly and not in any jerky efforts of acceleration, you might be shocked to notice that you are doing 75 mph when you felt like it was still 55 mph.

For getting into that mental zone, there usually can't be much if any acceleration taking place per se. Any rapid or jumpy acceleration can potentially snap you out of the fluid mindset. The zone seems to most often occur when you are simply maintaining a nearly constant fast speed. A driver's perceptions when acceleration enters into a driving journey is commonly known as accelarousal.

Okay, we've got the notion established that you can become complacent about your speed and feel as though you are not moving as fast as you really are. You might perceive your speed to be slower, possibly a lot slower, than the actual speed underway.

So what?

Well, this is where the dynamics and dangers of velocitation come to play.

Imagine that you've been driving like this for quite a while. Getting across town takes about 45 minutes or so of driving time. During the entire driving journey, you have had the good fortune of wide-open traffic and a constant full-throttle speed of about 70 miles per hour.

Easy-peasy.

Up ahead is the freeway exit that you want to take.

The posted speed limit for the offramp is 45 mph. This means that you are supposed to make sure that when you are engaged into the offramp that you try to be at 45 miles per hour or less (as suitable to existing roadway conditions). For example, if it is raining and the roads are slick, you would likely want to be going much slower, perhaps 35 mph or whatever makes sense for the situation at hand.

Let's pretend that you were going 55 mph on the freeway and began to take the offramp. At that juncture, you are doing about ten miles per hour faster than the posted speed. That's probably okay, as long as you are in the midst of reducing your speed to the indicated 45 mph. We are assuming in this scenario that it is a sunny day, the roads are nice and dry, etc.

Even if you remain at 55 mph for a tad long, you are probably still doing satisfactorily. You might find yourself getting a bit overstretched as you near the end of the offramp. Of course, if the offramp has a sharp curve to it, you will undoubtedly feel the heightened speed by the pulling forces of physics that will be trying to take the vehicle afield of the offramp. You don't want that to happen.

All in all, being around 5 to 10 miles per hour over the posted speed of the offramp might be livable, though certainly not recommended and you are perilously asking for potential troubles.

Let's recast the scenario and have you going at say 70 miles per hour.

I think you know what this is going to produce. If you take a 45 mph offramp at 70 mph, and for which you are now doing a strident 25 miles per hour excess speed, the world is not going to take this kindly. The odds are that you'll end up doing a massive heart-stopping braking action when you reach the end of the offramp. You might skid into the intersection or streets that are abutting the offramp. This is a car crash in the making.

Equally worse, when the offramp has a curved shape, you are playing with fire in that the car can go flying off the offramp. That might sound exciting, but it is not. It is a path to severe injury and potential death. You are encouraged to look online at the numerous news reports about drivers that misjudged a curved offramp and the deadly catastrophe that ensued.

You might be tempted to say that nobody in their right mind would end up taking an offramp at such an abundant speed. Only those that are drunk drivers would do so. Possibly a drowsy driver might also make that blunder. A distracted driver that is watching cat videos on their smartphone could potentially find themselves doing the same mistake.

Certainly not any rational driver that has their mind devoted to the driving task and that is diligently paying attention to the roadway.

Regrettably, I dare say, velocitation can take a chunk out of that assertion that a rational driver of a diligent nature would never misjudge an offramp in the manner heretofore depicted.

Your mind can sometimes fool you, as you likely know. Have you ever seen someone in a crowd that looked like an old friend that you haven't seen for years? You are absolutely sure it is the same person. Turns out that when you get closer, you realize that it is not the same person. An active and aware mind can potentially take what it sees and mishmash it into something else.

With velocitation, you are so accustomed to the fast speed that has become routine during a driving journey that you no longer adequately can judge your actual speed. The 70 mph feels like 55 mph, or maybe even 45 mph. Your eyes are on the roadway and the offramp, and not looking at the speedometer. You feel like there is no need to look at the speedometer since you can feel the existing speed in your bones (so you falsely believe).

After you get immersed in the offramp, you are now going to begin to realize that there is something askew about your speed and the confines of the offramp.

Oops, you realize, I'm going much too fast for this offramp. Time to bleed down some speed.

Most of the time, you probably can squeak through and get enough speed off the vehicle to still complete the offramp without a devastating result. It can be a moment though of sheer terror. Assuming you safely finish the offramp, you are sweating profusely and probably swear an oath that you will never let yourself be taken in again.

The thing is, velocitation is somewhat insidious.

Some people don't know that such a phenomenon exists. They are oblivious to the possibility of it. The instances of taking an offramp too fast are usually chalked up as a kind of oddity or quirky circumstance. Those drivers that are unfamiliar with this mental perception issue are assuming that any such occurrence is a fluke, a one-time occasion.

Other people know about the aspects of velocitation, perhaps vaguely so, and might not realize there is a word devoted to this particular manner of concern. Yet, despite the awareness of the potential for misjudging their speed, they make the same error repeatedly.

That's oftentimes because drivers tend to overrate their own driving prowess.

Sure, maybe you got caught by velocitation a month ago, but you are better than that and know that this won't grip you ever again. Lo and behold, a trip across town happens and perhaps the same thing occurs a second time.

What can help to break out of that mental zone would be any foul memories about that particular offramp. Thus, if you were to take that same offramp at a later date, your mind might flashback to the terror of previously using that offramp.

In that case, you might slow down adequately. In fact, you might overcompensate and essentially take your car to a crawling speed on that exit.

Your mind might not generalize the matter to other offramps. This suggests that if you drove across town and decide to take a *different* offramp, you could get tricked again. You have flagged in your mind the dangers of the other offramp. This newly being used offramp is clean in terms of your memories and not bound to spark any concerns.

Another factor that comes to play is the nature of your car.

In the earlier days of automobiles, the engine noise would be a key differentiator about your prevailing speed. While driving a car, you could pretty much gauge the speed by listening to the sound of the engine. No need to look at the speedometer. Your hearing was enough to tell you all that you needed to know about your pace.

Likewise, cars might rattle or prattle as your speed got faster. This added an additional sound as a clue to your speed. Furthermore, you could feel the speed rattling your entire body. When your driver's seat was shifting back and forth or shaking, that was a sign of your speed. Your body and limbs could feel the essence of the speed.

Modern cars are usually built so solidly that few if any of those cues are still identifiable. You probably won't hear the sound of the engine as you get to higher and higher speeds. There is plenty of specially designed soundproofing materials that deaden the sounds from coming into the interior of the vehicle. The shock absorbers and other contraptions are provided to ensure a smooth ride.

All in all, you would be hard-pressed to ascertain your speed via something that the car is doing, other than by looking at the speedometer.

As mentioned earlier, you would have other important clues as evidenced by the other traffic around you. When nearby traffic is going at a widely varying array of speeds, you are probably going to be a lot more cognizant of your speed.

If there isn't any other traffic, you can be embraced by velocitation, and similarly if there is constant and seamless traffic the same can occur.

I trust that you are willing to agree that velocitation exists and that drivers need to be mindful about getting sucked into the void of misjudging their vehicle and its speed.

Let's next consult our crystal ball and gaze into the future.

Consider that the future of cars consists of AI-based true self-driving cars.

There isn't a human driver involved in a true self-driving car. Keep in mind that true self-driving cars are driven via an AI driving system. There isn't a need for a human driver at the wheel, and nor is there a provision for a human to drive the vehicle.

Here's an intriguing question that is worth pondering: *Is it conceivable that AI-based true self-driving cars might be susceptible to velocitation, and if so, what can be done about this?*

I'd like to first further clarify what is meant when I refer to true self-driving cars.

Understanding The Levels Of Self-Driving Cars

As a clarification, true self-driving cars are ones that the AI drives the car entirely on its own and there isn't any human assistance during the driving task.

These driverless vehicles are considered Level 4 and Level 5, while a car that requires a human driver to co-share the driving effort is usually considered at Level 2 or Level 3. The cars that co-share the driving task are described as being semi-autonomous, and typically contain a variety of automated add-on's that are referred to as ADAS (Advanced Driver-Assistance Systems).

There is not yet a true self-driving car at Level 5, which we don't yet even know if this will be possible to achieve, and nor how long it will take to get there.

Meanwhile, the Level 4 efforts are gradually trying to get some traction by undergoing very narrow and selective public roadway trials, though there is controversy over whether this testing should be allowed per se (we are all life-or-death guinea pigs in an experiment taking place on our highways and byways, some contend).

Since semi-autonomous cars require a human driver, the adoption of those types of cars won't be markedly different than driving conventional vehicles, so there's not much new per se to cover about them on this topic (though, as you'll see in a moment, the points next made are generally applicable).

For semi-autonomous cars, it is important that the public needs to be forewarned about a disturbing aspect that's been arising lately, namely that despite those human drivers that keep posting videos of themselves falling asleep at the wheel of a Level 2 or Level 3 car, we all need to avoid being misled into believing that the driver can take away their attention from the driving task while driving a semi-autonomous car.

You are the responsible party for the driving actions of the vehicle, regardless of how much automation might be tossed into a Level 2 or Level 3.

Self-Driving Cars And Velocitation

For Level 4 and Level 5 true self-driving vehicles, there won't be a human driver involved in the driving task.

All occupants will be passengers.

The AI is doing the driving.

One aspect to immediately discuss entails the fact that the AI involved in today's AI driving systems is not sentient. In other words, the AI is altogether a collective of computer-based programming and algorithms, and most assuredly not able to reason in the same manner that humans can.

Why is this added emphasis about the AI not being sentient?

Because I want to underscore that when discussing the role of the AI driving system, I am not ascribing human qualities to the AI. Please be aware that there is an ongoing and dangerous tendency these days to anthropomorphize AI. In essence, people are assigning human-like sentience to today's AI, despite the undeniable and inarguable fact that no such AI exists as yet.

With that clarification, you can envision that the AI driving system won't natively somehow "know" about the facets of driving. Driving and all that it entails will need to be programmed as part of the hardware and software of the self-driving car.

Let's dive into the myriad of aspects that come to play on this topic.

The first place to start this discussion consists of clearly acknowledging that today's AI driving systems are not sentient and therefore cannot be subject to velocitation in the same manner as human beings. In short, if you strictly assert that velocitation *requires* human eyes and a human brain, we can summarily then reject the possibility of self-driving cars as being susceptible to velocitation.

Case seemingly closed.

But wait for a second, perhaps we can use the velocitation conceptually to glean some insights into what might go awry with self-driving cars.

Is it possible that a self-driving car could take an offramp at too high a speed?

Yes, absolutely so.

Let's explore the various ways that this could happen.

One obvious aspect would be that the AI driving system could potentially fail to have an accurate indication of what the speed for a given offramp is supposed to be. If that were the case, it is conceivable that the self-driving car could be moving along at the prevailing freeway speed as it comes onto and uses the offramp. The AI driving system would be awaiting some other indication that the speed should be lessened, otherwise the existing speed prevails.

I'm sure you are already clamoring that the AI driving system ought to have digital maps that include the offramp and therefore would have a stated speed that is associated with the offramp. As such, the odds are that the AI driving system would be able to readily direct the driving controls to reduce the freeway speed of the self-driving car accordingly as it utilizes the offramp.

Though most automakers and self-driving tech firms are indeed making use of extensive digital maps, this is not always necessarily the case. In addition, there is a chance (admittedly slim) that the digital map has an inaccurate indication about the offramp speed.

Okay, you might say, but certainly, the self-driving car is going to detect a roadway sign that showcases the allowed speed for that offramp.

Yes, it would normally be the case that the sensors of the self-driving car would presumably detect such a roadway sign. This would principally be done via the use of video cameras. Upon the video camera images being examined via Machine Learning (ML) and Deep Learning (DL) technologies, those computational pattern matching algorithms are apt to discern that there is a posted sign and also determine that the sign provides an indicated speed.

In the future, the expectation is that much of the roadway infrastructure will be making use of V2I (vehicle-to-infrastructure) electronic communications. There will be various devices such as IoT (Internet of Things) and edge computing units all over our highways and byways. Traffic signals will be beaming out electronic signals that self-driving cars can receive and ergo be alerted to whether the light is red, green, or yellow. Bridges can send out V2I that indicates when the bridge is closed or otherwise unavailable. Etc.

You can anticipate that roadway signs such as posted speed limits will also be part of the V2I efforts. Those signs will be beaming out an electronic signal indicating the speed in that area. In addition, the speed could be variable so that at some times of the day it has a "posted" speed of say 35, while at other times of the day a different speed is stated.

Anyway, that's more about the future and not what we have in hand today.

We were discussing that the self-driving car ought to be using its sensors to visually discern the offramp stated speed via capturing images of the driving scene and looking for an appropriate posted sign. This would seem to dispense with any reliance on a digital map since the posted sign would seemingly be the final arbiter of what the speed is.

The problem with relying solely on a posted sign is that the sign might be rigged or it might not be there. In the case of not being there, suppose the posted sign got struck by a wayward car and got knocked down to the ground, and has not yet been reposted. That means there isn't any posted sign to be readily discovered (it is laying in the dirt and marginally visible).

In terms of being rigged, there are ongoing concerns that self-driving cars can be potentially tricked in rather simple and highly dangerous ways. By masking a stop sign or altering the numbers on a speed limit sign, it is feasible to fool the AI driving system into making mistakes about the driving conditions. A human driver uses common sense (most of the time) to realize when something is amiss.

Efforts to imbue AI systems with common sense are ongoing but have been sorely lacking so far.

All in all, the emphasis is that a self-driving car might not have a proper indication about the offramp permitted speed. It might even have a false indication that was purposely crafted by evildoers to beguile self-driving cars. Generally, this is seemingly unlikely at this juncture and we can assess that it won't happen with any frequency.

Nonetheless, it can happen and sadly will happen.

Another possible way to have a self-driving car falter when using an offramp would be to have the AI driving system fail to ascertain that the offramp is an offramp.

How so?

Consider something that maybe has happened to you.

You might have been using your GPS and mapping software to drive in an area that has lots of freeway lanes and offramps and noticed that sometimes the system gets somewhat confounded. For example, a lane that branches off the freeway onto a different freeway can be the target lane that you are supposed to take. Imagine that you inadvertently don't make it into that lane. You've perhaps seen instances when the GPS and mapping system portrayed your location as though you were on that branching lane, even though you were still on the regular lane of the freeway.

In the case of a self-driving car, suppose the GPS and mapping were showcasing the autonomous vehicle as though it was still on the freeway, despite the fact that the AI driving system is maneuvering the self-driving car onto the offramp. This momentarily can create some difficulty for the AI driving system. Presumably, the sensors are indicating that the self-driving car is no longer on the freeway per se, meanwhile, the map is indicating to the contrary.

This could lead to the potential of the self-driving car not reducing speed as matching to the needs of the offramp.

Here's yet another possibility.

Some self-driving cars are programmed to do what insiders refer to as a follow-the-leader driving approach. The AI driving system detects a car ahead of it. If the car ahead slows down, the AI driving system will slow down the self-driving car. If the car ahead speeds up, the AI driving system will speed up the self-driving car.

Envision a human-driven car that opts to take the offramp and the human driver is experiencing a bit of velocitation and going too fast. A self-driving car is immediately behind the human-driven car and also taking the same offramp.

At that juncture, the AI driving system might calculate that it is okay to match the speed of the car ahead. Whether the AI driving system also has detected the posted speed sign or maybe has digital maps, could get the algorithm to computationally ascertain that following the human driver in this manner is inappropriate. Thus, the follow-the-leader is momentarily overridden.

On the other hand, it is also possible that the follow-the-leader is the "best" data that the AI driving system has. In that case, like lemmings going off of a cliff together, there is a danger that the self-driving car will follow the human-driven car into potential doom.

Numerous other possibilities could get the self-driving car into trouble about the offramp.

Suppose the self-driving car has some kind of bug or error in the software. This can happen. Keep in mind that there are going to be perhaps millions upon millions of lines of code, ostensibly hundreds of millions, and there are lurking errors that have yet to show themselves.

A bad bug at the wrong time could get the self-driving car into an out of sorts status as it proceeds down the offramp.

Conclusion

I've somewhat focused on velocitation when it comes to using a freeway and taking an offramp, but that's just a particular use case (a quite common one).

Velocitation can arise in other ways.

You might be on a lengthy highway. You might be on a long stretch of streets.

Those two have the same potential issues involving getting accustomed to a speed and misjudging what your actual speed is. If you are at some juncture wanting to make an upcoming left or right turn, your realization of your present speed versus the speed required for the turn can be askew.

For humans, velocitation can readily arise and catch us quite off-guard. Surprisingly, those that know about this vexing mental perception vulnerability can still fall into its dangerous and potentially deadly trap. That is the very definition of being insidious, it would seem.

AI self-driving cars can have similar kinds of difficulties, which we would not want to especially label as velocitation, due to the desire to avoid anthropomorphizing the AI. That being said, it is useful to consider the myriad of human foibles at driving and see what we can learn from how humans make mistakes while at the wheel.

Those human guffaws are surely helpful for trying to make AI driving systems be the best drivers that they can be.

CHAPTER 11
USERS BANNED FROM SELF-DRIVING CARS

People keep getting banned for doing the darndest and seemingly dumbest of acts.

Oftentimes getting banned for the rest of their entire life.

You might have heard or seen the recent brouhaha in major league baseball when a spectator in Yankee Stadium seated above leftfield opted to throw a baseball down onto the field that then struck the Boston Red Sox player Alex Verdugo in the back. He was not hurt, but you can imagine the personal dismay and shock at suddenly and unexpectedly having a projectile strike him from behind, seemingly out of nowhere.

Turns out that Alex had earlier tossed the same baseball up into the stands as a memento for a young Red Sox cheering attendee. By some boorish grabbing, it had ended up in the hands of a New York Yankees fan. Next, after some hysterical urging by other frenetic Yankees to toss it back, the young man did so. Whether this act of defiance was intentionally devised to smack the left-fielder is still unclear and it could have been a happenstance rather than a purposeful aim.

Regardless, this can instigate a highly dangerous slippery slope as sparked by the wayward or calculated act of an individual fan. If one person can get away with this, you can bet that others will soon thereafter try doing the same. It starts with an errant baseball and the next thing you know there is all manner of debris and piercing objects being rained down upon the players on the field.

As later on officially stated by the Yankees organization, this act by the attendee was considered a reckless, disorderly, and dangerous form of behavior and simply will not be tolerated.

Period, full stop.

Plus, this declarative condemnation is more than mere talk.

To showcase a serious and somber resolve to enforce the presumed walk-with-the-talk, as it were, this particular fan has been banned from attending any further games at Yankee Stadium. On top of that, the rest of the major league also agreed to ban the fan. And on top of that, this is a lifetime ban.

Presumably, the fan can never again attend in-person any major league baseball game for the rest of his life.

If the young fan is perhaps in his early 20s right now, this means that he cannot attend any major league baseball games when he is in his 30s, nor in his 40s, 50s, 60s, 70s, 80s, 90s, and however long he lives.

Think about that.

For example sixty years from now, in the year 2081, he still won't be able to attend such a game. What will the future world be like in that year? Will we all be finally traveling around via the use of jetpacks on our backs? Will we already be living on Mars? Say, you wonder, if major league baseball starts to play on Mars, will this particular ban still apply or is it only relegated to games played on Earth?

I suppose cynics might say this latest ban is not much of a penalty and point out that the wrongdoer can still watch the baseball games from home or anywhere else on TV, including possibly finding a position outside a stadium that allows him to directly peer into the field of play. He might also personally decide that he never wants to watch a major league baseball game again, anyway, and thus the penalty is rather mute from his perspective.

Still, it does seem like there has got to be a bit of a sting to know that he'll always be banned from attending all those baseball games for the rest of his time on this planet. We might assume he was something of a baseball fan, to begin with. Furthermore, the now declared ban might get him into the fevered mood of eagerly wanting to attend future games, as much or more so than before having gotten the ban placed upon him (a classic response to the enactment of the forbidden fruit).

Some wonder about the practical nature of enforcing the ban.

The assumption is that the major league baseball organizations all have his name and can seek to stop him from buying a ticket using his name. That of course is under the logic that he would use his real name to purchase a ticket. Also, unless attending baseball games goes the route akin to flying on airplanes, including having a TSA-like check-in to see your formal ID and ascertain whether you can proceed accordingly, it seems like this ostensibly banned fan can likely skirt around the sanction.

Speaking of the TSA, the notion of banning someone is especially known via the ongoing and seeming increasing efforts to ban people from flying that have performed some notable transgression.

We daily witness online videos of flying passengers that go berserk during a flight or while getting onto a plane. The particular airline involved then announces that the person is being banned from all further flights on that airline. This can sometimes be taken up too by other airlines that agree to equally enforce the ban.

The federal government officially has the famous (or infamous) no-fly list, assuredly one of the most widely known types of bans when it comes to nearly anything that is banned. News outlets indicate that the feds no-fly list has around 3,000 names on it. Some people are considered banned forever, while others are banned on a timed basis that might consist of months or years in duration.

You would naturally expect that this type of ban has some teeth to it since getting onto a commercial flight takes quite a bit of identification checking. The belief is that a person would not readily be able to find a means to evade the ban. That being said, as it is with humans and their altogether devious ways, where there is a will there is a potential means of circumvention.

Where else might people find themselves getting banned?

Self-driving cars.

Consider that the future of cars consists of AI-based true self-driving cars.

There isn't a human driver involved in a true self-driving car. Keep in mind that true self-driving cars are driven via an AI driving system. There isn't a need for a human driver at the wheel, and nor is there a provision for a human to drive the vehicle.

Here's an intriguing question that is worth pondering: *Is it conceivable that AI-based true self-driving cars might rally together to ban particular passengers from ever riding again in a self-driving car?*

I'd like to first further clarify what is meant when I refer to true self-driving cars.

Understanding The Levels Of Self-Driving Cars

As a clarification, true self-driving cars are ones that the AI drives the car entirely on its own and there isn't any human assistance during the driving task.

These driverless vehicles are considered Level 4 and Level 5, while a car that requires a human driver to co-share the driving effort is usually considered at Level 2 or Level 3. The cars that co-share the driving task are described as being semi-autonomous, and typically contain a variety of automated add-on's that are referred to as ADAS (Advanced Driver-Assistance Systems).

There is not yet a true self-driving car at Level 5, which we don't yet even know if this will be possible to achieve, and nor how long it will take to get there.

Meanwhile, the Level 4 efforts are gradually trying to get some traction by undergoing very narrow and selective public roadway trials, though there is controversy over whether this testing should be allowed per se (we are all life-or-death guinea pigs in an experiment taking place on our highways and byways, some contend).

Since semi-autonomous cars require a human driver, the adoption of those types of cars won't be markedly different than driving conventional vehicles, so there's not much new per se to cover about them on this topic (though, as you'll see in a moment, the points next made are generally applicable).

For semi-autonomous cars, it is important that the public needs to be forewarned about a disturbing aspect that's been arising lately, namely that despite those human drivers that keep posting videos of themselves falling asleep at the wheel of a Level 2 or Level 3 car, we all need to avoid being misled into believing that the driver can take away their attention from the driving task while driving a semi-autonomous car.

You are the responsible party for the driving actions of the vehicle, regardless of how much automation might be tossed into a Level 2 or Level 3.

Self-Driving Cars And Banning Bad Passengers

For Level 4 and Level 5 true self-driving vehicles, there won't be a human driver involved in the driving task.

All occupants will be passengers.

The AI is doing the driving.

One aspect to immediately discuss entails the fact that the AI involved in today's AI driving systems is not sentient. In other words, the AI is altogether a collective of computer-based programming and algorithms, and most assuredly not able to reason in the same manner that humans can.

Why is this added emphasis about the AI not being sentient?

Because I want to underscore that when discussing the role of the AI driving system, I am not ascribing human qualities to the AI. Please be aware that there is an ongoing and dangerous tendency these days to anthropomorphize AI. In essence, people are assigning human-like sentience to today's AI, despite the undeniable and inarguable fact that no such AI exists as yet.

With that clarification, you can envision that the AI driving system won't natively somehow "know" about the facets of driving. Driving and all that it entails will need to be programmed as part of the hardware and software of the self-driving car.

Let's dive into the myriad of aspects that come to play on this topic.

First, you might be curious as to why someone would potentially be banned from riding in a self-driving car.

We currently think of self-driving cars as exciting and a novelty. There are plenty of posted videos of people riding in an existing self-driving tryout. They seem to be happy. They seem to relish being inside a self-driving car. This is like tasting a piece of the future by getting a chance now to early-days glean what the world will inevitably become.

The thrill though won't last.

I've exhorted repeatedly that the excitement of being a passenger inside a self-driving car does not have a particularly lengthy stasis.

Once you've gotten used to the idea that there isn't a human seated in the driver's seat, you begin to be less caring about the fact that there is a hidden AI driving system that is pulling all the strings and operating the driving controls. It becomes an old hat and loses its allure as a novelty.

My strident prediction is that self-driving cars are going to face some pretty fierce competition.

The competition is whether prospective passengers will choose to ride in a self-driving car versus a human-driven car. You assume that of course, everyone will pick a self-driving car, but I would advise caution on that core belief.

If the price to use a self-driving car is less than the comparable human-driven car, you would likely be on relatively safe ground to claim that riders will clamor toward using self-driving cars. The hope is that the cost of self-driving cars is going to be lowered due to the lack of human-driver labor, and as such, the per-mile pricing will be quite inexpensive.

On that basis, pundits are predicting an era of mobility-for-all, whereby those that cannot afford to use a car today will be able to use self-driving cars.

Suppose though that the price to use self-driving cars is on par with human-driven cars, or possibly even more costly. What then? Other than taking a self-driving car as a first-time experience, you would need to weigh the cost difference for each subsequent ride. Paying attention to your wallet is probably going to be more vital than simply taking a mundane everyday ride in what just so happens to be a self-driving car. There are even voiced concerns that self-driving cars might be only usable by the extremely wealthy and special celebrities.

In any case, let's take at face value that self-driving cars will gradually become prevalent and the pricing will be moderate, ergo people will often make use of self-driving cars over selecting instead a human-driven car.

So, we are going to have all kinds of people in all kinds of places in all kinds of life circumstances that will be passengers inside self-driving cars.

You certainly have to anticipate that humans will do unruly things.

Especially since there isn't a human driver at the wheel, whereby the human driver is usually a type of craziness inhibitor that keeps passengers from going wild. The driver can tell riders to stay still. The driver can give the passengers a mean look that tells them to behave themselves. The driver can potentially tattle on bad behaving passengers, perhaps by calling the police or other authorities.

What might unfettered passengers do while inside a self-driving car?

The sky is the limit.

Some passengers might be quiet and respectful, staying properly seated during the entire driving journey. I'd like to think that will constitute the preponderance of passengers. Give that a smiley face view of the world.

Then there are the outliers (give that a frown face emoji).

While inside a self-driving car, you might as well party it up. Have a ruckus of a time. Roll down the windows and stick your head and other limbs outside the autonomous vehicle. Wave at people. Scream at people. You can do all of this because there isn't that onerous human driver trying to urge you to get back into the car. You are finally free.

I am even anticipating that we might still have variants of road rage.

Yes, despite not having anyone at the wheel, it is conceivable that some passengers will anyway wield a gun and opt to potentially use it. This seems unimaginable simply due to the obvious factor that they cannot then command the AI driving system to sprint away and escape from the scene of the crime. Though this lack of being able to dart away ought to stop any such shenanigans, don't bet on it.

A decidedly sinister act would be a cyber crook that gets into a self-driving car and tries to reprogram the AI driving system. By being inside the autonomous vehicle, the evildoer hacker can potentially crack into the onboard processors and enact some villainous scheme. This is the kind of person that we might all agree should be banned from being a "rider" inside a self-driving car.

The overall point is that it is certainly possible that some passengers will do bad things while riding in self-driving cars. Besides doing something outrageous that alarms those around the self-driving car, other adverse actions would entail doing destructive acts to the interior of the self-driving car. You can envision some shady people that might decide to rip up the seats or spray paint graffiti within a self-driving car.

For any of a myriad of reasons, a fleet operator of a set of self-driving cars might likely decide they want to ban a particular rider from using their fleet again. This ban might be time-based such as for the day, a week, a month, or for several years. It could also be a lifetime ban.

How will this ban be enforced?

This is actually easier to do and more stringent than nearly all the other types of banning circumstances of today.

Keep in mind that self-driving cars will be loaded with lots of sensory devices. There are video cameras, radar, LIDAR, ultrasonic units, thermal imagining, and the like. When a self-driving car comes to pick you up based on your request, it can "see you" and scan to try ascertaining who you are. For example, facial recognition would be an obvious form of detection and identification.

Someone that had been a prior rowdy passenger could readily be added to a self-driving car fleet database that is the equivalent of a localized no-fly list. This fleet database would be accessible by all of the self-driving cars in the fleet, doing so by using OTA (Over-the-Air) electronic communications. The database would presumably be in a cloud that is maintained by the fleet operator. All of the self-driving cars in the fleet would routinely download the no-fly data into the onboard computers of the autonomous vehicle.

Thus, any of the self-driving cars in that fleet could seek to directly determine whether a prospective passenger has been banned from using those autonomous vehicles. This detection could occur when the person walks up to get into the self-driving car.

If somehow the person can skirt past that detection, there are other secondary means of scrutinizing the person. Once the person gets into the self-driving car, the sensors can continue to examine the person.

There are likely inward-facing video cameras and microphones, usually intended to allow for being able to do fun and useful things while riding in a self-driving car. One expectation is that people might take online training courses that they can complete during their daily commute to work. You get into a self-driving car on your way to work in the morning, do part of an online training class, and then when you head home at night you continue the coursework. This turns your "wasted" or idle time of being inside a car as a rider into something personally fruitful.

Well, it is possible that the video cameras and microphones could be on even if you weren't necessarily aware of their presence. Assume that in some prior ride you had messed around and the circumstance was entirely recorded on video and audio, subsequently stored into the cloud database of the fleet operator. The AI could then analyze that video and audio, such that upon being in a self-driving car at a later date, the AI driving system could potentially pinpoint that it is you again, based on the prior visual images and the audio signature of your voice.

In short, it is going to be a lot easier to try and enforce a ban due to the chockful of state-of-the-art sensors on a self-driving car. The sensors are there mainly for purposes of self-driving, though they can be used for a variety of other purposes too.

As an important aside, there is a hornet's nest of privacy intrusion issues that this is going to bring to the fore, I refer to this as the "roving eye" of self-driving cars.

Conclusion

Note that I've emphasized that the ban would seemingly be initiated by a particular fleet operator. I mention this because the belief generally is that self-driving cars will be deployed in fleets.

A company might decide that they are going to purchase or lease a large bunch of self-driving cars from a particular automaker or self-driving tech firm, and then deploy those in a specific area. They are then a fleet operator in that area.

There might be other companies that do likewise and also opt to put their fleet in that same area. You then have a multitude of fleets operating in the same geographic area. Each of the fleets is considered distinct, likely having their own cloud-based systems to keep track of data collected by their respective fleet.

Okay, so one of the fleets decides to ban a passenger. This ban might be only effective for that specific fleet in that particular geographic area. If the company perchance has other fleets in various other cities or towns, perhaps the company might notify those other allied fleets too. In addition, the fleets in a given area might have a cooperative agreement amongst themselves. They might opt to share the various disparate no-fly lists.

If that happened, the person listed would presumably not be able to get any self-driving car as a rider anywhere that those fleets operate.

All told, this could radiate outwards extensively and a person would essentially be banned from using any self-driving cars anywhere throughout the country. Depending upon how far the fleets extend, this could end up being a worldwide ban.

Now, to be clear about this, the whole arrangement of having banned lists that are shared and traded back and forth by the numerous fleet operators of self-driving cars is a bit of an overstretch in that this doesn't yet exist. Nonetheless, the technological facets are relatively trivial and it would mainly be a matter of the cost to put such a program in place. The cost might be worth it, attempting to keep the bad apples of unsavory passengers out of the self-driving cars of the numerous fleets.

You can imagine that any especially unruly or outrageous rider could indeed be a bad apple that spoils the entire barrel of self-driving cars in society. If the over-the-top foul acts grab headlines, which you can be assured would happen since they touched upon the advent of self-driving cars, there would be a potentially pulling back from self-driving cars. People might be worried about what nutty passengers are going to do.

There is a chance too that regulators would get into the ballgame, as it were. There readily could be a federally maintained list of those that are not to be allowed to ride in self-driving cars. This kind of overarching no-fly list then would presumably be observed and obeyed by all self-driving cars being operated nationwide.

There are numerous twists and turns on this, which I won't cover fully herein, but will proffer a few prominent ones.

Passengers that get embroiled in the self-driving car rider banning might believe they are falsely accused or might assert that they were somewhat deserving but that the time length of the ban is overly burdensome and uncalled for. Someone that gets a lifetime ban could argue that being banned for a year would be sufficient rather than for the rest of their life. That kind of thing.

Thus, one aspect you can pretty much guarantee about banning people from riding in self-driving cars is that it will ultimately and nearly immediately land into our courts. Lawyers are likely going to be eager to fight these battles.

Yet another twist is something that I slightly glossed over earlier, and that you might have caught out of the corner of your eye.

I had stated that passengers will possibly go wild and do crazy things while inside self-driving cars because there isn't a human driver present to give them the evil eye and tone them down. That makes indubitable sense that without humans overseeing other humans, misbehavior can result.

In the same breath, I mentioned that self-driving cars will likely have inward-facing video cameras and microphones. This would allow for recording the misbehaviors of passengers. Noted too is that this could be construed as a potential privacy intrusion.

The point now is that the AI driving system could potentially use inward-facing cameras and microphones to detect in *real-time* that someone is misbehaving while inside the self-driving car. Based on that suspected misbehavior, the AI driving system might instruct the rider to immediately quit monkeying around. If that didn't do the trick, the AI driving system could indicate it will come to the soonest feasible safe stop and will not proceed with the ride.

And if that didn't solve the matter, the AI driving system could alert the authorities, such as dialing 911 and reporting the offending passenger to the local police. You could even have the AI driving system take the passenger to a nearby police station or at least rendezvous with a dispatched police car.

I bring up this somewhat scary portrayal (scary because some liken this to a Big Brother overlord scenario), due to the assertion by some pundits that nobody is ever going to get riled up while riding inside a self-driving car. The passengers will realize that doing so is going to be instantly detected and they can find themselves either no longer able to ride or being delivered to the authorities.

What do you think?

Perhaps these usage safeguards assure that nobody will consider doing anything untoward while riding in a self-driving car. We will all be respectful and civil during our self-driving car rides. Yes, all of society will be compliant and no one will try to step out of line.

That's going to be quite an interesting future to see. No bans are presumably needed, at least in the use case of self-driving cars. You can gleefully go your entire life riding in self-driving cars and won't have to second-guess whether you are allowed to be riding in one or not.

And you can take a self-driving car to the ballpark, though it is conceivable you might be banned at the stadium gates there, but, hey, at least the self-driving car didn't ban you.

That's assuredly taking you *out* to the ballgame.

CHAPTER 12
TEEN SWERVES AND SELF-DRIVING CARS

Honest Abe.

That was the moniker given to our famous statesman and sixteenth president of the United States, namely Abraham Lincoln.

He well-earned the nickname. Furthermore, the catchy phrase became widely known and popularized during his lifetime and of course, was everlasting too.

There are plenty of stories about Abe's honest ways.

Some are large-scale examples and others are seemingly trivial but nonetheless telling. The small ones are ostensibly as important as the big ones if nothing else as evidence that this was a trait that was through-and-through and not merely by happenstance or when the right moment perchance presented itself.

For example, one tale is that when he was working as a store clerk a customer paid for some items and left the store, and upon further reflection, Abe ascertained that the customer had inadvertently been overcharged by six cents. Six cents isn't much money today, and even back then it wouldn't have been a fortune, though the fact that the customer was overcharged was the pivotal matter at hand. Apparently, once the store closed for the day, Abe walked several miles to the home of the customer and returned the overpaid six cents.

As they say, honesty is the best policy.

Of course, a cynic might point out that if Abe had not returned the six cents, and if the customer discovered the error on their own, the customer could have made quite a ruckus. And a store in a small town could be nearly put out of business if local customers thought it was some kind of a rip-off operation. In that sense, it was the practical and prudent thing to right away return the overpaid amount, averting a potential for a dire and adverse consequence to the liveliness and survivability of the local store.

Be that as it may, let's go ahead and stick with the stout remark that honesty is nonetheless still the best policy and leave things there for now.

I bring up Abe Lincoln due to a recent errant car incident that unintentionally plowed into the historic Samuel Lincoln Cottage located in Hingham, Massachusetts.

This is a longstanding home that was built in 1650 and occupied by Abe's great-great-great-great-grandfather (according to historical records). For those of you that are savvy history buffs, rest assured that this is not the same as the Samuel Lincoln House, which is just a bit down the street from the revered cottage. There are quite a number of vital structures in that same Hingham geographic locality that are all part of the Lincoln Local Historic District.

Anyway, here's what happened.

A teenager was driving an everyday car there in the Lincoln Local Historic District and minding their own business when (according to the driver) a squirrel suddenly ran into the street. The teenager did not want to strike and potentially harm or outright kill the squirrel. Thus, the teenager opted to swerve and try to avoid the bushy-tailed little creature.

In the act of swerving, the teenager generally lost control of the car and went up and over the curb of the street. Continuing forward, the car then skirted across a small sidewalk and rammed into the side of the Samuel Lincoln Cottage.

Bam! Bash! Crash! Smash!

Pictures released by the Hingham Police Department are quite revealing as to the amount of damage done. The vehicle seems to have gone sideways into a major wall that is adjacent to the front door of the home. The right side front area of the car slammed into the wooden wall and created a massive opening. In addition, pictures of the interior showcase a lot of debris such as shattered wood tables, chairs, and other items.

To clarify, the cottage was not destroyed. It still stands.

We can though likely agree that there is a lot of damage and will be costly to repair. On top of that, one could have some despair that this is historically an important home and that making repairs might undermine the original nature of the structure. That being said, it is hard to imagine that this cottage of some hundreds of years of age hasn't already had plenty of retrofits and fixes during those many years of standing tall.

Beyond the historical elements, we can rejoice that nobody was hurt in this car crash.

The teenage driver seemed to be fine and was sitting on the sidewalk awaiting the arrival of the local constables (per the official police report that was later formally filed). None of the residents inside the cottage were injured. This is nearly a miracle since anyone that might have been seated or standing in that part of the house would certainly have gotten struck, either by the wayward vehicle or by flying debris.

You can almost envisage that the driver would not have been seriously injured due to the aspect that this was a relatively modern car that had various contemporary safety features (it was a 2014 Audi Q7). The vehicle should have pretty much protected the driver. Also, it seems that the speed at impact could not have been particularly high, thus the forces involved were less so than a car crash on an open highway or freeway.

The teenage driver was issued a citation for unlawfully staying in the marked lanes. Assuming too that the driver perhaps lives at home with parents, it stands to reason that perhaps the scolding upon getting home was nearly worse than receiving the citation. The apparent damages done to the car appear to be somewhat modest and repairable.

You might be thinking that this is an interesting news item about a car crash but that other than the coincidental fact that the vehicle struck a venerated Lincoln ancestry structure, there isn't much else of noteworthiness involved.

Well, truthfully, you'd be somewhat mistaken in that assumption.

Here's the first twist.

Social media immediately questioned the claim that a squirrel was the culprit in this car crash.

Aha, some caustically stated, the old blame-it-on the squirrel trickery. Skeptics roundly asserted that the teenage driver was probably using a smartphone and texting, or maybe watching cat videos (perhaps, ironically, watching videos of cats chasing squirrels!).

This altogether presumed distracted newbie driver sought to pin the blame on an imaginary furry animal, those naysayers contend. Doing so makes indubitable sense. If you were the driver and divulged freely that you were driving while distracted, the nature of the citation is seemingly going to get more severe. The beauty too is that by having saved the life of an innocent squirrel, the driver appears to be a heartwarming person that was doing whatever they could to spare the tiny creature, including putting their own human life at risk.

What would Honest Abe say?

If Abe had been at the wheel, we would of course presume that whatever he said was the gosh-darned honest and unbridled truth.

In this recent case, there do not seem to be any witnesses to the car crash and nor any video captured that would show precisely what happened. As far as can be discerned, the teenage driver is the only one that knows exactly what occurred.

I suppose you could suggest that the squirrel knows.

If indeed there is one that was involved.

I'm not sure how we could sufficiently interview the squirrel to find out what it has to say. Maybe someday we'll have animal-to-human AI-based machine translators that can figure this kind of thing out. Hey, Alexa, translate that squirrel chirping over there (that kind of thing). Not today.

I'd vote that we give the teenager a kindly break in life and assume that there was a squirrel and that the incident entailed avoiding squashing one. That seems like the right thing to assume. Nobody ended up getting hurt and the damages to the car and the cottage can be repaired.

Matter closed.

But wait for a second, there's more.

Did the driver really do the proper driving act?

Most of us would undeniably agree that squirrels can be endearing, there's little doubt about that. On the other hand, if you are at the wheel of a car and driving along, and you have to choose between hitting a squirrel and perhaps hitting a pedestrian by swerving, which would you choose? All else being equal, you'd better be choosing to strike the squirrel over striking the human (some might disagree, but would likely find themselves on feeble ground when explaining their choice).

Now, to be abundantly clear, the squirrel versus pedestrian dilemma was not an aspect of this particular car crash case.

The hidden factor that maybe you might not have considered is that there could have been, and it turns out that there were, people inside the house that was struck. Thus, even though pedestrians were not at risk, the innocent people residing in that cottage were definitely at risk.

The point is that other people besides the driver were intertwined into the driving action and had a stake in how the driver made their choice. These "bystanders" weren't as obvious as when you see pedestrians walking along on a sidewalk. They were simply and quietly residing in the house that it turns out was summarily rammed into.

None of us would likely be thinking about that at the moment of swerving.

In other words, you might swerve to avoid the squirrel and be anticipating that you can maintain control of the vehicle. This would then entail going erratically onto the sidewalk, driving ahead a bit, and then coming back into the street.

Nobody would be hurt, assuming there aren't any pedestrians nearby.

We can guess that perhaps the reason the car rammed into the house might be as a result of striking the curb on the way up onto the sidewalk. It could be that the sharp blow to the tires and the swerving vehicle made it very hard to control the trajectory. The car was somewhat an unguided missile as it came into contact with the side of the house. The driver likely jammed on the brakes at that time, and there were therefore multiple forces bringing the car ultimately to a halt (the emergency use of the brakes and the strength and fierce resistance of the structure).

In theory, the driver should have been mentally calculating that there was a chance that swerving to avoid the squirrel could lead to the car going into the structure that was immediately adjacent to the sidewalk.

This same logic should also have included that there is a chance that people might be inside that structure.

If you knew beyond a shadow of a doubt that the cottage was empty, you could then simply weigh the concern of saving the squirrel against the costs and concerns of slamming into the cottage. We would certainly want to assume that the driver is also considering the risk to themselves. So, in the instance of an empty structure, the driver needs to be figuring out the risk of their own injury or death as a result of potentially swerving into the house.

Again, with special attention to those of you that are devoted squirrel fans, what is the acceptable risk level for potentially harming yourself as the driver and damaging an empty structure?

That would be one estimation of risk.

Suppose you did not know for sure that the house was empty. There is some probability that people are inside. There is some additional probability that those people inside are somewhere near where the car is potentially going to impact the house. There is yet another probability associated with the consequent danger associated with the car crashing into the house, such as other parts of the domicile collapsing or perhaps a stovetop gas line ignites. And so on.

You see, that's seemingly a lot more risk involved.

I dare say that few humans use that kind of mental reckoning or mindfully calibrated probabilities when they are trying to decide what driving action is "best" to undertake.

We might though have different expectations if a car was being driven by a machine.

Say what?

Consider that the future of cars consists of AI-based true self-driving cars.

There isn't a human driver involved in a true self-driving car. Keep in mind that true self-driving cars are driven via an AI driving system. There isn't a need for a human driver at the wheel, and nor is there a provision for a human to drive the vehicle.

Here's an intriguing question that is worth pondering: *Should we expect that AI-based true self-driving cars will figure out a full set of potential risks when making day-to-day and special case driving choices?*

I'd like to first further clarify what is meant when I refer to true self-driving cars.

Understanding The Levels Of Self-Driving Cars

As a clarification, true self-driving cars are ones that the AI drives the car entirely on its own and there isn't any human assistance during the driving task.

These driverless vehicles are considered Level 4 and Level 5, while a car that requires a human driver to co-share the driving effort is usually considered at Level 2 or Level 3. The cars that co-share the driving task are described as being semi-autonomous, and typically contain a variety of automated add-on's that are referred to as ADAS (Advanced Driver-Assistance Systems).

There is not yet a true self-driving car at Level 5, which we don't yet even know if this will be possible to achieve, and nor how long it will take to get there.

Meanwhile, the Level 4 efforts are gradually trying to get some traction by undergoing very narrow and selective public roadway trials, though there is controversy over whether this testing should be allowed per se (we are all life-or-death guinea pigs in an experiment taking place on our highways and byways, some contend).

Since semi-autonomous cars require a human driver, the adoption of those types of cars won't be markedly different than driving conventional vehicles, so there's not much new per se to cover about them on this topic (though, as you'll see in a moment, the points next made are generally applicable).

For semi-autonomous cars, it is important that the public needs to be forewarned about a disturbing aspect that's been arising lately, namely that despite those human drivers that keep posting videos of themselves falling asleep at the wheel of a Level 2 or Level 3 car, we all need to avoid being misled into believing that the driver can take away their attention from the driving task while driving a semi-autonomous car.

You are the responsible party for the driving actions of the vehicle, regardless of how much automation might be tossed into a Level 2 or Level 3.

Self-Driving Cars And Those Squirrels On The Roadways

For Level 4 and Level 5 true self-driving vehicles, there won't be a human driver involved in the driving task.

All occupants will be passengers.

The AI is doing the driving.

One aspect to immediately discuss entails the fact that the AI involved in today's AI driving systems is not sentient. In other words, the AI is altogether a collective of computer-based programming and algorithms, and most assuredly not able to reason in the same manner that humans can.

Why is this added emphasis about the AI not being sentient?

Because I want to underscore that when discussing the role of the AI driving system, I am not ascribing human qualities to the AI. Please be aware that there is an ongoing and dangerous tendency these days to anthropomorphize AI. In essence, people are assigning human-like sentience to today's AI, despite the undeniable and inarguable fact that no such AI exists as yet.

With that clarification, you can envision that the AI driving system won't natively somehow "know" about the facets of driving. Driving and all that it entails will need to be programmed as part of the hardware and software of the self-driving car.

Let's dive into the myriad of aspects that come to play on this topic.

First, an important aspect of exploring this topic entails being straightforward and proffering an Honest Abe-like perspective.

Here's why I mention that emphasis.

There are some pundits and vendors that keep insisting that self-driving cars will be utterly *uncrashable*. This is rather bold and turns out an entirely misleading and incorrect claim.

I bring up the uncrashable notion because those promulgating that rather false opinion about self-driving cars would also argue vehemently that a self-driving car would never get into a car crash akin to the story of the teenage driver that averted hitting the squirrel. If self-driving cars will never get into car crashes, there doesn't seem to be any need to discuss the nature of such matters.

Case closed, as they say.

But wait for a second, do not be led down a path of falsehoods. We need to look more closely and see the truth. We can do so by examining the squirrel-avoiding situation to see how the "uncrashable" viewpoint seems to magically (and untruthfully) arise.

Envision a car that is cruising down an everyday street at a speed of 35 miles per hour, which is about 51 feet per second. If the brakes are instantaneously applied the car will continue a distance of about 60 feet before coming to a complete halt.

When human drivers apply the brakes with brute force, we would usually need to add several additional seconds to account for the mental time required to figure out the need to apply the brakes and then the physical activity time of applying one's body and limbs to carry out that braking action. Thus, this would be an additional 80 feet or so on top of the 60 feet, meaning that the car will have gone a total of around 140 feet.

A squirrel can run at about a speed of 12 miles per hour, which is nearly 18 feet per second. Squirrels are relatively small in stature. They can easily hide in bushes, tall grass, and the like. All told, I think we would all agree that squirrels can seemingly dart here or there quite quickly and can seemingly appear out of nowhere.

Imagine that a squirrel is hiding in tall grass that is adjacent to the roadway. A self-driving car is coming along. With nary any substantive distance involved, the squirrel opts to scramble out of the hiding spot and directly into the street, perhaps trying to get to the other side of the road, and has not sufficiently figured out that the car is an impending threat to its existence.

The self-driving car uses its sensors and perchance detects the presence of the squirrel. The distance between the squirrel and the nearing self-driving car is about 10 feet. Assume that the AI driving system nearly instantaneously detects the squirrel and applies the brakes of the self-driving car. The car comes to a firm stop at a distance of approximately 60 feet later.

What happened to the squirrel?

For those of you that are squeamish, please skip to the next paragraph. The answer about what happened to the squirrel is rather apparent, it is a goner. The self-driving car would have run over the furry animal, even if we are assuming that almost no time was taken to compute the need to undertake a braking action. The physics of the world as we know it will overtake any make-believe notions about being uncrashable.

Okay, if the self-driving car in that scenario indeed struck the squirrel, we can declare that a crash has occurred. Ergo, the self-driving car in this instance is decidedly not uncrashable. Those of you that are smarmy might try to argue that hitting a squirrel is not tantamount to a "car crash" since it is only a squirrel and the damage to the car itself is going to be minimal.

Well, I don't see how the amount of damage is especially pertinent to whether a car crash occurred or not. A crash is a crash. Some crashes are worse than others, certainly. At the same time, when a car rams into something, this seems clearly a form of a car crash, big or little, massive or minuscule.

If you are still stuck on the demure size of the squirrel, we can change the scenario and substitute a deer in the place of the squirrel. A deer is hiding in the brush that is adjacent to a roadway. The deer scoots out of the hiding spot and directly into the path of the self-driving car. Once again, we have a car crash. I won't go into the details of what happens to the deer, but you get the picture.

As an aside, one aspect of an interesting cultural and ethical matter is the programming of AI driving systems and the striking of animals that might dart into the roadway.

If a rat darts into the street, we probably would be somewhat mollified if the self-driving car ran it over, assuming that no other viable choice was feasible. Suppose though a chicken ran into the street? We might be less sanguine. Suppose it was a dog or cat? You can readily anticipate that this rundown would be considered outrageous and somehow derelict.

Back to the squirrel.

There is a real possibility that a self-driving car could ram into a squirrel. There isn't any magic wand that will negate that possibility. AI driving systems are not going to be all-seeing and all-knowing. In fact, you could easily make the case that the sensors of the self-driving car might fail or falter in detecting the squirrel.

Depending upon the circumstances, the video cameras of the self-driving car might not capture sufficient visual imagery to discern the presence of the squirrel, and nor might the radar, LIDAR, and other sensory devices. We would also need to include the prevailing weather conditions. There is also the matter of daytime versus nighttime. Etc.

Even if the sensors do provide data that seems to include the presence of the squirrel, the added question is whether the AI programming has been crafted to determine that a squirrel is there. In other words, the AI might only be computationally able to identify that an object is present and it is moving along on the street. Being able to also identify what kind of object is there, and what the significance of the object is, such as a squirrel versus say a child's toy that has rolled onto the roadway, that's an entirely separate matter and differing capability.

All in all, we ought to reasonably agree that a self-driving car could run over a squirrel. The next and particularly tough question is whether the AI driving system should attempt to avoid hitting the squirrel and if so, what other risks are satisfactory to take in the effort to avert striking the wondrous creature.

Would you want the AI driving system to intentionally swerve the car, similar to the action of the teenage driver, such that the squirrel would live?

I hope that we would all acknowledge that the answer depends upon what the swerving action might produce. Swerving into a house that might have people inside would seem like a really bad computational choice by the AI driving system.

This then lays at the feet of the automaker and self-driving tech firm that devised that kind of AI programming (remember, the AI is not sentient).

Conclusion

There are numerous other added twists and turns (I'll touch upon just a few more for now).

Conventional human-driven cars always presumably have at least one human inside them while being driven, obviously so, because a human driver must be at the wheel. A self-driving car can be entirely empty and have no humans in it whatsoever.

I bring up this fact because the choice about what to have a self-driving car do or not do can weigh into the equation the potential lack of presence of a human inside the autonomous vehicle.

The teenage driver had to consider their own potential injury as a factor in what to do. An AI driving system does not seem to have that same difficulty. If the AI driving system makes a computed choice that wrecks the self-driving car and yet saves others, this would seem a readily agreeable option to all.

There is a well-known and controversial thought experiment known as the Trolley Problem that comes to bear here. In short, the Trolley Problem posits the thorny issue of having to make life-or-death choices (or, more aptly, deaths versus deaths choices). This raises all sorts of ethics-oriented considerations.

Some in the self-driving cars industry decry the Trolley Problem and assert that it is entirely unrelated to the advent of self-driving cars. I politely and stridently disagree with that sentiment.

You see, there is a hidden Trolley Problem in the case of the teenage driver, the squirrel, and the ramming of the Abe Lincoln ancestry cottage. If the teenage driver had chosen to run over the squirrel, the car would seemingly not have swerved, and the people residing in that house would have not been in any immediate danger. By swerving to avoid the squirrel, the chances of things go awry began to pile up.

Would a self-driving car be calculating those odds?

Some technoids might contend that the AI driving system could have swerved and yet not subsequently rammed into the cottage. Maybe yes, maybe no.

We do not know for sure that mishandling of the car was the basis for the post-swerve resulting in striking the house. It could be that anyone or anything at the driver's wheel would have been unable to avert the cottage ramming once the choice was made to swerve in that direction.

Overall, I trust that you are now aware that we cannot assume that AI driving systems are going to miraculously avoid all car crashes.

In addition, there is a vacuous indication as yet about how AI driving systems will be computing the tradeoffs and risks of taking evasive driving actions. This is all being done in a very proprietary way right now.

Even scarier, this is oftentimes being done without any explicit realization of what is being assumed or taken for granted. Few are asking open and honest questions about how these AI driving systems are being programmed and what kind of Trolley Problem type of decision algorithms are being put into place.

That's honestly quite disconcerting..

CHAPTER 13
FREEWAY PHOBIA
AND
SELF-DRIVING CARS

The joys of riding in a car.

When I was a youngster, my grandparents delighted in taking me for a trek in their car, especially on the weekends. They would come to visit during the summers. A car ride included rolling down the windows of the vehicle and we would all relish the rushing cool breeze on those hot and muggy summer days as we drove leisurely along.

Since I wasn't old enough to drive, they instead did all the driving activity. I did though have a hand in where we went. Let's go to the store, I would clamor. Let's drive past the school ground and wave at anyone there. Let's go driving around the local park and see all the trees and the ducks in the pond.

There was one place that they would not go. No matter how often I asked, no matter how hard I implored them. They were defiant and professed utter and outright refusal.

They would not drive on the freeway.

It turns out that they overtly and vehemently were opposed to driving on the freeway. Any freeway. All freeways.

To avoid getting onto a freeway, they were willing to drive on local roads and even out-of-the-way highways, despite the journey taking sometimes twice as long. The moment that I saw an onramp to the freeway, I would enthusiastically point at it and urge vociferously that we try going that way. Meanwhile, they would quietly dismiss my exhortations and continue to stridently stay off the freeway entirely.

I wasn't exactly sure at the time why they were so reticent about using the freeways.

Later on, there was speculation that they did not like the fast speeds involved. This was a time period when the freeways were wide open (if you can wildly imagine that possibility). Any cars that traversed the freeway were the equivalent of taking a spaceship at lightspeed. Just like the sci-fi movies of that era, you could seemingly get from planet to planet by jumping into lightspeed or hyperdrive via the use of the multi-lane super-duper fast freeway.

But not for my grandma and grandpa.

Nope.

They were fine without the freeways. Take your time, they would sagely say. Be safer and stick to what works, namely anything and everything other than the freeways. You would need to have your head examined if you opted to take a freeway to get to wherever you wanted to go.

I admit then when I finally reached the age to start driving, their recalcitrant resistance and stern hesitation about using freeways initially carried into my mind and my driving efforts. Here's a taste of what happened.

My driver training class included how to drive on the freeways. We used to have several students in our school-provided training car and we would go driving around together, with the instructor in the front passenger seat, of course. Numerous trips included practicing driving on the freeways.

When it came to my turn to be sitting behind the wheel, I would look at the instructor with a pained expression when told to proceed onto a freeway. Since a sour look wasn't sufficient, I then pointed out that there really was no need to drive on the freeway since we were going to only go a few miles and then immediately get off at the next available exit.

What a dumb trip, I asserted. Let's practice some more U-turns and parallel parking, I politely pleaded.

This instructor was no fool. It was obvious that I was seeking to avoid learning about freeways and how to best traverse them. Not only did he have me get onto the freeway, but it also became a kind of focus of his. Whenever I got to be in the driver's seat, he would make an explicit point of mentioning that it was probably about time that we got some more freeway driving under our belts.

What is somewhat ironic or at least notable is that I eventually for my working efforts ended up driving on the freeways each workday, typically commuting to an office that took a couple of hours per day of back and forth on the freeways. Eventually, driving on freeways seemed like an old hat. This gradually encompassed taking freeways when there was little advantage in doing so. I guess I had completely gone freeway bonkers or freeway favoring, something like that.

There is the other end of that spectrum too.

Freeway phobia.

It is a real thing.

Some people have a phobia associated with driving on a freeway. Do not confound that predilection with necessarily having a phobia of driving. In other words, someone can be perfectly fine with driving, and yet nonetheless have a phobia about specifically driving on freeways.

Before we dig into the phobia of driving on freeways, you might be familiar with other kinds of phobias and we can consider them as a suitable warm-up on this topic.

Most people have heard about arachnophobia, a fear of spiders and other arachnids. Something kind of similar is ophidiophobia, the fear of snakes. You might remember the fictional character Indiana Jones famously having a fear of snakes.

Gosh, there have even been snakes on a plane, which certainly seems to attest to the basis for disliking and dreading snakes.

The reason I liken the fear of spiders with the fear of snakes is due to those both involving fear of animals. I think we can all sympathize with fearing certain types of animals, especially ones that seem evil or at least have been portrayed that way in movies and TV shows.

Here's another well-known phobia, acrophobia.

That's the fear of heights.

This is abundantly another type of fear that we can all sympathize with. I dare say that nearly everyone has had a moment of standing at the top of a mighty cliff or looking over the thin railing of a tall building and experienced a semblance of height trepidation. Those social media videos of people willingly jumping off tall pinnacles while wearing the flimsiest of parachutes or minuscule flying gear are enough to give the rest of us the willies.

Note that acrophobia is not an animal-based phobia. You could suggest that it is a situational form of a phobia that encompasses being up high. Furthermore, the heights involved are likely subjectively assessed. One person's sense of a sharp height might seem like nothing notable by someone else. If you've ever seen the infamous and altogether classic movie *Vertigo* by Alfred Hitchcock, you know what I mean.

Do you know what this phobia entails: Aerophobia or pteromerhanophobia?

You might have known or made an educated guess that it is the fear of flying. This used to be a pretty big topic. Airlines plentifully provided free classes to help people to overcome aerophobia. I realize that seems somewhat absurd by today's standards.

In any case, we certainly have a lot of trouble nowadays with rambunctious people while on commercial flights, though this seemingly has little to do with having aerophobia.

Since we are talking about flying, this brings up another type of situational-related phobia. Aerophobia encompasses the act of transit while in the air. I'm betting that you might not realize there is something similar for what is construed as ground-based traveling.

Amaxophobia or motorphobia.

Generally, that's a phobia about either riding in or driving a motorized vehicle such as a car. Some would focus on the driving aspects and tend to downplay the qualms of those that exhibit the phobia while merely riding inside a vehicle. Others assert that both possibilities are to be given equal weight.

There are indeed contrasting theories about the riding versus driving-related phobia aspects. For example, you might make the argument that a passenger is experiencing a loss of control over their destiny when riding inside a car. The driver is the one that is in control. As such, part of the fear of the rider variant is that they lack control of the vehicle.

In terms of the driver aspects, some drivers seem to exhibit a phobia only when particular driving circumstances arise. Driving into a tunnel is one prime example. This might be explained by underscoring that you don't know what might be inside the tunnel. Unlike driving on open roadways, the tunnel offers a foreboding possibility of ill will.

To be clear about this, a momentary expression of concern or dismay is not really what conventionally constitutes a phobia per se. Though people can have brief episodes, the traditional view about expressive phobia is that it is persistent and carries substantive fear and anxiety. Some people have an intense and outwardly demonstrative physiological and mental reaction and the phobia can be severely debilitating.

There is a slew of informative research and medical science that you can explore if you are further interested in the details of phobias and including the motorphobia instance.

For our purposes here, consider what could happen if someone does have a phobia or pronounced fear of riding in a car or a fear of driving a car.

A driver that gets behind the wheel and is filled with distressing levels of fear and anxiety is not what we might seek to have taking place on our public roadways. The person could react in adverse ways, doing so while commanding a multi-ton vehicle that can bring about costly damages or possibly cause life-or-death consequences.

You might say that the easy solution is to simply not have the person ever drive a car. Though that does exist as a possibility, it also can dramatically undercut one's existence. In our society, we often relate the notion of being independent as being able to drive a car. Someone that cannot drive a car has historically been somewhat stinted, though in more recent times this attitude has changed.

It might seem that the person that has a phobia about riding in a car is less worrisome to the rest of us since they are presumably not going to put themselves in the driver's seat. In that sense, they might react adversely if inside a car, but at least they are not at the driving controls. Of course, the concern is that the rider might take disruptive actions that could adversely affect the driver. A rider that starts reacting frantically can cause a driver to go awry.

What about that freeway phobia, you might be wondering?

Some drivers will steadfastly not drive on a freeway or exhibit phobia responses while driving on a freeway.

Things would seem somewhat safer if the person opted to not go on a freeway, especially if we are to assume that they are generally comfortable in driving while off the freeway. Such a driver could seemingly have an uneventful driving history by simply refraining from getting onto a freeway.

There are hardly any situations where the only means to get from point A to point B requires the use of a freeway. It might be more convenient to do so, and take less time or entail shorter driving distances, but rarely the only way to proceed (exceptions do apply).

For those people that have a phobia associated with riding in a car but that is only manifested when the car is on a freeway, well, that might be somewhat tolerable. In theory, they would be comfortable riding in a car that goes on regular streets and perhaps even highways. They just need to make sure that the driver doesn't take any freeways. This would seem generally like a feasible way to be a rider, assuming that you could either direct a driver in that manner or would know beforehand which rides to avoid because they are going to take a freeway.

Getting back to my grandparents, I am still to this day unclear as to whether they had such a phobia. And if they did, it is unclear too as to whether it was driving oriented or riding oriented, or both, when it came to going onto the freeways.

I remember at the time that some relatives said they had *freeway phobia*, while others preferred to use the expression *freeway fright*. Speculation was that they had perhaps experienced a jack-knifed truck or some unimaginably nightmarish car crash on a freeway, and therefore vowed to never get onto a freeway again.

One leading theory about this kind of phobia is that it might be tied to agoraphobia. That's the fear of being trapped and having no ready means of escape.

The logic is that when you get onto a freeway, you are somewhat locked into the roadway activities and have no immediate form of escape. With a normal street or avenue, you can easily see that there is a right turn or left turn ahead to get you off that particular pathway. On a highway, you usually can pull over or somehow relatively quickly get off the highway. For freeways, there is usually a semblance of being stuck on the freeway until that next exit perchance is neared.

I'm guessing you've had that type of experience, somewhat.

I remember one time when my children were toddlers and we were on the freeway, driving to someplace fun, I'm sure, and they just had to suddenly go to the bathroom. Unfortunately, the traffic was bumper to bumper and crawling at a snail's pace. The next available exit was about two miles ahead, and yet it seemed like it was thousands of miles away. We moved at a glacial speed, meanwhile, the kids were hollering for relief and clamoring for me to find the nearest restroom.

The gist of that scenario is that you are somewhat locked into place while on most freeways. The next exit is sometimes a long way away. Recall those famous signs by the side of the freeway that caution you that the next gas station is some distance ahead. I think that all of us can understand that feeling of being trapped while on a freeway.

We've been ruminating quite a bit about what can happen if a driver of a car has a freeway phobia, and likewise covering the ridership aspects too.

Consider that the future of cars consists of AI-based true self-driving cars.

There isn't a human driver involved in a true self-driving car. Keep in mind that true self-driving cars are driven via an AI driving system. There isn't a need for a human driver at the wheel, and nor is there a provision for a human to drive the vehicle.

Here's an intriguing question that is worth pondering: *How might car-related phobias arise in an era of AI-based true self-driving cars?*

I'd like to first further clarify what is meant when I refer to true self-driving cars.

Understanding The Levels Of Self-Driving Cars

As a clarification, true self-driving cars are ones that the AI drives the car entirely on its own and there isn't any human assistance during the driving task.

These driverless vehicles are considered Level 4 and Level 5, while a car that requires a human driver to co-share the driving effort is usually considered at Level 2 or Level 3. The cars that co-share the driving task are described as being semi-autonomous, and typically contain a variety of automated add-on's that are referred to as ADAS (Advanced Driver-Assistance Systems).

There is not yet a true self-driving car at Level 5, which we don't yet even know if this will be possible to achieve, and nor how long it will take to get there.

Meanwhile, the Level 4 efforts are gradually trying to get some traction by undergoing very narrow and selective public roadway trials, though there is controversy over whether this testing should be allowed per se (we are all life-or-death guinea pigs in an experiment taking place on our highways and byways, some contend).

Since semi-autonomous cars require a human driver, the adoption of those types of cars won't be markedly different than driving conventional vehicles, so there's not much new per se to cover about them on this topic (though, as you'll see in a moment, the points next made are generally applicable).

For semi-autonomous cars, it is important that the public needs to be forewarned about a disturbing aspect that's been arising lately, namely that despite those human drivers that keep posting videos of themselves falling asleep at the wheel of a Level 2 or Level 3 car, we all need to avoid being misled into believing that the driver can take away their attention from the driving task while driving a semi-autonomous car.

You are the responsible party for the driving actions of the vehicle, regardless of how much automation might be tossed into a Level 2 or Level 3.

Self-Driving Cars And Those Pertinent Phobias

For Level 4 and Level 5 true self-driving vehicles, there won't be a human driver involved in the driving task.

All occupants will be passengers.

The AI is doing the driving.

One aspect to immediately discuss entails the fact that the AI involved in today's AI driving systems is not sentient. In other words, the AI is altogether a collective of computer-based programming and algorithms, and most assuredly not able to reason in the same manner that humans can.

Why is this added emphasis about the AI not being sentient?

Because I want to underscore that when discussing the role of the AI driving system, I am not ascribing human qualities to the AI. Please be aware that there is an ongoing and dangerous tendency these days to anthropomorphize AI. In essence, people are assigning human-like sentience to today's AI, despite the undeniable and inarguable fact that no such AI exists as yet.

With that clarification, you can envision that the AI driving system won't natively somehow "know" about the facets of driving. Driving and all that it entails will need to be programmed as part of the hardware and software of the self-driving car.

Let's dive into the myriad of aspects that come to play on this topic.

For those people that have a freeway driving phobia, the advent of self-driving cars should alleviate their concerns, hopefully so. The AI driving system will be doing the driving for them. Thus, whatever qualms they have about doing driving should presumably be washed away. Simply stated, they won't need to be in the driver's seat anymore.

That being said, it is imaginable that the freeway driving phobia could transform to one of having pronounced anxiety and fear about the AI driving system doing the driving on the freeway. We don't know if that will occur. In theory, too, it could be that only some people incur that realm of a phobia if any at all.

Another twist is the possibility that somebody that did not previously have a phobia about driving on the freeways might somehow garner such a phobia due to realizing that self-driving cars are driving on the freeways with them. In essence, similar in some respects perhaps to reluctance to drive into a tunnel, it could be that the seemingly mysterious nature of self-driving cars could cause someone to react negatively accordingly. Or something else about self-driving cars leads to that realization.

What about the phobia of riding in a self-driving car while on a freeway?

Sure, that could certainly be a possibility.

If someone already has that particular phobia for conventional human-driven cars, it seems somewhat unlikely that replacing the human driver with an AI driving system will necessarily relieve the rider of their corresponding anxiety and fear. But, perhaps it might alleviate those severe qualms in some cases, thus we should consider the notion that having an AI driving system in lieu of a human driver might help to cope with their otherwise incurred phobia.

And meanwhile, one supposes that some people might newly develop such anxiety by the aspect that the self-driving car is explicitly being driven by an AI driving system.

All told, the point being that we have the potential of numerous changes in status about freeway phobia by introducing self-driving cars into the calculus. In some cases, the self-driving cars will aid in mitigating the phobia, while in other cases it is conceivable that the use of self-driving cars will stoke or provoke a phobia, possibly giving rise to new variants.

Specifically, a self-driving car phobia of one kind or another.

Time will tell.

Keep in mind that things are still quite early on in the emergence of AI self-driving cars and so we don't yet have much mileage to consider what will or will not transpire. People's reactions to self-driving cars are relatively muted right now. Once self-driving cars are roaming on our highways and byways and going down your neighborhood streets, we'll need to see how people react.

The reactions that we normally anticipate are about being an outside observer and watching self-driving cars traversing our communities. The other less often discussed aspect is how people will react by being a rider inside a self-driving car.

Returning to the earlier point about having control as a human driver, this is something that some human drivers are not going to willingly give up to an AI driving system. There are already some that have indicated you will only take away their driving when you have pried their cold dead hands from the wheel of the car.

The efforts so far of making use of self-driving cars are somewhat skewed and not especially fruitful for exploring these heady topics.

We have so few self-driving cars being tried out on our public roadways that the odds are we won't yet encounter those people that might have a phobia related to self-driving cars. Essentially, right now, the people voluntarily choosing to experience using a self-driving car are doing so, and thus they are pre-selecting themselves as presumably avidly preferring to go in a self-driving car.

When self-driving cars are widely prevalent, how people will respond is up in the air, as one might say.

Conclusion

Suppose that there are people that won't ride in a self-driving car that goes onto a freeway.

What then?

Well, the AI driving system could be programmed to take into account such a preference of not using the freeway. This would be relatively easy to attain. The rider would indicate they don't want the self-driving car to take any freeways. The AI driving system would plot out a navigational path accordingly.

There would probably need to be clear-cut communication about this. I say that because the trek might end up taking longer or possibly cost more than if the freeway was an allowed means of transit. A person might discover that someone else took the same ride as they did, at least in terms of going from point A to point B, and yet the cost and time were much lower for that other person. This might suggest something duplicitous has taken place, yet it might simply be due to the wishes of the passenger that stated no freeways were to be utilized.

This interestingly brings up an intriguing offshoot of this matter about avoiding freeways.

Before I jump into that topic, realize that we are going to have a mixture of both human-driven cars and self-driving cars on our roadways for a long time to come. We will not suddenly overnight replace all convention human-driven cars with self-driving cars. In the United States alone, there are about 250 million conventional cars and they aren't simply going to be tossed onto the junk heap on a whim.

Here's where I am headed on this.

Suppose that self-driving cars are actively using the freeways. In theory, AI driving systems should be especially adept at driving on freeways. There are a lot fewer moving objects to be dealt with, particularly erratic ones such as jaywalking pedestrians.

What we need to though take into account is how human drivers are going to react to self-driving cars that are on the freeways with them.

If the AI driving system begins to pick up on a pattern that human drivers are on edge when self-driving cars are on the freeways, it is possible that the AI driving systems might start to eschew driving on freeways. This is a simple computational pattern matching aspect and has nothing to do with sentience.

In short, if each time a self-driving car gets onto a freeway there is a heightened amount of human-driven cars that seem to swerve toward, rush up upon, and otherwise seemingly endanger impacting with the self-driving car, it is a pattern that would readily be detected. In that case, the AI driving system might calculate that it is safer to stay off the freeways, if possible.

I would expect that the fleet operator would discern that this is taking place. At that juncture, the question would arise as to what to do about it. Should self-driving cars generally stay off the freeways or not in those circumstances?

You can bet that there would be a backlash against human drivers for their having fostered this kind of thorny situation.

Some might even falsely try to claim that self-driving cars have derived a presumed *freeway phobia* or *freeway fright* about driving on the freeways. That is assuredly *not* a proper characterization. As mentioned earlier, we need to avoid anthropomorphizing AI.

For those of you that relish driving on freeways, you might want to consider self-driving cars as a helper rather than a hindrance. By and large, AI driving systems aren't going to be programmed to do the kinds of a daredevil and road rage acts that human drivers do.

We can be thankful for that and perhaps worry about other things in life, such as having a phobia about phobias.

CHAPTER 14
DITCH LEVEL 5 OF SELF-DRIVING CARS

Standards are important.

That is a general truism and backed up by the tremendous value we place on a myriad of existing and worldwide standards. It's hard to argue with such a seemingly self-evident statement.

Yet there are always qualms about whether a particular standard is up to the task at hand. Perhaps a standard is obstructing further progress or becoming haggard and no longer especially productive.

Indeed, a valid argument can be made that sometimes a standard gets in the way and has to be revised or potentially entirely revamped. Out with the old, in the with new, as they say. A standard might have outlived its usefulness or at least need some hefty repainting and well-needed shop repairs for it to continue forthrightly as a guiding light of sorts.

There is one particular standard that has been attracting attention lately, though you might not be aware of the slowly rising din unless you are acutely watching the tea leaves. Yes, bubbling in the inner circles are some grumbling insiders and outspoken pundits that are starting to overtly rankle aloud about whether the time has come to do something about this particular standard.

Remarkably, proposing that something quite dramatic must be done.

It has to do with self-driving cars.

And, some would say, it has to do with chopping off the head.

Well, that is, excising or summarily cutting off the topmost level known as Level 5 that constitutes the pinnacle of the autonomous levels for self-driving cars.

Say what?

Yes, there is an increasing undercurrent that is pushing to get rid of the Level 5 part of the scale. Cast aside that darned thing, they are clamoring. Get rid of it. No replacement is needed and nor desired. The new topmost pinnacle would become the existing Level 4. Thus, whereas today there are six levels of autonomy, scored from zero to five, the total number would drop down to just five levels and the shinning apple at the top would become Level 4.

Congrats would go to Level 4 for having survived the toppling of the seemingly controversial and purportedly unwanted Level 5.

I realize that some of you might not know what in the heck this is all about.

Perhaps you are unfamiliar with the various levels. Even those that are deeply rooted in autonomous vehicles and that are quite knowledgeable about the levels of autonomy might not have any inkling that some are seeking to oust the existing topmost level.

A mystery, a conundrum, and a potential fisticuffs prized boxing match are quietly in the making.

Let's back up and make sure we are all on the same page about the nature and scope of the prevailing standard regarding the levels of autonomy for ground-based surface vehicles (i.e., self-driving cars). Once we've gotten all of you up-to-speed, we can then dig into the gripes, complaints, and at times heartfelt qualms about that revered Level 5 and the contention that we need to heave-ho with it.

In my intrepid efforts as an ongoing self-driving cars whisperer, you might be aware of my numerous in-depth analyses of the existing and firmly implanted standard concerning the levels of autonomy for driverless cars, also referred to as self-driving cars or at times simply as robo-taxis. For my closeup assessment of the latest and recently released version of the venerated standard, see my column coverage.

In brief, some adamantly assert that the Rosetta Stone for defining the nature of self-driving capabilities is the esteemed SAE International standard formally as the "Taxonomy and Definitions for Terms Related to Driving Automation Systems for On-Road Motor Vehicles." Those that are in the know refer to the standard by its official designation, namely J3016.

Why is this standard so important?

You see, there is little doubt and altogether relatively unanimous agreement that the future of cars consists of AI-based true self-driving cars. There isn't a human driver involved in a true self-driving car. Keep in mind that true self-driving cars are driven via an AI driving system. There isn't a need for a human driver at the wheel, and nor is there necessarily a provision for a human to drive the vehicle.

It sure would be nice to have a means to across the board make use of an established scale or rating system that would enable us to all collegially gauge the degree of autonomy that a vehicle has achieved.

Thus, this is a key genesis for the crafting and subsequent promulgation of the SAE J3016 standard.

By having a codified standard, we can all talk the same lingo, as it were, and be relatively assured that there is something substantive and tangible about the terminology that we are using. Without such a standard, we would all be likely talking past each other and using our own idiosyncratic vocabulary that could radically mean one thing to some and mean something entirely different to others.

By having a standard that delineates the levels of autonomy, we can all readily discuss and discern the status of self-driving car efforts.

In theory, by using the provided scale, we can separate the wheat from the chaff.

That being said, please be aware that some vendors have blurred the lines by using questionable naming for their wares and conspicuously avoid citing the scale to apparently avoid getting pinned down on what their vehicles actually achieve. See my columns for indications in which I take to task those purveying such unsavory efforts.

Added to that devious morass is the underhanded ploy of using the scale by ascribing an existing vehicular capability to what the vendor hopes their vehicle will someday become, rather than getting jammed up with the otherwise demoting connotation of what it can actually do today.

Here's how that trickery works.

I might only have in hand today a bologna sandwich for you, but one day aspires to proffer a splendorous and complete meal. Rather than stating that you are being handed a baloney sandwich, instead, you are led to believe that the sandwich is going to transmogrify into a complete meal. You are told in rather fine print that the thing in your hand is merely a baloney sandwich, thus presumably protecting the purveyor from claims of not being forthright, and meanwhile touting boisterously to the world that this is going to be the most incredible meal ever imagined. The assumption is that people will buy into this line of thought in an akin manner to the philosopher's stone turning into gold.

Anyway, that somewhat of a side tangent isn't so much about the levels of autonomy standard as it is about how some can attempt to sidestep or exploit a standard in beguiling ways. Having a standard is handy. But how particular people decide to use it, including doing an end-around or other hanky maneuvers is something that we all need to be watchful of and hopefully be wary about.

Okay, that's a bit of helpful grounding on this topic.

Here's an intriguing question that is worth pondering: *Why are some carping about the standard for autonomous levels and seeking to jettison the topmost Level 5 from the widely known self-driving cars scale?*

First, I'd like to quickly further clarify what is meant when I refer to true self-driving cars.

Understanding The Levels Of Self-Driving Cars

As a clarification, true self-driving cars are ones that the AI drives the car entirely on its own and there isn't any human assistance during the driving task.

These driverless vehicles are considered Level 4 and Level 5, while a car that requires a human driver to co-share the driving effort is usually considered at Level 2 or Level 3. The cars that co-share the driving task are described as being semi-autonomous, and typically contain a variety of automated add-on's that are referred to as ADAS (Advanced Driver-Assistance Systems).

There is not yet a true self-driving car at Level 5, which we don't yet even know if this will be possible to achieve, and nor how long it will take to get there.

Meanwhile, the Level 4 efforts are gradually trying to get some traction by undergoing very narrow and selective public roadway trials, though there is controversy over whether this testing should be allowed per se (we are all life-or-death guinea pigs in an experiment taking place on our highways and byways, some contend). Even worse so is the concern surrounding the circumstances involving Level 2 or Level 3 vehicles that are being improperly touted as ostensibly being at Level 4.

Since semi-autonomous cars require a human driver, the adoption of those types of cars won't be markedly different than driving conventional vehicles, so there's not much new per se to cover about them on this topic (though, as you'll see in a moment, the points next made are generally applicable).

For semi-autonomous cars, it is important that the public needs to be forewarned about a disturbing aspect that's been arising lately, namely that despite those human drivers that keep posting videos of themselves falling asleep at the wheel of a Level 2 or Level 3 car, we all need to avoid being misled into believing that the driver can take away their attention from the driving task while driving a semi-autonomous car.

You are the responsible party for the driving actions of the vehicle, regardless of how much automation might be tossed into a Level 2 or Level 3.

Self-Driving Cars And Pointing Fingers At Level 5

For Level 4 and Level 5 true self-driving vehicles, there won't be a human driver involved in the driving task.

All occupants will be passengers.

The AI is doing the driving.

One aspect to immediately discuss entails the fact that the AI involved in today's AI driving systems is not sentient. In other words, the AI is altogether a collective of computer-based programming and algorithms, and most assuredly not able to reason in the same manner that humans can.

Why is this added emphasis about the AI not being sentient?

Because I want to underscore that when discussing the role of the AI driving system, I am not ascribing human qualities to the AI. Please be aware that there is an ongoing and dangerous tendency these days to anthropomorphize AI. In essence, people are assigning human-like sentience to today's AI, despite the undeniable and inarguable fact that no such AI exists as yet.

There is something else important that you need to know and it entails the significant and hugely crucial difference between Level 4 and Level 5.

Level 4 relies upon an important concept known as an ODD (Operational Design Domain).

Here's the formal definition of ODD from the SAE J3106 standard: "Operating conditions under which a given driving automation system or feature thereof is specifically designed to function, including, but not limited to, environmental, geographical, and time-of-day restrictions, and/or the requisite presence or absence of certain traffic or roadway characteristics."

In short, the notion is that a Level 4 self-driving car is devised to operate in a particular operational domain and the vehicle is presumed to only be viably able to be driving while staying within the constrained setting. I guess you could say it is a kind of carve-out. Rather than blankly stating that a self-driving car is able to pretty much go wherever instead the emphasis is to clarify where and under what circumstances it has been devised to operate.

These ODD's are entirely up to an automaker or self-driving tech firm to individually decide what it should be for their wares, such as saying that their self-driving car won't work at night time and only works during the day, or works only in one city but not in another. Meanwhile, some other automaker offers a self-driving car that will work both during nighttime and daytime, but maybe it won't work in the rain.

And so on.

This can be quite confusing to the public and the media too, namely that these ODD's aren't defined in a standardized way (see my column coverage about efforts underway to standardize ODD's).

In other words, an automaker or self-driving tech firm can decide to divine their own proprietary ODD's.

This means that if you see a self-driving car driving past you, there's no immediate way to know what its scope consists of. Maybe it has been devised to go only in a 10-block radius of where you happen to see it, or maybe it can go across your entire state to other states and other cities. Perhaps it can work in the rain, but not in snow. You have no direct or immediate way of discerning what the ODD is.

In a moment, I'll be digging more deeply into the Level 4 and the Level 5 general aspects.

The key to have in mind is that Level 5 is somewhat akin to the set of all ODDs, loosely so.

In other words, in theory, it could be somewhat said that a Level 5 self-driving car has no particular ODD and encompasses all other ODDs, suggesting that a Level 5 can go just about anywhere, though that is a bit of an overstatement and technically imprecise. I will right away herein provide clarification since many both outside and even inside the industry misunderstand and misstate the definition of Level 5, sadly so.

Here's a useful quote from the SAE standard that helps indicate the Level 4 versus Level 5 capabilities of the Automated Driving System (ADS):

- Level 4: "Permits engagement only within its ODD"

- Level 5: "Permits engagement of the ADS under all driver-manageable on-road conditions"

I'll come back to this in a moment.

Now that we've laid the stage appropriately, time to dive into the myriad of aspects that come to play here.

Why are some intimating or outright calling for the abolishment of Level 5?

I'm glad you asked.

Here's the deal.

Some assert that Level 5 is simply not attainable.

I will try to convey their sentiment as best feasible and hope that my indication does proper service toward their devout belief on this matter. Please know that I will need to be somewhat brief due to word constraints and the desire to keep this discussion readily digestible.

Okay, the rub is that Level 5 is argued as being unattainable.

Level 5 is a mirage. A false idol. Fakery. An aspiration that cannot be realized.

And a core crux to the problem, they would say, involves the misguided attempts to reach Level 5.

According to these contentions, automakers and self-driving tech firms are pursuing something that gives them and everyone else false hopes. This, therefore, raises expectations. The expectations are out of whack with reality. Nobody is going to achieve Level 5, and it is a fool's errand to think otherwise.

The problem is compounded by using resources and attention that ought to be going toward Level 4, they would contend. But the race to attain Level 5 distorts what is being done. Instead of putting all your eggs into the ostensibly practical and level-headed Level 4 attainment, there is a leakage of valuable efforts toward garnering a Level 5 that isn't going to happen.

Stop messing around and get your act together by going all-in on Level 4.

Furthermore, there are additional and quite serious concerns about providing a ready-made open door for deviousness by those that wish to distort reality, shamelessly exploiting the Level 5 formalized status.

Shady characters can claim that Level 5 is their goal and showcase snippets of evidence that seem to suggest they are on their way to Level 5. They presumably could not do this if there wasn't a Level 5 definition, to begin with. The very presence of the false idol opens Pandora's box for those that wish to dreamily assert that whatever they are doing is for the goodness of ultimately achieving the acclaimed Level 5.

As long though as Level 5 sits there in the entrenched standard and keeps gloriously shining that altogether breathtaking and songstress beckoning light, there is little chance to bring self-driving car pursuits off the precarious ledge and back to focusing solely and appropriately on Level 4.

Regrettably, they would stridently argue, the Level 5 is firmly implanted in the standard which anoints it with officialdom that will continue to be a deceptive allure like that of a Venus Fly Trap.

The solution then is patently obvious, they would say, namely, kick out that troublesome and overinflated Level 5 from the standard.

Erase it.

Knock it off the lofty perch.

We would then all realize that Level 4 is where we ought to be looking. No more wasted time or money on that darned Level 5. Hopefully, everyone would gradually forget that Level 5 ever even was stipulated. Indeed, future developers might be shocked to discover that there had been a Level 5 and chuckle when the old-timers tell them that we used to think that Level 5 was possible. A hearty laugh and lots of headshaking ensue.

Now, before I provide the other side of the coin on this particular line of thinking, I'd like to mention that there are lots of variants of that aforementioned argument.

For example, one common variant is that Level 5 is not necessarily unattainable and instead the qualm is instead that it isn't attainable *anytime soon*. Thus, rather than making a blanket statement that we won't ever achieve Level 5, this variant posits that it might be many decades or more away, and therefore for the foreseeable future it is entirely out of reach.

You might wonder why those in that variant niche would also go along with ditching Level 5. They seem to agree that Level 5 is potentially possible. Why not keep it intact?

Their logic is somewhat akin to the ones that say Level 5 is never attainable, namely that in the short run it is inadvertently acting as a distractor and can be deceptively used by those that wish to take advantage of its existence in the standard.

Take out Level 5 right now, and maybe someday in the future consider bringing it back into the realm of possibilities.

There are other variants of this overarching argument too (see my columns for further details).

Let's for now take a mindful glance at the primary counterarguments to this line of logic.

First, some would contend that you cannot un-ring the bell. Level 5 has already been specified and promulgated. Even if you got it out of the SAE standard, Level 5 would still be floating around and likely cited.

Some people would not realize that Level 5 had been removed. Too much history about Level 5 is laying around and easily found on the Internet. All that would happen is mass confusion. Is there a Level 5? Was there a Level 5? Why did it get removed? Is it coming back?

Thus, the key counterargument is that you cannot undo that which has already been done.

Sure, you could perhaps persuade enough insiders to get it removed, but society is not going to likely give up on Level 5. In addition, those devious people that you are trying to avert, well, certainly they would make sure that Level 5 continues to be alive. Perhaps even inventing some nifty conspiracy theories about why Level 5 was removed. That could stoke even greater interest in Level 5, one supposes.

Second, there is a position taken that we do not know for sure that Level 5 is in fact unattainable.

Speculation on the achievability is strong on both sides of the question. For those providing compelling reasons that Level 5 is someday attainable, they would believe it nonsense or worse to remove it from the standard on the basis that it is proclaimed as presumably being unattainable. They would likely fight tooth and nail on that supposition.

Third, not having a Level 5 in the standard would be like omitting a vital part of the scale and render the standard horrendously incomplete, diminished, and inadequate, ergo undercutting any due respect or conformity.

This also dovetails into the aspect that Level 5 provides a lofty goal and inspires researchers, inventors, and everyone involved toward achieving something greater than might otherwise be envisioned. Some liken this to earlier postulating that we can get humans to the moon, which at the time seemed potentially improbable. Nowadays the equivalent might be getting humans to Mars. As a side note, the Level 5 opponents would say that's an improper analogous situation and that you would need to say that we are aiming to get humans to some really far away planet well-beyond our universe somewhere in the multiverse.

Anyway, I trust you get the sense that there are those on the other side of tossing out Level 5 that would stoutly argue that Level 5 ought to remain in. The horse is already out of the barn on that, they would strongly contend.

Meanwhile, I believe that even the most ardent believers in keeping Level 5 would all pretty much be open to making refinements and adjusting Level 5, as indeed the standard is regularly being updated and revised.

There is another tack that some take in the rumblings about booting out Level 5.

This angle is a bit easier to unpack and alas is based on misleading or outright misunderstandings about the standard and Level 5. I say that this is unfortunate since it happens to simultaneously postulate a position that seems relatively untenable and meanwhile incorrectly portrays the elements of Level 5 as clearly stated in the standard.

Here we go.

Some have stated that their major issue with Level 5 is that it supposedly aims at having self-driving cars driving anywhere at any time in any manner whatsoever. This is portrayed as an eyebrow-raising slippery slope that leads inexorably to assured doom.

This is perhaps brought about by a mistaken comprehension of ODDs. The argument goes that since Level 4 has ODDs, it won't get into dangerous driving environments, while Level 5 since it has no ODDs per se, would seemingly get itself into some knotty and dire binds.

Ugh, time to set the record straight on that.

The usual way this is portrayed is by asserting that a self-driving car of a Level 5 is going to proceed onto precarious cliffs while off-roading or in other highly dangerous settings such as driving around in the midst of monsoon, all of which is seemingly and undeniably bad.

Apparently, in contrast, a Level 4 would have a defined ODD that would prohibit this kind of reckless and wayward type of driving.

Sorry to say, that doesn't compute.

Let's briefly return to the definition of Level 5 (as stated earlier, from the SAE standard): "Permits engagement of the ADS under all driver-manageable on-road conditions."

Take a close look at that wording.

I'll help.

Notice that the wording refers explicitly to *on-road* conditions.

The Level 5 definition specifically and unequivocally refers to on-road driving only. Period, full stop, drop the mic.

Allow me to quote further from the standard: "On-road refers to publicly accessible roadways (including parking areas and private campuses that permit public access) that collectively serve all road users, including cyclists, pedestrians, and users of vehicles with and without driving automation features."

As I've repeatedly exhorted, the existing standard considers off-road driving to be out of scope.

Anyone that attributes off-roading to Level 5 is misstating the standard and improperly expanding what Level 5 is. That being said, you are welcome to argue about whether off-roading should or should not be included in the standard, and you are equally welcome to aid in fostering off-roading autonomous levels or something like that.

But please don't misstate the standard as it sits today.

Next, take a look again at this wording from the standard (I realize that I've already shown this, but you'll see it is worth taking yet another look-see): "Permits engagement of the ADS under all driver-manageable on-road conditions."

I'd like to point out that the wording refers to *driver-manageable* conditions.

That's quite important phrasing. It intends to indicate that the driving action of the AI driving system would be adherent to what human drivers can manageably do when driving. The standard refers to the Level 5 unconditional or not ODD-specific driving as nonetheless still being bounded by that which is only also drivable by a human driver.

Here's a further indication in the SAE definition: "Unconditional/not ODD-specific means that the ADS can operate the vehicle on-road anywhere within its region of the world and under all road conditions in which a conventional vehicle can be reasonably operated by a typically skilled human driver. This means, for example, that there are no design-based weather, time-of-day, or geographical restrictions on where and when the ADS can operate the vehicle. However, there may be conditions not manageable by a driver in which the ADS would also be unable to complete a given trip (e.g., white-out snowstorm, flooded roads, glare ice, etc.) until or unless the adverse conditions clear."

Okay, the point is that the AI driving system is presumably going to be driving when the circumstances are warranted such that if a human driver was at the wheel would be able to drive in that setting. I'll readily grant that this is still somewhat ambiguous. Some human drivers do stupid things and try driving in settings that are unwise. No doubt about that.

But if you are going to twist the standard and argue that it *forces* the AI driving system of Level 5 into driving in unwarranted settings, that's a distortion and not per se the indication.

You could somewhat reasonably argue that there is a kind of macro-ODD that exists for Level 5, namely that a Level 5 self-driving car is only supposed to be devised to drive in driver-manageable on-road conditions. That might not seem like an ODD as is defined for Level 4, and it might seem like a quite open-ended ODD of a sort, but it nonetheless smacks of the underlying conceptual underpinnings that there are indeed conditions or restrictions associated with Level 5.

No mayhem per se. No wide-eyed frenetic driving is being proffered by the standard. Some make Level 5 out to seem like it is utterly without bounds and going to be wanton and drive in an indubitable maniac fashion in the craziest and nuttiest of ways.

It will be that of which we make it, if you will.

Conclusion

There are a lot more twists and turns on this topic, but I'll save those for another day.

Well, a quick taste of one seems especially noteworthy.

If the ODDs of Level 4 are supposedly going to keep Level 4 out of the potential driving troubles that are purportedly in Level 5, what is it that somehow magically makes the self-defined ODDs of Level 4 so attributable to seemingly safer driving?

The answer is that there is no such guarantee.

Here's again the SAE standard definition for ODD (we covered this earlier, but it is handy to repeat it again here):

> "Operating conditions under which a given driving automation system or feature thereof is specifically designed to function, including, but not limited to, environmental, geographical, and time-of-day restrictions, and/or the requisite presence or absence of certain traffic or roadway characteristics."

One could presumably craft an ODD for Level 4 that is as dangerous or perhaps more so dangerous than Level 5, though we would not expect anyone to do this.

The assumption by some is that ODDs are going to be nicely and neatly devised into rather tight quarters that are assuredly safe boundaries, which is what most of today's efforts are seeking to do. That doesn't though stop someone from doing otherwise.

One would hope that this isn't a direction taken, but it is conceivable.

Now that we've covered the ongoing jawing about whether to ditch Level 5, you get to be the judge.

Ought Level 5 be dropped like a hot potato from the standard?

Should Level 4 reign supreme?

Some suggest that the insiders stoking such flames are just trolling everyone and are having a bit of fun.

Though, there is an inherent downside to crying wolf, even in jest and especially when doing so on the sly. Others are said to be trying to provoke deep thoughts and get some renewed energy into postulating what the levels ought to be. If so, one supposes that at least it might be helpful to ensure that the facts are on par and suitably sketched.

What will happen next, you might be mulling over.

As Sun Tzu famously stated, it is prudent to ponder and deliberate before you make a move. Then again, he also proffered that to be quick is to survive and that if not quick then all shall be lost.

CHAPTER 15
LINE IN SAND FOR SELF-DRIVING CARS

Deadlines.

You either love them, hate them, or experience both sentiments at the same time.

A deadline can be handy as a focal point that aids in rallying together everyone towards achieving something great. On the other hand, a deadline can turn each person against the other and fester a bitter fight that leaves all involved forever scarred and upset due to a seemingly arbitrary and reprehensible line in the sand.

Deadlines do decidedly set expectations, though at times the expectations are out of whack with reality.

There are those crazy deadlines that just cannot be met.

These are the outsized and wildly chosen deadlines that are so ridiculous that they are nearly laughable, except of course if you are part of the team that is supposed to make it happen. In that case, you are supposed to tough it out and make sure that the deadline is achieved. The deadline might not be based on any semblance of knowing what is reasonably feasible and was selected at the whim of some lofty character, but by gosh, it is the proclaimed deadline and no one dare challenge it.

Maybe the deadline declarer knows something you don't know.

Perhaps the deadline is indeed thoughtfully chosen and can be achieved. There is always that self-doubt that others might be better at setting deadlines than you give them credit for. Meanwhile, it sure appears that the deadline has about a zero chance of being attained.

And, like a punch to the stomach, you'll be bearing all that endless effort leading up to the deadline as though the deadline is a must-do, when you are sure all along it is absurd and completely unattainable.

Another angle is that the deadline is secretly known to be unattainable and the declarer is purposely using it as a rallying cry, despite the inner realization that it is not viable. The declarer merely wants to set a marker for everyone to see. Sure, it would be nice if that deadline could be achieved, but the declarer knows fully beforehand that the deadline is outrageously outlandish. This though won't be stated aloud. Just use the deadline as a means to an end, getting the troops to work hard and believe they are seeking a doable deadline, regardless that it is pretty much hogwash.

That is a bit hard to take by some.

Working tirelessly under a knowingly calculated false deadline is something that few would later on agree was a wondrous idea. They will feel cheated. They might also never believe any future deadlines that are proffered by the declarer. People will realize that there was a prior crying of the wolf, as it were, and won't fall for the same trickery twice. Thus, they will seem to be on board with the latest deadline, while in their hearts they are unwilling to do the death march that they once thought made sense to undertake.

Whoa, say those that relish deadlines, you are missing the boat, or perhaps missing the point about having a deadline.

Deadlines strip out complexity. The world is a much simpler place when you have a deadline. This is when things need to be finished. Period, full stop. No need to think further about that. Just take it as a given. Your aim is simplified now, keep your eye on that deadline.

Resources can be channeled accordingly. You can also keep track of progress. How far do we have yet to go toward the deadline? Are we behind? Are we ahead? A sense of urgency can be fostered by the deadline looming at the end of the rainbow. Go, go, go.

Prioritization comes to play too.

If the deadline is going to be met, which it has to be, you need to prioritize the efforts underway. Some say that deadlines bring forth creativity. Yes, the idea is that while under the pressure of a deadline, people will have creative thoughts about how to get things done soonest. Without that purposefully applied pressure, the creative juices would not have been otherwise flowing (well, others contend that those outsized pressures clamp down on creativity and suppress it since you don't have the latitude of playful avenues to be creative when confronting a harsh and unrelenting deadline).

Some assert that deadlines are necessary to get people off their duff. The unwavering heat from having to achieve a deadline will turn lackadaisical into the furiously hard-working. We all have an innate notion of seeking to arrive at the finish line. Getting to the finish means the glory of victory.

But wait for a second, all this talk about achieving deadlines begs a rather blatant and yet unstated question, namely what happens if there isn't a deadline at all.

- Does chaos reign?

Without a deadline, there is a solid chance that whatever is taking place will meander, some would say. Take your time would be the outspoken mantra. There's no rush. However long it takes, it takes. Don't get yourself all wound up and wrapped into a tizzy when no one has put their foot down about a rock-solid deadline.

So, we have the tradeoffs associated with sensible deadlines versus ostensibly nonsensical ones, plus we have the other side of the coin that deals with the lack of any deadline whatsoever.

Dizzying.

Some say that you *especially* cannot put deadlines on achieving new inventions or brand-new innovations.

When attempting to do something that has never been done before, the use of a deadline is argued as being entirely misplaced. Deadlines are only rightfully established when you are doing something that is generally known to be accomplishable. Endeavors treading onto new territory that is essentially unmappable would be construed as unwisely tied down by presumed wild-guess off-the-cuff deadlines (so it is intimated).

Is that really the case that deadlines are wholly incompatible with seeking outstretched innovations?

You would get quite a pushback on that contention. There are plenty of examples, notable ones, that seem to showcase that a deadline was instrumental to making progress in circumstances that were abundantly new, unproven, and for which the path forward was fraught with innumerable unknowns.

Use this quote as a basis for thinking about that brazen point (can you guess who said this?): "I believe this nation should commit itself to achieve the goal, before this decade is out, of landing a man on the moon and returning him safely to the Earth." You might recognize that quote as being the famous words of President John F. Kennedy. He made that remark on May 25, 1961, during a joint session of Congress.

As you know, this became one of the most controversial and outstretched "new innovation" deadlines of all time.

Yes, to be clear, it was a deadline. Maybe at first glance or initial mention, it was inclined toward being a hoped-for hazy notion. Over time, it became a deadline. A deadline that gripped an entire nation. A deadline that riveted the entire world.

Many at the time thought this was unmitigated crazy talk.

There was no tangible path to attaining the deadline. It seemed as though this was plucked out of the air and had no basis in reality. Yet, as we all know, ultimately, the Apollo 11 mission successfully landed on the moon in July 1969, and two astronauts walked upon the moon at that historic time. The before-the-decade-is-out aspirational deadline was attained.

By the way, some cynics or malcontents today try to claim that the moon landing was all doable from day one (i.e., knowing so in 1961, when JFK made his speech) and that this was entirely obvious at the get-go. I can only say that this ranks up there with those that believe we never reached the moon and harbor those conspiracy theories about the matter. Anyway, believe as you will.

Would we have reached the moon and put humans on the moon if we had not had a deadline?

Seems like a deadline was crucial.

You can argue about whether the deadline was a reasonable one, such that maybe JFK should have said that by the end of the following decade was the goal or something later than picking the end of the decade such that a wee bit more wiggle room was allowed for. The entire activity during the 1960s was continually focused by the end of the decade declaration, for which some might well argue pushed past obstacles that might have otherwise become quagmires.

In essence, each time an obstacle arose, there was dedicated attention toward overcoming the obstacle, in the soonest feasible manner. If the deadline had provided an additional say ten years, perhaps the same type of energy and drive would not have arisen. It is hard to say and we can only speculate about such matters.

This does though remind me of a noteworthy quote by Henry Ford, the venerable maker of cars: "Obstacles are those frightful things you see when you take your eyes off your goal."

I suppose that goes hand-in-hand with another one of his indubitably quotable lines: "If you think you can do a thing or think you can't do a thing, you are right."

Speaking of cars, consider that the future of cars consists of AI-based true self-driving cars.

Allow me a moment to tie together the topic of self-driving cars and the theme of setting deadlines.

For AI-based true self-driving cars, there isn't a human driver involved. Keep in mind that true self-driving cars are driven via an AI driving system. There isn't a need for a human driver at the wheel, and nor is there normally a provision for a human to drive the vehicle.

Here's an intriguing question that is worth pondering: *Do we need an all-in steadfast deadline for attaining AI-based true self-driving cars, which today there isn't any such overarching deadline?*

I'd like to first further clarify what is meant when I refer to true self-driving cars.

Understanding The Levels Of Self-Driving Cars

As a clarification, true self-driving cars are ones that the AI drives the car entirely on its own and there isn't any human assistance during the driving task.

These driverless vehicles are considered Level 4 and Level 5, while a car that requires a human driver to co-share the driving effort is usually considered at Level 2 or Level 3. The cars that co-share the driving task are described as being semi-autonomous, and typically contain a variety of automated add-on's that are referred to as ADAS (Advanced Driver-Assistance Systems).

There is not yet a true self-driving car at Level 5, which we don't yet even know if this will be possible to achieve, and nor how long it will take to get there.

Meanwhile, the Level 4 efforts are gradually trying to get some traction by undergoing very narrow and selective public roadway trials, though there is controversy over whether this testing should be allowed per se (we are all life-or-death guinea pigs in an experiment taking place on our highways and byways, some contend).

Since semi-autonomous cars require a human driver, the adoption of those types of cars won't be markedly different than driving conventional vehicles, so there's not much new per se to cover about them on this topic (though, as you'll see in a moment, the points next made are generally applicable).

For semi-autonomous cars, it is important that the public needs to be forewarned about a disturbing aspect that's been arising lately, namely that despite those human drivers that keep posting videos of themselves falling asleep at the wheel of a Level 2 or Level 3 car, we all need to avoid being misled into believing that the driver can take away their attention from the driving task while driving a semi-autonomous car.

You are the responsible party for the driving actions of the vehicle, regardless of how much automation might be tossed into a Level 2 or Level 3.

Self-Driving Cars And Deadlines

For Level 4 and Level 5 true self-driving vehicles, there won't be a human driver involved in the driving task.

All occupants will be passengers.

The AI is doing the driving.

One aspect to immediately discuss entails the fact that the AI involved in today's AI driving systems is not sentient. In other words, the AI is altogether a collective of computer-based programming and algorithms, and most assuredly not able to reason in the same manner that humans can.

Why is this added emphasis about the AI not being sentient?

Because I want to underscore that when discussing the role of the AI driving system, I am not ascribing human qualities to the AI. Please be aware that there is an ongoing and dangerous tendency these days to anthropomorphize AI. In essence, people are assigning human-like sentience to today's AI, despite the undeniable and inarguable fact that no such AI exists as yet.

With that clarification, you can envision that the AI driving system won't natively somehow "know" about the facets of driving. Driving and all that it entails will need to be programmed as part of the hardware and software of the self-driving car.

Let's dive into the myriad of aspects that come to play on this topic.

First, please be aware that there is no overarching deadline associated with attaining true self-driving cars. There is assuredly an amorphous desire to *soonest possible* achieve true self-driving cars, but no specific deadline.

You might already know some of the reasons cited for seeking to produce self-driving cars.

For example, it is assumed that self-driving cars will essentially save lives by reducing the number of annual fatalities associated with car crashes. Right now, in the United States alone, there are about 40,000 deaths due to car crashes. Many of those car crashes are attributed to driving while drunk, driving while drowsy, driving while distracted, and so on. Self-driving cars should not exhibit those same human foibles during the act of driving.

There is also the strident belief that we will potentially arrive at an era of mobility-for-all via the advent and prevalence of self-driving cars. Those that today are mobility disadvantaged or that are mobility marginalized will be able to affordably make use of self-driving cars. It is assumed that the cost per mile or price per mile for using self-driving cars is going to be a lot less than that of conventional human-driven cars, principally due to excising the need for the human labor of the driving chore.

Okay, the point is that the sooner we can bring about self-driving cars and have them roaming our public highways, byways, and streets, the better off we will be. As a side note, not everyone agrees with that heralded viewpoint.

Soonest is best, one might nonetheless ardently argue.

What kinds of deadlines have been proffered?

There are a plethora of them. And they pretty much are vacuous. Each automaker and each self-driving tech firm is able to freely decide upon whatever deadline they wish to establish.

They can have a deadline or choose to not have a deadline.

They might opt to have an internal deadline that is kept secret and have no outwardly stated deadline. They might have an outwardly stated deadline that they believe internally, or it is merely a prop or display to the outside world and an entirely different deadline exists inside the company.

Many of the deadlines have come and gone.

Amazingly, this doesn't seem to phase most people. An outspoken top executive or founder makes a bold indication about a deadline by which they will have perfected self-driving cars, and when the deadline passes, they seem to get a hall pass and are not held accountable for their missed deadline.

This at times happens because of short memories. You can get away with setting a deadline to the outside world and at the moment of the announcement, it is a big splash. Later on, perhaps years later, no one seems to remember that the big splash occurred. Or, bringing up the long-ago big splash is no longer worthy of a big splash.

Indeed, you could almost mockingly assert that making overt and splashy deadlines is the best thing you could do as someone in the self-driving cars niche. It gets you rapt attention at the time. Furthermore, you get almost no penalty for later on having been wrong. Sure, it will occasionally come back to haunt you by those that quote those prior deadline splashes, but this is not of much concern.

One can always contend that they were caught up in the excitement of self-driving cars. Thus, you are supposed to give them their due as someone that was an enthusiastic supporter, setting aside the misguided or mistaken deadline. They were optimistic. Don't we relish optimism?

Plus, it is easy to blame something or someone else for having failed to attain the deadline. This is a deflection that seems to work most of the time. As I've discussed in my columns, using governmental regulations as a bogeyman is the seemingly slipperiest and most cunning of current deflections.

Anyway, getting back to the overarching question, if we don't have any overarching deadline then maybe we ought to have one.

Similar to the landing on the moon deadline, perhaps we need to put a foot firmly planted down on terra firma and collectively come up with a deadline for the attainment of true self-driving cars. We need to provide a finish line goal. We need to rally the troops. We need to glean all the advantages and early stated benefits of having a looming and clear-cut deadline.

No more playing around. No more of those puffery deadlines that have no stake in the ground. Stop the incessant conga line of concocted deadlines that come and go.

Create a national deadline for the achievement of true self-driving cars.

And then work the heck toward achieving it.

Whoa, that's potentially crazy talk.

How could that be done?

One concern is that this would potentially force together governmental interests and commercial sector interests in a manner that we might regret. Imagine too the aspects of what is the prize for meeting the deadline and how would the monies be expended toward the deadline seeking efforts. It would be a morass within a quagmire of an abyss.

Some vehemently argue that we should leave things as they are. Let the efforts continue and see what happens. Companies will make deadlines, and the deadlines will come and go. So be it. The marketplace will eventually sort things out. If there is profit to be made from achieving self-driving cars, the market will find a path there.

Others believe that true self-driving cars are of such a vaunted and revered nature that we need to find a better way to reach attainment. The comings and goings of the marketplace have shown that we aren't doing this right, they contend, and we need to try something new.

You might know that there are many comparisons often made to the moon landing and the achievement of self-driving cars.

It is claimed by some that the incredible feat of being able to go into outer space and reach the moon is analogous to the brashness and newness of being able to attain true self-driving cars. Breakthroughs will be required.

Those breakthroughs will not only be vital to the goal of achieving self-driving cars but will have tons of spillover, entailing all kinds of breathtaking AI advances and high-tech mechanizations.

In short, the need for a deadline is larger than just attaining self-driving cars per se, though that by itself is undeniably praiseworthy and essential.

Conclusion

There are a lot more twists and turns on this topic (lamentably, space limitations only allow a few more remarks herein).

Suppose that somehow the notion of setting a deadline for self-driving cars is actually undertaken.

One question is how will we know that self-driving cars have been achieved?

In short, are we going to say that Level 5 is the functionality associated with the deadline? Or would we be willing to accept some variation of Level 4? Etc.

The emphasis is that without squaring down the functional meaning, we would have a deadline that has little value. You would have everyone coming out of the woodwork to claim that they achieved the deadline and ergo showcase their alleged self-driving car as evidentiary proof. That would be a nightmare. We would need to pin down the rules beforehand.

Here's another potential head-scratcher.

What date should we pick for the deadline?

It could be the kind of date that is plucked from thin air. That doesn't though seem very sensible. Maybe we gather a herd of experts and get them to derive a date, allowing as much fisticuff activity (intellectually, of course) as needed to arrive at a consensus deadline. Anyway, some means would have to be devised and agreed upon.

Maybe *you* would like to partake in coming up with the deadline.

Sure, that seems fine. We can crowdsource the date.

Pick a year.

We all usually like to choose years that seem to be shapely and consist of round numbers, along the lines of 2025, 2030, 2035, 2040, 2045, or 2050.

Do any of those strike your fancy?

I haven't listed the years after the year 2050, since we'll all be flying around with jetpacks by then and we won't especially care about what is happening with those ground-based surface-going vehicles and whether they are autonomous or still being driven the old-fashioned human-driven way.

I forgot, please remind me, what again was the deadline for jetpacks.

CHAPTER 16
LEFT LANE BLOCKERS AND SELF-DRIVING CARS

Left lane hog!

I'm referring to those darned drivers that sit in the left lane nearly forever, cruising leisurely along without a seeming care in the world, backing up traffic as they do so.

You've undoubtedly been stuck behind such a driver.

Indubitably many times.

It is exasperating, infuriating, and altogether makes you want to bust a gasket.

They get into the left lane and occupy the lane as though it is owned by them. On top of this, they decide to be the unofficial determiner of the allowed speed for the rest of nearby traffic. For example, even though the posted speed limit might be 65 miles per hour, the left lane hog will opt to go at say 55 miles per hour.

Why so slow?

There are lots of frequently cited reasons or excuses for this type of behavior.

One claim is that they are going at the safest appropriate speed. This is based on the logic that the posted speed is the maximum allowed speed, which is not necessarily the safest allowed speed. Indeed, the driver's handbook clearly states that you should never assume that the posted speed is the speed that you are to be driving at.

A driver is required to go at a speed that is safest for the conditions and circumstances of the roadway, and presumably no faster than the posted speed limit.

All of this translates into some drivers that believe they are an excellent judge of what the appropriate speed is.

Thus, they are more than happy to sit in the left lane and prevent other traffic from moving faster than their self-divined safety speed. The drivers that are behind this obnoxious lane hog are probably going to get riled up and angry at the pace being established. But in the mind of the left lane hog, that's of no consequence since anyone not obediently abiding by the now enforced speed threshold is plainly wrong and needs to clearly and vigorously be put in their place.

The vaunted rule of thumb that we all live by is that you are to use the left lane as the "fast lane" and that you are to also use the left lane as a passing lane. Otherwise, get out of the left lane.

This is an inherently efficient way to do things. By rigorously adhering to those golden rules, traffic can be more neatly undertaken. It is like trying to get water to flow through a bunch of plumbing pipes. The right lane might get clogged up, but the left lane should not get equally plugged. The left lane should always be generally open and available.

Sure, there are moments when the left lane has a car getting into it from the right lane, and then the vehicle has to get up-to-speed and at some point get back into the right lane. This should be done expeditiously and all drivers ought to learn how to do this with proficiency.

That being said, a lot of drivers do not seem to have figured out how to make that transition into and then out of the left lane.

They botch the maneuver. They cut off traffic that is already in the left lane and disrupt those drivers, potentially sparking a car crash. They sit way too long in the left lane before opting to get out and back into the right lane.

When they get back into the right lane, they mess up that act too, including causing the left lane traffic to come to a crawl and trying to squeeze into the right lane in a manner that disrupts those law-abiding drivers.

Okay, so there are left lane hogs that earnestly believe they are helping mankind by being the speed regulator. They presumably are thinking with their heart. Unfortunately, this is shortsighted and actually illegal if they are unduly upsetting the prevailing traffic. You can imagine their shock at getting a ticket for their presumed heroic efforts, mindlessly unaware that they are not somehow magically ordained as the designated speed police or unofficial traffic cop on our highways and byways.

Taking the law into your own hands is a dangerous play.

We certainly see and hear lots of stories about road rage that began with these kinds of situations. A person gets stuck behind a lollygag in the left lane. This leads to horn honking. The drivers of both cars think they are completely doing the right thing. They agree to pull over to the side of the road. After shouting obscenities and insults, they go to fisticuffs. Nutty human behavior, that's for sure.

There is a multitude of ways that hogging the left lane can produce car crashes or at least fender benders. A car coming up from behind the hog in the left lane might decide to try and pass around the blocker by darting into the right lane. This is generally an unexpected move. Traffic in the right lane will get summarily cut off. Bam, a car collision occurs.

The driver that ducked into the right lane will try to point fingers at the other car that was holding the left lane hostage. Sorry, no dice. You are not going to wiggle out of bad driving by simply pointing at another bad driver. Two wrongs do not make a right. No matter how upset you get with a presumed wrong driver, you aren't given a green light to do something untoward. That's not how things work in the real world.

Keep in mind too that some left-lane hogs are clueless about what they are doing. They perhaps never heard about the left lane as being the fast lane and nor that is a passing lane. It seems bizarre that they have a driver's license and do not know this, or even without a driver's license they surely would have gleaned this rule of thumb by having driven on the roadways.

Anyway, inexplicably, the driver is oblivious to this.

It is tempting to then aid those drivers by awakening their driving sensibilities. That's why those that honk their horn at such a driver do so, trying to get them out of their mental fog and into the driving realm. Another tactic involves riding on the bumper of the hog. You can turn your headlights on and off, perhaps using your high beams. There is even the roll down your window and wave your arm tactic.

I think you might already know that all of those actions are pretty much a dangerous gambit and should not be employed.

Some left-lane blockers will react to those exhortations in ways that make the situation worse. They will become preoccupied with making sure that you don't get past them. The driver might intentionally go slower, wanting to show you that they are in charge.

Oddly enough, when you switch lanes to the right, doing so to try and get around the left lane hog, they might opt to also get into the right lane. At first glance, this seems like they have finally gotten the message and realize they were hoarding the left lane. Maybe so.

On the other hand, sometimes the left lane hog wants to block you while you are trying to use the right lane as a passing lane. They will get into the right lane as you do so. The moment that you realize that the left lane is apparently now available, and you begin to aim back into the left lane, they will do the same.

This is scary driving.

Cars moving along at around 60 miles per hour should not be playing a game of tag. The back-and-forth shenanigans sometimes stretch out over several miles of driving distance. The drivers are in a frame of mind that entails a winner-take-all mindset. They are so immersed in their own competition that they fail to realize there is other traffic on the roadway too. All in all, this type of adverse oppositional driving can produce a cascading car incident that causes a multitude of vehicles to collide.

Drivers often get into their own mental cocoons while driving. They begin to disconnect the reality of being in a multi-ton machine that has tremendous speed and power, becoming numb to the physics of what they are doing. In a manner of speaking, they almost seem to believe they are playing a video game.

The thing is, there are assuredly life-and-death consequences in this case.

One complaint that some have about the public roadways in the United States is that we do not have a federally mandated one-universal standard about how to use the left lane across all of the states. Instead, each state sets up its own rules.

Some states have no specific indications about how a left lane is to be used. Other states have a written rule that you are okay to use the left lane continuingly until you need to make an exit (thus, at that juncture, needing to get into the right lane for those right lane oriented offramps). Those states usually don't say anything about using the left lane for passing purposes.

Some states are clearer about the passing aspects. For example, the rule might be that you must move to the right if a car behind you is desirous of proceeding past you. Usually, this rule has a caveat that you do not need to undertake this allowed passing if you are already at the maximum posted speed or at an otherwise optimal safe speed. Some make added caveats such as this kind of rule only applies on roads that are at the speed limit of 65 mph.

The point being that supposedly you can be sympathetic to your fellow drivers about the left lane usage due to the confusion of overlapping, conflicting, or unstated rules that occur across each of the states throughout the USA. When you drive in a particular state, the left lane usage is like the proverbial box of chocolates, namely you never know what you are going to get.

Others would scoff mightily at that contention. If you are driving anywhere in the United States, you ought to know what the correct driving action is. Do not drive in a given state if you aren't versed in their driving laws. Furthermore, everybody knows about the left lane as a cultural phenomenon about how to properly drive. You don't need to read a state-by-state driving guide to know what to do.

For those of you who have driven the autobahn in Germany, you've certainly seen how the left lane is rigorously treated there. By and large, drivers know to get the heck out of the left lane and keep it clear for other drivers. Any meandering tourists that either does not realize the rule or that decide they are going to flout the rule, well, they'll find out soon enough the err of their ways.

Meanwhile, here in the US, we are still struggling day-to-day and mile-by-mile with the left lane usage.

In Arkansas, they recently put in place a new set of rules about the left lane. The old rule said this: "Motor vehicles shall not be operated continuously in the left lane of a multilane roadway whenever it impedes the flow of other traffic."

That seems relatively clear-cut.

Does it seem straightforward to you?

After mulling things over, Arkansas has revised their vehicle code and it replaced that single sentence with this longer passage: "Except as otherwise provided in this section, a vehicle shall not be driven upon the left lane of a multilane highway, except as follows: (1) When overtaking and passing another vehicle proceeding in the same direction under the rules governing that movement; (2) When all other lanes for traveling in the same direction are closed to traffic while under construction or repair; (3) When all other lanes for traveling in the same direction are in disrepair or are in an otherwise undrivable or unsafe condition; or (4) When a vehicle is preparing to exit the multilane highway on the left."

You could suggest that the more verbose version is an improvement because it adds specificity. Some though are concerned that it is too much for drivers to know, especially when in the heated battle of driving on public roadways.

Another concern is that it includes seemingly nebulous language. For example, what does "undrivable or unsafe condition" truly mean? This could be a loophole for a driver that asserts the right lane was assuredly undrivable or unsafe (their contention could be entirely arguable or fictionalized). All you've done is given those left-lane hogs a handy ready-made excuse and rendered things easier for them by adding phrasing to embolden their outlandishly outstretched driving proclivities.

The lengthy passage also has gotten some to question the scope of the language.

Here's how.

I've previously covered the move-over slow-down laws that are essential for safety on our roadways.

If a driver decides to get into the left lane while in Arkansas due to the desire to do a move-over and avoid an emergency vehicle that is partially in the right lane, where does that fit in this wording?

This use case does not appear to be in any of the four stated rules. At best, you would do a squeaker and claim that the right lane was "unsafe" at that moment and therefore the third rule applies. Others decry that the move-over isn't explicitly called out in one of the rules or stated as a fifth rule.

All of this has to do with something known in the driving world as having *lane discipline*.

Drivers in some locales have rather strict and overtly top-notch lane discipline. In other locales, lane discipline is lax and confounding. The problem comes to the fore in those locales with the mishmash of lane discipline. When drivers do not have the same understanding of how to drive, it can produce chaos and car crashes. Plus, having the same understanding is the first essential part, while the second and equally or more essential part is stridently employing the agreed lane discipline.

Being loosey-goosey with human drivers is fraught with troubles.

To reduce car crashes, you need to make the driving rules and conditions patently apparent and vociferously enforced. Without that kind of discipline, lane discipline is out the window. Drivers will still do wild and endangering driving acts regardless of rules, but the hope and assumption are that any willy nilly opens the floodgates for horrific driving.

We've been ruminating quite a bit about driving in the left lane and the role of lane discipline.

Consider that the future of cars consists of AI-based true self-driving cars.

There isn't a human driver involved in a true self-driving car. Keep in mind that true self-driving cars are driven via an AI driving system. There isn't a need for a human driver at the wheel, and nor is there a provision for a human to drive the vehicle.

Here's an intriguing question that is worth pondering: *How might left lane usage change in an era of AI-based true self-driving cars?*

I'd like to first further clarify what is meant when I refer to true self-driving cars.

Understanding The Levels Of Self-Driving Cars

As a clarification, true self-driving cars are ones that the AI drives the car entirely on its own and there isn't any human assistance during the driving task.

These driverless vehicles are considered Level 4 and Level 5, while a car that requires a human driver to co-share the driving effort is usually considered at Level 2 or Level 3. The cars that co-share the driving task are described as being semi-autonomous, and typically contain a variety of automated add-on's that are referred to as ADAS (Advanced Driver-Assistance Systems).

There is not yet a true self-driving car at Level 5, which we don't yet even know if this will be possible to achieve, and nor how long it will take to get there.

Meanwhile, the Level 4 efforts are gradually trying to get some traction by undergoing very narrow and selective public roadway trials, though there is controversy over whether this testing should be allowed per se (we are all life-or-death guinea pigs in an experiment taking place on our highways and byways, some contend).

Since semi-autonomous cars require a human driver, the adoption of those types of cars won't be markedly different than driving conventional vehicles, so there's not much new per se to cover about them on this topic (though, as you'll see in a moment, the points next made are generally applicable).

For semi-autonomous cars, it is important that the public needs to be forewarned about a disturbing aspect that's been arising lately, namely that despite those human drivers that keep posting videos of themselves falling asleep at the wheel of a Level 2 or Level 3 car, we all need to avoid being misled into believing that the driver can take away their attention from the driving task while driving a semi-autonomous car.

You are the responsible party for the driving actions of the vehicle, regardless of how much automation might be tossed into a Level 2 or Level 3.

Self-Driving Cars And Left Lane Usage

For Level 4 and Level 5 true self-driving vehicles, there won't be a human driver involved in the driving task.

All occupants will be passengers.

The AI is doing the driving.

One aspect to immediately discuss entails the fact that the AI involved in today's AI driving systems is not sentient. In other words, the AI is altogether a collective of computer-based programming and algorithms, and most assuredly not able to reason in the same manner that humans can.

Why is this added emphasis about the AI not being sentient?

Because I want to underscore that when discussing the role of the AI driving system, I am not ascribing human qualities to the AI. Please be aware that there is an ongoing and dangerous tendency these days to anthropomorphize AI. In essence, people are assigning human-like sentience to today's AI, despite the undeniable and inarguable fact that no such AI exists as yet.

With that clarification, you can envision that the AI driving system won't natively somehow "know" about the facets of driving. Driving and all that it entails will need to be programmed as part of the hardware and software of the self-driving car.

Let's dive into the myriad of aspects that come to play on this topic.

First, the good news.

For whatever left lane usage rules that we might come up with, the odds are pretty high that the AI driving system can be programmed to abide by those rules. If each of the various US states does things its own way, that's fine too. When a self-driving car enters into a US state from another one, it would merely swap out the rules being used from that other state and swap in the rules for the state being entered.

Easy-peasy.

Furthermore, essentially all AI driving systems across all of the various brands and models of self-driving cars could readily include the same sets of rules. This would mean that the self-driving cars on our public roadways would all have the same basis for how they will utilize left lanes. Unlike the haphazard nature of human drivers, self-driving cars could consistently and reliably implement those rules.

This saliently points out the fact that the rules would not only be stored in the AI driving system but also be carried out rigorously by the driving efforts, nearly to the letter. The problem with human drivers is that they might forget the rules, or decide to undercut the rules or do whatever they darned well please to do. Assuming that the programming of the AI driving system is written to strictly adhere to the rules, this would algorithmically be applied and occur with relatively precise enactment.

Before we get overly carried away with the AI somehow being perfect at the left lane adoption, we need to be realistic and revisit the nature of the rules that are likely to be used.

Recall that earlier the Arkansas driving law indicated that the left lane can be used whenever the right lane appears to be undrivable or in an unsafe condition.

There is a lot of ambiguity amidst the notion of being undrivable and also the aspects of being unsafe.

Assuming that this vague phrasing is not viably tied down to specifics, it means that each of the AI driving systems as developed by their respective teams of AI developers will likely have different ways of ascertaining the conditions of being undrivable or being unsafe. This lack of consistency means that a particular brand of a self-driving car that is using a particular AI driving system might assign the labels of undrivable or unsafe to a situation that some other AI driving systems might not.

You see, a lot of how we drive has to do with probabilities and figuring out estimates of what might happen. We somehow do this in our human noggins. For self-driving cars, the AI driving system is programmed to explicitly calculate the likelihoods and chances of things that are happening or might happen. All in all, the efforts by a specific brand of a self-driving car and its version of the AI driving system can arrive at different formulations about what driving actions to take, subject to how the algorithms have been devised.

In any case, despite that variability, you can generally rest assured that self-driving cars would be more consistent and reliable about how to deal with left lanes than the capricious nature of everyday human drivers.

We can pat the back of self-driving cars by also bringing up another advantage they will have while on the public roadways, namely the use of V2V (vehicle-to-vehicle) electronic communication.

This has to do with self-driving cars being considered as *connected* in addition to working autonomously. They are connected via several means, the most notable perhaps being V2V.

An AI driving system of a self-driving car will be programmed to send electronic messages to other nearby self-driving cars.

Suppose that a self-driving comes upon a piece of debris lying in the middle of a lane on the highway. The AI driving system, upon detecting the debris, might be designed to start broadcasting a V2V message so that any nearby self-driving cars will get notified about the debris. Those other self-driving cars would then take into account the handy warning. This might then have those AI driving systems opt to get out of the lane that contains the debris or takes an earlier exit to avoid coming upon the debris.

The beauty of using V2V would be the possibility of coordinating the actions of a multitude of self-driving cars when they are near each other in traffic.

Returning the left lane usage, whenever a self-driving car wanted to maneuver from the right lane into the left lane, it could send out a quick V2V message to other self-driving cars that are already in the left lane. Those AI driving systems would then presumably aid the other self-driving car in making the lane change, doing so by providing a sufficient gap among the vehicles or taking other helpful actions.

We oftentimes hope that human drivers will do the same for us when we are on the highways. There are those courteous and supportive drivers out there that sometimes act in that selfless manner.

Unfortunately, and though this might seem a bit pessimistic about humanity, most drivers seem to act in a dog-eat-dog way and the last thing they would ever do is give another driver a beneficial hand involving left lane usage. I hope that doesn't appear caustic, and maybe it is only me that seems to abundantly come across those unhelpful and altogether meanspirited drivers.

Here's yet another big plus for self-driving cars and the *lane discipline* considerations.

In theory, we could come up with a zillion more rules about numerous other variants entailing how to properly perform the left lane usage. We could also come up with a ton of rules about the right lane usage. Add as many as you like. For humans, this would go straight over their heads and they would shrug their shoulders and lament that it is impossible to abide by so many rules.

Not so with the AI driving systems.

We can just keep piling on rules to our heart's content.

Plus, the rules could readily be changed from time-to-time, and then electronically pushed out to the AI driving systems, doing so using the OTA (Over-the-Air) updating communication components that self-driving cars will be outfitted with. This will be nearly seamless. In contrast, as you know, changing driving rules for human drivers is a nightmare and some will get wind of the changes and others will not. In a sense, one push of the button and all self-driving cars could be updated (this, sorry to say, has some potential downsides).

Conclusion

This all adds up to a wonderful world of self-driving cars readily cooperating with each other and using the left lane in the manner that we might dream it should be used.

Wait for a second, there is a fly in the ointment, as they say.

What is the kicker that will make things not quite so hunky-dory?

The straightforward answer in two words: *Human drivers.*

Allow me to briefly elaborate.

There are some proponents of self-driving cars that have their heads in the Utopian clouds and oftentimes forget about those pesky and innumerable human drivers. The wistful belief is that we will only have self-driving cars and do away with any human driving. Maybe so, but that's a somewhat farfetched vision of the future and not in the cards for now.

Keep in mind that there are currently about 250 million conventional human-driven cars in the United States alone. Those won't be tossed into the junk heap overnight. It will take decades upon decades for self-driving cars to be gradually rolled out, and increasingly dispense with human-driven cars. We will also need to contend with those human drivers that insist they will only give up their driving upon the day that you pry their cold dead hands from their steering wheels.

Why does it matter that there will be a mixture of self-driving cars and human-driven cars?

Because the AI driving systems are going to try and abide by the left lane usage rules, and most likely be stymied or messed up by human drivers that aren't doing so. In the same manner that you might today get blocked or otherwise confounded in your driving due to a left lane hog, the same issues are facing self-driving cars.

It gets worse too, in a manner of speaking.

Human drivers are already starting to bully self-driving cars. They do so because they can.

In essence, the AI driving systems are programmed to be relatively polite and civil at driving. When human drivers encounter other human drivers that are kind and considerate, this is usually "punished" by taking advantage of those generous drivers. Remember, it is a dog-eat-dog world. Or, more aptly, the viewpoint is that if there are drivers that are sheep, while the drivers that are the wolves will surely and axiomatically sheer them.

And the self-driving cars right now look like sheep to many of those overbearing take-no-prisoners human drivers.

You can bet your bottom dollar that once self-driving cars become prevalent, there will be hordes of human drivers that will rejoice. The cause for their jubilation is that those self-driving cars in traffic all around them will be easily bamboozled. Easily bullied. Easily taken advantage of.

In total, this could spell disaster for left lane usage. You'll have some human drivers that want to overtake self-driving cars. Those human drivers are probably already doing the same to human drivers and will continue as such toward the remaining human drivers on the roadways. Meanwhile, some human drivers won't realize what is going on, or some human drivers are trying to be helpful to self-driving cars.

Could be a colossal mess.

I don't want to end on such a sour note.

I could on and on about this topic, but let's end it for now on this key and a rather upbeat facet if you will.

Self-driving cars will have all kinds of sensors, such as video cameras, radar, LIDAR, and so on. They can record the antics of those scheming human drivers. Presumably, those recordings could electronically be beamed directly to the driving enforcement authorities and those human drivers would get nailed for their driving recklessness.

Self-driving cars might hold the upper hand, you see, being able to tattletale on despicable human drivers and do so in real-time.

Take that, you ruffian human drivers, and score a point for the AI..

CHAPTER 17
TECHNICAL DEBT AND SELF-DRIVING CARS

Getting in over your head.

That's what often happens when people take on debt.

Shakespeare famously warned us about the dangers of going into debt, stating that "neither a borrower nor a lender is; for loan doth oft lose both itself and friend." For some people that become swamped by debt, they find themselves sinking into an all-encompassing abysmal abyss. The debt sorely and adversely impacts them, their loved ones, their friends and acquaintances, and otherwise bodes for indubitably rotten tidings.

Sometimes, a person is oblivious to their mounting debt.

I know that seems nearly impossible to imagine. What can happen is that the person starts making zillions of charges on their credit cards and they meanwhile delude themselves into not realizing there will ultimately be unfavorable consequences. The piper though will eventually need to be paid.

Credit card agencies often make life especially easy for those that wantonly are apt to spend. Charge this, charge that, and it all seems like free money. You have a seemingly endless credit limit, so why not keep spending. Little or no thought goes toward how this is going to get paid for.

Some people realize what they are doing but are insidiously hooked on spending recklessly. It is said to at times be like a gambling addiction. They might overtly know that what they are doing is racking up a debt that they can never afford to repay.

Turns out that the urge to go into debt is seemingly greater than the stopping forces to prevent it.

More variations arise.

Some people know they are getting themselves into a lot of debt and do so straightforwardly. They are anticipating that the money being borrowed will provide a sizable payoff. Taking on debt could be highly profitable, and there are lots of instances where this has been a proven strategy.

They say that at times the debt rainbow can lead to a pot of gold at the end. That's at least the grand hope unless of course the payoff never happens.

Oopsie.

Why all this talk about debt?

Because there is another kind of debt that few know about, a type of debt that arises in the software development realm and has been coined as *technical debt*.

To be clear, technical debt can arise in any engineering or technological endeavor. I'm going to focus on the nature of technical debt in the context of software systems. Please do though keep in mind that the same notions can be applied to lots of other tech-oriented contexts.

Here's how technical debt in software arises.

A software engineer is working night and day on a programming project. It is a hard-fought battle. A timeline has been established for getting the code done and put into production by the end of the month. This is a ridiculous deadline and the programmer is at their wit's end as to how the coding can be finished by that rapidly approaching date.

Most seasoned programmers are used to these kinds of scenarios, which seem to happen overly frequently. Rather than receiving a deadline that is based on what can be done, there is a tendency for others to assign deadlines simply based on other whims that have nothing to do with the actual programming required. Get things done by this date is the mantra, regardless that the date was plucked from thin air or based on a dreamy whimsy.

Anyway, a programmer is apt to decide that to meet the deadline will require doing a bit of flimflam on the coding. Good programming practices dictate that you ought to build in error handling so that your code will be resilient and able to handle gotchas that occur once the program is put into use.

Nice idea, but that's going to get placed aside, for now, the hectic programmer decides. The programmer doubts there are many errors in the code and thus the error handling won't especially ever be needed. So, skip it, for now.

Score a foul point for the entry of technical debt into this scenario.

In essence, the program has taken on a form of debt. The debt is a future cost that for the moment seems worthwhile. Put off for today that which can be dealt with at some later unspecified date.

Nobody will presumably notice the debt for now. It is hidden from view. The programmer knows about it. Whether the managers overseeing the project know about it is another question. Sometimes they do, and they encourage the debt, aiming to attain the touted and prized deadline on time. Sometimes the debt is only known to those that are creating it. Others that are presently unaware will on a later occasion find out to their dismay that such debt is laden inside the code.

Returning to the scenario, the programmer determines that omitting the error handling is not going to be enough of a jettison to reach the deadline.

Something else has to be tossed over the side of this boat. After giving the matter some pronounced thought, the programmer stops documenting the code and goes into a heads-down mode of churning out lines upon lines of code.

Yes, that's another kind of technical debt that has been added to this mounting stack or heap.

The programmer figures that since they personally produced the code and ergo know the code by heart, there is no need to document it. No need to write down what the code does. No need to proffer inline explanations. The programmer believes that the code is so transparent and so obvious that anyone coming along to later update or modify the code will immediately understand it. Plus, documentation is not much fun and won't aid in meeting the deadline of having a running app that works.

For those of you that aren't programmers, you might not realize this is a rather common refrain by some alleged purists of coding. They don't want to mar their code with commentary, nor waste their precious mind on doing something considered mundane. The thing is, these same programmers will often curse themselves later on when called back to revise their prior code since they no longer remember what was in their minds when they generated the code.

In addition, any programmer that has ever had to take over someone else's code will undoubtedly tell you that it can be a nightmare to try and divine what the other programmer was trying to do. The code itself is insufficient to showcase what the purpose is. Without some documentation, albeit even meager or scant documentation, the code can be an enigma that either takes an excessive amount of time and effort to figure out or sometimes you end up having to summarily chuck out the code and start anew.

We've now got two variants of technical debt in this situation. There is a lack of error handling as one form of technical debt. The other technical debt is the paucity of documentation.

You might be tempted to assume that this is marginally any semblance of debt. It seems like nothing of great consequence is being owed.

Sorry, that's akin to playing the odds at the roulette wheel.

Let's assume that those incurred technical debts are able to allow the programmer to attain the end of the month deadline. Hurray! The deadline was achieved and all are happy and delightfully pleased with the now underway app.

Lurking though in the shadows is the ominous technical debt.

Imagine that after the app is in use for a week or two, when all of a sudden, the code reaches an unexpected error. Yikes! Without the error handling capabilities, the app has no provision about what to do. The app shuts down each time that the error occurs.

People using the app are furious.

What the heck is going on with this crazy app. One minute it seems to be working just fine, and the next moment it inexplicably closes down. Carping about this bizarre behavior spreads quickly across the vastness of social media and the Internet. Those that at first hailed the app as a tremendous breakthrough are now warning that you cannot count on it. At the worst of times, it can get flakey and die on you.

You see, the debt is now being paid, rather involuntarily one might say.

The cost to pay this technical debt could be enormous. Perhaps the app is no longer used by anyone and languishes as a useless or haphazard app that should be avoided entirely. On top of that, whoever developed the app and fostered it into becoming available could face reputational ruin. You might anticipate lawsuits too, assuming that those using the app might believe that they suffered some form of losses due to the flakiness of the app.

In short, the cost to cover this technical debt might be many times more than the perceived debt value at the time it was initially incurred.

We can go further and make this a rather sad tale of woe. A different programmer is quickly brought in to resurrect the app. Upon looking at the code, the programmer is dismayed and taken aback that there is absolutely no documentation. The code is inscrutable. It is going to take weeks or maybe months to decipher this murky mound of enigmatic code.

The technical debt of not having documentation now rears its ugly head. This was not apparent by those that were earlier running the app as they had only encountered the other technical debt (i.e., the error handling technical debt).

As a rule of thumb, some technical debt will be readily witnessed or experienced, while other kinds of technical debt can remain hidden and elusive.

There is also the concept of garnering interest on technical debt, similar to incurring interest on financial debt. Suppose the programmer that is brought in to modify the code can successfully do so, and meanwhile doesn't document what they are doing. You could say that the technical debt associated with the lack of documentation is growing in interest or being further piled onto.

One other aspect to be aware of is that technical debt can happen at any stage of software development. I've focused for the moment on code debt, which is ostensibly the most popularly discussed instance of software technical debt.

You can also have software design debt. That's when you scrimp or incur technical debt during the design stage or phase of developing a system. This happens quite frequently, whereby there is angst to move right away into coding and so the design efforts are shortchanged. The shortchanged design elements are a form of technical design debt that will someday need to be repaid.

Another stage or phase of software technical debt consists of testing debt.

Developers do this all the time. When deadlines are nearing, the seemingly easiest thing to do is shorten or narrow the amount of testing that is going to be done. There is that infamous Silicon Valley mindset that it is best to move fast and break things. This includes a willingness to forgo extensive testing and just let the end-users become the testers.

That can be sensible or it can be a horrendous choice.

If an application is going to be used in simple ways and not be a life-or-death matter, you can potentially get away with piles of technical debt. Those that use the app might shrug off the problems of the app. They might be excited to be able to use the app, perhaps being in a beta group that gets access sooner than others.

The problem is that any life-or-death software that has technical debt is like a ticking timebomb. Depending upon the nature of the software technical debt involved, the consequences of that underlying debt might cause notable damages or harm.

One area that is already starting to encounter the throes of technical debt includes AI-based systems.
I refer to this as *AI technical debt.*

Though you might be assuming that AI systems are surely developed with the utmost of heightened stringent controls and capabilities, you'd be sadly and utterly mistaken. Indeed, as I've often pointed out, the pell-mell rush toward crafting AI systems has regrettably led to a goldrush that is ridden with software that is unreliable, poorly tested, and waiting to fail.

Let's then combine the overall software technical debt aspects and the AI goldrush, tying this amalgamation to matters entailing real-time life-or-death types of systems.

Where can such facets converge?

Answer: *AI-based self-driving cars.*

That might seem surprising, perhaps shocking to some. Well, get used to it. There is AI technical debt right now being incurred in the development of AI self-driving cars.

The piper will someday need to be repaid.

This is an alarming realization when you somberly consider that the future of cars consists of AI-based true self-driving cars. There isn't a human driver involved in a true self-driving car. Keep in mind that true self-driving cars are driven via an AI driving system. There isn't a need for a human driver at the wheel, and nor is there a provision for a human to drive the vehicle.

Here's an intriguing question that is worth pondering: *How might AI technical debt potentially undermine the advent of AI-based true self-driving cars?*

I'd like to first further clarify what is meant when I refer to true self-driving cars.

Understanding The Levels Of Self-Driving Cars

As a clarification, true self-driving cars are ones that the AI drives the car entirely on its own and there isn't any human assistance during the driving task.

These driverless vehicles are considered Level 4 and Level 5, while a car that requires a human driver to co-share the driving effort is usually considered at Level 2 or Level 3. The cars that co-share the driving task are described as being semi-autonomous, and typically contain a variety of automated add-on's that are referred to as ADAS (Advanced Driver-Assistance Systems).

There is not yet a true self-driving car at Level 5, which we don't yet even know if this will be possible to achieve, and nor how long it will take to get there.

Meanwhile, the Level 4 efforts are gradually trying to get some traction by undergoing very narrow and selective public roadway trials, though there is controversy over whether this testing should be allowed per se (we are all life-or-death guinea pigs in an experiment taking place on our highways and byways, some contend).

Since semi-autonomous cars require a human driver, the adoption of those types of cars won't be markedly different than driving conventional vehicles, so there's not much new per se to cover about them on this topic (though, as you'll see in a moment, the points next made are generally applicable).

For semi-autonomous cars, it is important that the public needs to be forewarned about a disturbing aspect that's been arising lately, namely that despite those human drivers that keep posting videos of themselves falling asleep at the wheel of a Level 2 or Level 3 car, we all need to avoid being misled into believing that the driver can take away their attention from the driving task while driving a semi-autonomous car.

You are the responsible party for the driving actions of the vehicle, regardless of how much automation might be tossed into a Level 2 or Level 3.

Self-Driving Cars And AI Technical Debt

For Level 4 and Level 5 true self-driving vehicles, there won't be a human driver involved in the driving task.

All occupants will be passengers.

The AI is doing the driving.

One aspect to immediately discuss entails the fact that the AI involved in today's AI driving systems is not sentient. In other words, the AI is altogether a collective of computer-based programming and algorithms, and most assuredly not able to reason in the same manner that humans can.

Why is this added emphasis about the AI not being sentient?

Because I want to underscore that when discussing the role of the AI driving system, I am not ascribing human qualities to the AI. Please be aware that there is an ongoing and dangerous tendency these days to anthropomorphize AI. In essence, people are assigning human-like sentience to today's AI, despite the undeniable and inarguable fact that no such AI exists as yet.

With that clarification, you can envision that the AI driving system won't natively somehow "know" about the facets of driving. Driving and all that it entails will need to be programmed as part of the hardware and software of the self-driving car.

Let's dive into the myriad of aspects that come to play on this topic.

There is AI technical debt aplenty amidst the AI driving systems and related code of today's budding self-driving cars.

First, some estimates are that there could be around 100 million lines of code or more that exist to empower and enable the capabilities of a self-driving car. This includes proprietary code that a particular automaker or self-driving tech firm has devised for their self-driving cars. Also included are the reams and reams of third-party code, such as the use of open-source code that is intermixed into the AI driving systems and other components.

Scarily, many firms are unaware of how much AI technical debt they are sitting atop.

This is somewhat akin to those people that take on financial debt and aren't aware that they are doing so. It just kind of happens. Debt is incurred and not noted or tracked. The same can be said for some of the AI development groups and their amazing efforts to craft AI driving systems. They are incurring AI technical debt here and there, right and left, above and below, yet there isn't an explicit effort toward noting that it is piling up.

Where might this AI technical debt reside?

One of the most significant arenas consists of the AI underlying the sensory suite and all of its machinations.

The sensors for self-driving cars are crucial. By and large, sensors are being used that encompass real-time video cameras, radar, LIDAR, ultrasonic detection, thermal imagining, and so on (the choice of which kinds of sensors to use is highly variable and differs from firm to firm).

The sensors are essentially the eyes and ears of the AI driving system. During a driving journey, data is streaming into the sensors and being computationally analyzed. A significant means of doing the needed computational pattern matching consists of utilizing Machine Learning (ML) and Deep Learning (DL). Besides analyzing the data directly, there is also the need to perform Multi-Sensor Data Fusion (MSDF), bringing together the data and seeking to align and triangulate the interpretations of the driving scene.

Hidden within all of the complex code for these sensory uses is all manner of AI technical debt.

Some of the debt has been incurred by a rush to pull together the AI driving system and try to get a self-driving car up and going for tryouts. Some of the debt exists as a result of putting a myriad of AI developers to the task of developing the code, stretching the skills of novice AI developers, or pushing to the brink the skills of savvy AI developers. In addition, this is at times being undertaken without rigorous tracking and software coding practices being set up and observed.

I've described previously that the AI development efforts for self-driving cars can be given an overly wide berth and allowed to do their "magic" without the typical rigors expected of similar real-time life-or-death systems of this nature.

There are relatively few self-driving car makers that are directly watching out for AI technical debt.

What they all need to do is take a comprehensive inventory of their enormous efforts and figure out where that AI technical debt is potentially lurking. This can be painstaking and painful to do. Finger-pointing and all manner of unsightly blame-game exhortations can arise.

The easier path is to just wait and see what happens.

Note too that the AI technical debt can arise throughout each of the stages or phases of a self-driving car and its life cycle.

It could be that there are design debt aspects that have yet to be uncovered, perhaps only gaining visibility once the self-driving car is underway on roadway trials. That's a bad time to be running into the skulking technical debt.

Conclusion

There are numerous additional twists and turns (I'll mention just a few more, given the space limitations herein).

Though the AI technical debt can be demonstratively bad, it can also be somewhat of a "necessity" in some cases, though this comes with a big caveat. If an AI team is at least aware of where the technical debt is being incurred, they can consider the tradeoffs of allowing it to exist. They can try to minimize the dangers of the debt. They can seek to reduce the amount of debt-related technical interest that will be accrued.

What should not happen is the outright hiding of any mounting AI technical debt. Trying to keep say upper management in the dark about the technical debt is going to be unseemly in the end, for everyone involved. Pressures to meet deadlines or to keep costs tapped down are certainly primal urges to go ahead and allow technical debt to soak into the AI driving system.

Lamentedly, those that are outspoken can find themselves internally blacklisted for decrying the generation of software technical debt, as per my discussion about the potential for whistleblowers to start appearing in the self-driving cars industry.

All told, if an existing self-driving car development effort isn't already on top of the AI technical debt phenomena, it is time to do something about it.

Better late than never.

And remember the immortal words of Benjamin Franklin in his 1758 treatise entitled *The Way To Wealth*: "The second vice is lying, and the first is running in debt."

Good old Ben knew what he was talking about back then, and which still applies in today's state-of-the-art AI-infused self-driving cars emergent world. This is undeniably sage wisdom worthy of posting on the cubicle walls of contemporary AI developers and their managers.

CHAPTER 18
HAWK DEER RABBIT AND SELF-DRIVING CARS

A recent viral video caused a lot of head-scratching and rapt wonderment.

It provides a breathtaking story, entirely seen visually and absent of any narration (thankfully so, allowing for our uninterrupted attention to the altogether moving pictorial saga itself).

Let me walk you through the action as though your perchance happened upon the video while otherwise perusing your usual dose of social media. Assume that you came upon the video on a random basis and opt somewhat leisurely to click on it, mainly out of curiosity about why it has garnered so many views.

The opening scene consists of a seemingly pleasant and innocuous green pasture that is surrounded by a lush forest. Grass in the untamed pasture has grown relatively high, providing for a bit of hiding coverage for any petite-sized animals that might opt to go out into this verdant open space.

A rabbit has ventured out into the grassy area.

If you are thinking what I think you are thinking, you are right that the rabbit is about to get a rather unpleasant surprise. Please prepare yourself accordingly for what happens next.

Out of view of the fixed-in-place video camera (affixed to a tree or some such supporting structure), a hawk must have been flying in the sky above the pasture. All that we know and catch a fleeting glimpse of is an ominous shadowy figure that shockingly and surprising swoops down upon the rabbit. It happens in an eye-blinking split second.

One moment the rabbit is hopping along without a care in the world, and the next moment it finds itself in the clutches of fearsome talons.

Yikes!

The hawk is doing what hawks do.

While this nimbly flying creature is now on the ground, it is trying to voraciously turn the rabbit into a tasty meal. A mighty struggle ensues. The prey is desperately trying to fight back against the determined predator. We hear the faint and frantic squealing of panicked cries coming from the rabbit as it does whatever it can to getaway. The odds though of escaping are extremely slim.

Hawks have fine-tuned this kind of predatory machination and the rabbit is presumably and inexorably not long for this earth, sadly so.

But wait for a second, this story has only just begun.

Out of nowhere, a young deer suddenly scampers into the pasture. We aren't sure what this deer has in mind. It sprints in a circular fashion around the engrossed hawk and rabbit. Is the deer going to take a close look at the life-or-death battle underway? Will the deer merely scamper back out of the pasture and leave the struggling pair to whatever ends that destiny or fate shall decide?

Get ready to drop your jaw and become utterly mesmerized by what happens next.

The young deer attacks the hawk.

Say what?

Yes, the deer attacks the hawk.

One kind of doubts that the hawk was giving much due to the deer, prior to that moment, and logically assumed that the deer would simply move along. It seems likely that hawks quite frequently might perform ferocious attacks on small animals and be amidst larger animals while doing so. It also seems likely that those larger animals would tend to scurry away and not want to get involved in someone else's fight.

Who can blame them? Self-preservation would seem to be the axiomatic approach for any nearby observing animals. Those larger animals have their own set of predators to be worrying about.

That being said, if an eagle was possibly flying around, it might relish seeing the hawk on the ground. Eagles are considered predators of hawks. We would not be especially surprised if an eagle took advantage of the hawk as the ground-based struggle was taking place. The eagle would be all too happy to catch the hawk unawares.

But a deer opting to intervene, well, you've got to admit that is something unexpected and assuredly astonishing.

But there's more!

The rabbit manages to escape from the hawk. This indubitably makes sense. That hawk is now being pounced upon and being ransacked by the young deer.

This is one heck of a beat down by the deer. As some have stated, we watch as Bambi seemingly transforms into Rambo. The hawk tries to get away, fluttering its wings and going toe-to-toe with the deer. Vicious fisticuffs are at work here.

If the deer had done this to simply distract the hawk, the job was completed. Excellent work. The rabbit was free and seemed to entirely get away, hopping anxiously back into the wooded area where the hawk would have little chance of rediscovering the prey. For the deer, it was time to call it quits, one would assume, and the deer could merrily move on and pat itself on the back for having done a good deed and preserved an itty-bitty rabbit's life.

And yet the battle further ensues.

For several long minutes, the hawk and the deer go at it, fiercely. This is far more than an attempt by the deer to scare the hawk or startle the hawk into having given up the rabbit stew that was on the plate for today's dining. We don't know for sure what the two have got going here. The deer is absolutely determined to do what it can to dispense with the hawk.

Think about that famous fictional character known as the Hulk, and how there is a sudden transformation from one moment being relatively withdrawn and reserved, which then metamorphizes into this muscular overpowering hulking thing. That's what seems to take place with this deer.

Eventually, we can see that the hawk is becoming less and less combative. The deer has clearly prevailed. Some have suggested that the hooves of deer can have sharpened edges that are akin to polished knives. The fact that the hawk was pinned to the ground by the deer and pummeled and slashed at by the hooves, you would certainly expect that the hawk would lose that kind of a streetfight skirmish.

Toward the end of the video, another similarly sized deer enters the pasture. As this newcomer approaches the conquering deer that has taken to task the hawk, the victorious deer momentarily moves menacingly toward the approaching interloper, getting the interloper to back off. This recurs a couple of times. One interpretation is that the triumphant deer does not want to share its hard-fought winning spoils. There are other possible interpretations too.

That is the gist of the video and we are then left to our own devices to decide what we have just witnessed.

I'd wager that it is a rock-solid bet that most people would be completely taken aback by the idea that a deer would not only attempt to shoo away a hawk that is already in the middle of a battle with a rabbit, but even more so that the deer would continue long after the initial disruptive action had succeeded. The myriad of posted comments reinforces that incredulous notion.

What's up with that?

We think of deer as herbivores. They love to munch on leaves and plants. We see them idly grazing around in pastures and forests. Perhaps that's what adds to our beloved adorability of deer. I dare say that nearly all of those Saturday morning cartoons and ongoing animated portrayals of deer seem to stridently abide by that preordained script.

Before you read the next paragraph, I will warn you that it isn't going to proffer pleasant news. You might want to skip around it.

Scientists emphasize that deer are considered omnivorous, and thus they will indeed eat meat (whoa, exalted gasp!). This is somewhat rare for deer to do. Usually, the deer would have to be quite hungry. Furthermore, the situation would typically need to present itself on a silver platter, such as if the deer came upon a ground-based bird's nest and realized there were defenseless hatchlings to be had. Generally, whatever meat might be eaten has to be easily made into munchable morsels since deer do not have the usual natural equipment for the arduous ordeal of eating raw meat.

Sorry if that ruins your dreamy imagery of deer.

We are now ready to take a running leap at how to interpret the video.

Some argue that the deer was aggressively hungry. It saw that the hawk was vulnerable and distracted. The deer calculated that this was the perfect moment to get a nearly free meal. All it had to do was a sneak attack on the hawk, thus the basis for going around at the first encounter, and the rest would be glorious history.

Maybe so, some concede.

But the hawk was still active, alive, and proving demonstrably that it could put up a fight. That's not at all like going after an animal that might be a hatchling or perhaps already injured and possibly feeble. Trying to go at a hawk that was amid battle status would seem poorly calculated and doesn't provide a convincing case, they counterargue. Plus, the grassy area and surrounding forest appeared to be replete with tons of food for the deer, unlike if it were the dead of winter and food sources were covered in deep snow.

Here's another take.

The deer heard the cries of the rabbit. It is conceivable that those cries are similar sounding to those of a fawn. The deer rushed to save what was believed to be a fellow deer. Running past the two, the deer realized it was simply a hawk and a rabbit. Nonetheless, now that the deer was close enough and judged that the upper hand was now at play, the deer decided to pounce on the hawk.

There are multiple variations of that version. Perhaps the deer and the rabbit were already friendly toward each other and had earlier bonded. If that wasn't the case, it could be a natural instinct that the deer and a rabbit would have toward each other, regardless if they had ever met before. And so on.

Hang onto your hat, there are more interpretations to be considered.

Maybe this particular deer was ticked off at hawks, either this specific one or at hawks in general. It could be that a hawk had previously attacked a fawn and this deer was either the one attacked or that it saw a fellow deer that got attacked. In any case, this deer has had a festering hatred for hawks. Hawks were on the list of creatures to be excised if possible.

Under that scenario, the deer ostensibly had come upon a situation of incredibly good luck. Finally, a hawk was in the right place at the wrong time. This deer, harboring for perhaps a long time the burning desire to someday right the wrongs of this planet by trouncing a hawk, finally got its wished-for chance. That's why this hawk was not ever going to escape from this now superhero deer. This was payback time, aplenty.

You can go on and on about the underlying rationale for the actions that transpired.

Before I get into the overarching theme that I want to explore herein, it is probably prudent to include another viewpoint about that video of the deer. Some lamented that the deer ever got into the fray. They pointed out that the hawk was merely seeking to survive and that part of the cycle of nature is that hawks will grab up rabbits. Life is tough that way. Making the hawk into the baddie is unfair, some would assert. The deer should not be made into a hero. It interfered. In addition, you ought to cast the deer in the same sour light as that of the hawk, in the sense that if the deer was trying to eat the hawk, this could be construed as equivalent to the hawk trying to eat the rabbit.

Just wanted to include that further perspective on the matter at hand.

What can we glean from all of these disparate interpretations?

First of all, there is something natively and intrinsically fascinating about having a situation involving a prey caught by a predator (the rabbit getting caught by the hawk), which then is summarily overturned when a different "predator" of a predator enters into the matter and takes out the initial attacker.

That being said, this is more than just fascinating when an unexpected overtaking occurs, such as by a deer that attacks a hawk. This is breathtaking since we would not expect a deer to take this stance and seeing this happen makes you stop in your tracks and think mindfully about the world around us.

Some of our most basic assumptions about how things work can suddenly become topsy-turvy.

This provides a handy lesson for us that we might find useful to employ in other contexts. Are you ready to shift gears and yet simultaneously apply the lessons learned from this endearing saga?

I hope so.

Let's talk about self-driving cars.

The future of cars consists of AI-based true self-driving cars. There isn't a human driver involved in a true self-driving car. Keep in mind that true self-driving cars are driven via an AI driving system. There isn't a need for a human driver at the wheel, and nor is there a provision for a human to drive the vehicle.

Here's an intriguing question that is worth pondering: *How might the saga of the deer and the hawk and the rabbit provide insights into the advent of AI-based true self-driving cars?*

I'd like to first further clarify what is meant when I refer to true self-driving cars.

Understanding The Levels Of Self-Driving Cars

As a clarification, true self-driving cars are ones that the AI drives the car entirely on its own and there isn't any human assistance during the driving task.

These driverless vehicles are considered Level 4 and Level 5, while a car that requires a human driver to co-share the driving effort is usually considered at Level 2 or Level 3. The cars that co-share the driving task are described as being semi-autonomous, and typically contain a variety of automated add-on's that are referred to as ADAS (Advanced Driver-Assistance Systems).

There is not yet a true self-driving car at Level 5, which we don't yet even know if this will be possible to achieve, and nor how long it will take to get there.

Meanwhile, the Level 4 efforts are gradually trying to get some traction by undergoing very narrow and selective public roadway trials, though there is controversy over whether this testing should be allowed per se (we are all life-or-death guinea pigs in an experiment taking place on our highways and byways, some contend).

Since semi-autonomous cars require a human driver, the adoption of those types of cars won't be markedly different than driving conventional vehicles, so there's not much new per se to cover about them on this topic (though, as you'll see in a moment, the points next made are generally applicable).

For semi-autonomous cars, it is important that the public needs to be forewarned about a disturbing aspect that's been arising lately, namely that despite those human drivers that keep posting videos of themselves falling asleep at the wheel of a Level 2 or Level 3 car, we all need to avoid being misled into believing that the driver can take away their attention from the driving task while driving a semi-autonomous car.

You are the responsible party for the driving actions of the vehicle, regardless of how much automation might be tossed into a Level 2 or Level 3.

Self-Driving Cars And Unexpected Aspects

For Level 4 and Level 5 true self-driving vehicles, there won't be a human driver involved in the driving task.

All occupants will be passengers.

The AI is doing the driving.

One aspect to immediately discuss entails the fact that the AI involved in today's AI driving systems is not sentient. In other words, the AI is altogether a collective of computer-based programming and algorithms, and most assuredly not able to reason in the same manner that humans can.

Why is this added emphasis about the AI not being sentient?

Because I want to underscore that when discussing the role of the AI driving system, I am not ascribing human qualities to the AI. Please be aware that there is an ongoing and dangerous tendency these days to anthropomorphize AI. In essence, people are assigning human-like sentience to today's AI, despite the undeniable and inarguable fact that no such AI exists as yet.

With that clarification, you can envision that the AI driving system won't natively somehow "know" about the facets of driving. Driving and all that it entails will need to be programmed as part of the hardware and software of the self-driving car.

Let's dive into the myriad of aspects that come to play on this topic.

I brazenly might begin by saying that a deer, a hawk, and a rabbit walk into a bar. Zing! That's a bit of tongue-in-cheek levity and I'll leave the rest of the curveball to your imagination.

Moving on to some serious considerations, one aspect that I just mentioned moments ago concerns the desire that we ought to not anthropomorphize AI. In that same vein, many scholars worry that we oftentimes anthropomorphize animals too.

There is an ongoing debate about how much thinking we can ascribe to animals.

Years ago, some argued vehemently that humans were thinkers while animals were not. This for example was claimed to be proven by the aspect that humans made use of tools, while (presumably) animals did not. Such a difference was held forward as a basis for asserting that humans think but that animals don't. Since then, the tools matter has been debunked in the sense that there are animals that indeed do make use of tools. Etc.

Anyway, the reason that I bring this up is that the viral video of the deer is an immediate kneejerk reacting possibility to ascribe all kinds of thinking processes to the animals involved in the intriguing struggle. Was the deer "angry" at hawks and thought mindfully about attacking the hawk, or did the deer simply react in some inherently preprogrammed way to the situation at hand? Will the rabbit possibly someday seek to save the life of the deer, doing so because it has contemplated the lifesaving efforts of the deer and therefore aims to intentionally repay that debt in the future?

You might find of further potential interest that there had been attempts at getting dogs to drive a car. Yes, you read that correctly. The question was whether a dog has sufficient intelligence to be able to drive a car. We all pretty much seem to accept that dogs do some amount of thinking, and if so, perhaps this could be directed toward driving a car.

That's enough on those side tangents. I'd like to focus for now on the earlier highlighted theme that sometimes the things that we think that we know are not entirely apt.

Here's how this applies to the advent of AI-based true self-driving cars.

One of the biggest and loudest debates about having self-driving cars doing tryouts on public roadways is that this should not be happening at this time. Some vehemently oppose those tryouts. They argue that until self-driving cars have been shown to be safe for our streets, they ought to not be on our highways, byways, and avenues.

The use of computer-based simulations is argued as being the right way to proceed, and only after the simulations are essentially completed would actual autonomous vehicles be deployed onto our roadways. Do the simulations first. If the simulations showcase that self-driving cars are safe to be on the roads, so be it. If the simulated self-driving cars are unsafe in the simulation, they aren't ready for being around us and nearby to us all.

When you drive your car and come upon a self-driving car, the thing is that you don't know what that self-driving car is going to do. Is the AI driving system up to snuff? Will it react in the proper way to all variants of driving settings?

Even if you aren't driving near a self-driving car, you might be a passenger in a human-driven vehicle that comes across a self-driving car, thus endangering you. You might be a passenger inside a self-driving car, and therefore endangered by what it will or might not do. Pedestrians are likewise in danger.

It would seem obvious that simulations ought to be undertaken.

And, they are, which is something that by and large the automakers and self-driving tech firms are glad to tout. They relish emphasizing the number of millions of miles that they have done in their simulations for their self-driving cars.

That would seem to shut the case closed on those decrying that simulations need to be undertaken.

Not so, the retort quickly arises.

Here's the rub.

The simulations are taking place and meanwhile, the self-driving cars are on our public streets. That's not the way things are supposed to work, say the simulation proponents. You do all of the simulations, and then, maybe you put self-driving cars on the roads. In essence, once all of the simulations are done, you look at what it showcases. If the results are demonstrable that self-driving cars are cleared to be on our roadways, sure, go ahead and ergo proceed.

Doing public roadway trials while simulations are ongoing is likened to building a skyscraper before you have figured out all of the architectural rigors. It's a bad idea to take a chance on something that has not yet properly been sounded out via simulations.

The cart has been placed in front of the horse, as it were.

The next aspect of the simulations-first argument is that the existing simulations also tend not to be fully realistic. A concern raised is that the simulations are computer-based mockups of what cars do and what happens on our streets. Some of the simulations have no direct bearing on the physics of the real world, and they are more akin to those fun playing video games about driving cars. Some simulations are much more robust and rigorous than the game-playing kind, but many of those are even still said to be a dollar short at fully portraying the realities of real-world driving.

There are various counterarguments to this simulations-first precondition.

One is that simulations are handy but cannot replace on-the-road driving and the consequent vital feedback that will be had from the real world. It is argued that only via having actual self-driving cars on actual roadways can you glean what you need to know to make self-driving cars viable.

Some would then say that you can get that real-world driving experience by using special closed tracks, also known as proving grounds. Take your self-driving cars there. Try them out to your heart's content. They are typically on private lands and completely fenced off from the public roadways (not always, some exceptions exist).

In that manner, you can use simulations and use real-world driving, though the real-world driving is being done separate and apart from the public, which protects the public from any endangerment while the self-driving cars are being put through their paces.

Now that I've dragged you through all of that, you might be curious about how that deer, hawk, and rabbit fit into this picture.

Remember that viewers of the viral video seemed to be quite surprised that a deer would opt to attack a hawk and continue the attack unabated and seemingly unashamedly so (well, let's not veer into anthropomorphic territory there).

An issue that is front and center about the use of simulations and likewise the use of closed tracks is that those are devised by mankind and are presumably and potentially constrained by what mankind thinks is worthy of including. In short, those that insist on public roadways tryouts are quick to emphasize that the real-world of open-ended driving will reveal various edge cases and unusual driving settings that by conventional thinking would not have been set up or tested in any simulation or proving ground settings.

What are edge cases?

The wild and shall we say unpredictable nature of the public roadways bring forth driving scenarios that nobody would have prior thought to include.

What we think that we know can be a blinder to what we need to know.

Those that advocate stridently for the public tryouts assert that encountering real-world "unpredictable" situations via the public roadways is the most sensible path toward discovering what we don't know and what we do need to know.

Of course, that's a debatable contention and one that doesn't sit well with the simulationists.

Conclusion

That whole topic about whether to be doing public roadway tryouts is a hornet's nest of contention. On that, we can likely all agree.

I've discussed additional twists and turns in my columns and won't cover those again herein.

The handy aspect of the deer story is that it reminds us that we at times might have preconceived notions that are not correct.

There is that old line about making assumptions is a slippery slope and you need to be cautious when doing so (since it makes one into the butt of the matter).

Another takeaway is that the next time you are wandering in the woods and see what seems like the cutest of Bambi deer, do not let your conditioning by cartoons and movie portrayals mislead you. Those deer can do one heck of an eye-opening awe-inspiring smackdown, so be dutifully be wary and give them some proper street cred.

I'd bet that any hawk reading this column and worth its salt is going to think twice the next time they see a rabbit that has a grazing deer nearby. Hawks, you've been forewarned.

CHAPTER 19

MOUSE BRAIN AND SELF-DRIVING CARS

Mighty mouse.

I'm referring to the aspect that mice can be amazingly smart, mightily so. We already all would likely agree that mice are quick on their feet and physically agile. That's a given.

I dare say, and you are welcome to argue about the contention if you wish, that they are also remarkably cunning.

On a personal level, I've dealt with mice that perchance decided to take up residence at my home and were seemingly determined to stay without my permission and without paying any rent. Upon witnessing a mouse running around in my domicile, I rushed over to the local store and got an everyday mouse trap.

Turns out that the mice were able to readily avoid the thing and probably got quite a laugh at my having set it up, to begin with. Let's refer to them as mocking mice, in addition to being mighty mice.

I then decided to copiously watch numerous popular online videos labeled as providing a myriad of guaranteed-to-work formulae about how to steadfastly catch a mouse. Those videos usually started by pointing out the futility and stupidity of trying those dime-store mouse traps. This made me cringe and feel embarrassed each time that such a video made such a proclamation, but I was determined to find the optimal means to snag the mice and would endure nearly any belittling to do so.

All told, I fervently tried many of the proffered solutions. Those darned clever mice seemed to escape each one. Sometimes the trap would remain untouched. Other times the cheese or other bait would be half-eaten, yet the ingenious creatures were not captured.

I finally threw in the towel and did what my colleagues and friends had kept adamantly suggesting all along.

I got a cat.

This nearly immediately solved the dilemma. It was also like striking two birds with one stone. I gained the joys of having a beloved housecat, plus the mice mysteriously disappeared. It was like a magic act of pulling a rabbit out of a hat, except this was the part of the magic performance that made things disappear.

I don't know if my beloved cat had summarily dispatched them directly or maybe they headed for the hills after realizing that there was a new sheriff in town. My cat never revealed to me the secret of the mice disembarking success. Either way, the house was now mice-free and had the warmth of a purring cat as protector and soulful playmate for the family.

Back to the claim that mice can be sharp cookies, as it were.

Scientists would generally say that mice are reasonably intelligent beings and are ostensibly worthy of rapt attention. A recent study has attempted to count up the number of mice that are used annually in the United States for biomedical research.

The number is staggering. Prepare yourself accordingly. The estimate is that there are about 107 million mice annually being used in scientific research and perhaps about another 4 million related rodents such as rats. That's a grand total of around 111 million, with mice being about 97% of the count.

Mice are kindly doing a great service to humanity. They are being analyzed and scrutinized on a daily basis. The assumption is that mice can reveal all sorts of insights about animals in general, and about mammals in particular, and hopefully provide a helpful glimpse into the nature of humans and human capabilities.

You've undoubtedly seen or read stories about those ubiquitous mouse-in-a-maze efforts.

The mice often appear to showcase a number of intelligence-oriented characteristics.

They can seem to demonstrate having short-term memory and also having long-term memory. The mice will figure out more expedient paths of a maze and seek to optimize their self-behavior. They also go beyond doing work individually or independently and seem to be able to work in teams, making use of various communications to coordinate their joint activities. It is believed that the communications take place via sound, touch, smell, urination, and even by the act of thumping via their appendages.

You can make a pretty good case that mice are inquisitive about the world around them. They are explorers. Yet they also do so with caution and can seem to identify situations that might be subtly menacing, such as a mousetrap that is waiting to be sprung. They can be seemingly tricky or even devious when you are trying to catch them (perhaps I am somewhat jaded due to the fact that they outfoxed me, though I used the ultimate ace card and invoked an overarching predatory strategy to win the war, even after having lost numerous momentary battles).

Anyone that has had a pet mouse knows that you can train them to learn a human-assigned name.

Let's be clear though that we don't know for sure what the name means or signifies entirely to the mouse per se. All that we can reasonably assert is that the mouse learns to associate the sound of the name to the rewards that you proffer, and thus is presumably mainly tracking the sound rather than having any grasp of what a "name" consists of. Humans have a robust understanding of what a name denotes, for which we cannot necessarily ascribe equally so to the inner noggin calculations of the mouse brain.

Speaking of brains, as you likely know, the usual measure for the size or magnitude of a brain is to estimate how many neurons there are. This is not especially the most revealing way to try and gauge the possibility of intelligence within a being, but it is handy and relatively easy to discuss. In addition to the number of neurons, another similar numeric count consists of the number of synapses that tend to interconnect the neurons. A neuron is usually connected with other neurons in a networking fashion.

Okay, let's consider some of the estimates about the number of neurons and the number of synapses there are in animals of keen interest herein.

It is said that the human brain has perhaps 86 billion neurons and around 125 trillion synapses, though these are only rough estimates and you can find a lot of other suggested counts throughout the scientific literature. We will take those counts with a grain of salt and merely use them as an order of magnitude indicator rather than any semblance of an exactitude.

What are the counts for those feisty mice brains?

Some estimates indicate that mice have perhaps 70 million neurons and around 1 billion or more synapses, but please do realize there are lots of other estimates in the scientific literature. Again, consider this merely as an order of magnitude indication.

Given the caveats that I've emphasized, we can perhaps be somewhat cautious but proceed to compare that human brains have approximately 86 billion neurons in contrast to mice that have a meager 70 million. And that human brains have possibly 125 trillion synapses to around 1 billion in mice brains. The gist is that there are a lot more of each in human brains versus mice brains, by leaps and bounds.

One reason to be cautious in making such a comparison is that the counts alone are not sufficient to fully portray whether intelligence-oriented behavior will arise or not, nor the degree of intelligence that will arise.

For example, some scientific studies altered a single gene of a set of mice and were able to produce seemingly much smarter mice than in comparison to everyday mice. These souped-up mice were shown to have more extensive short-term and long-term memory capabilities and be able to perform mazes at paces and in ways that everyday mice had not.

In any case, let's suppose that mice brains are demonstrably scaled-down versions of human brains such that if we could figure out how mouse brains function, we could potentially get a leg-up toward unpacking the nature of the human brain.

Start small, and then go big, as they say.

You could though readily argue that the human brain might not be functioning akin to the same manner that a mouse brain does. In that case, perhaps learning about the inner workings of the mouse brain will not substantively aid our quest toward unlocking the secrets of the human brain.

Sad face emoji.

Nonetheless, most would reasonably agree that whatever we can stridently figure out about mouse brains is going to one way or another further inform us about the intrinsic underpinnings about how brains seem to work.

That might or might not be crucial to reverse-engineering the human brain, though it seems a worthwhile try. Happy face ensues!

A recent study has done a yeoman's job in trying to push toward further mapping out the mouse brain.

A large-scale study done via the *Machine Intelligence From Cortical Networks* program (known as MICrONS), unveiled a high-resolution 3D mapping of a mouse brain segment. This consisted of about 120,00 neurons and another approximately 80,000 other kinds of brain-related core components. The scientific study was conducted by computational neuroscientists from the Allen Institute for Brain Science, Baylor College, Princeton University, and other entities.

The dataset of the mapping is available online and publicly accessible. Visualization tools are included. The data is housed in the repository known as the Neural Data Access (NDA) as part of the MICrONS research collection and encompasses the electron microscopy (EM) results. The work states that:

- "It is the largest multi-modal connectomics dataset released to date and the largest connectomics dataset by minimum dimension, number of cells, and number of connections detected (as of July 2021)."

- "It is the first EM reconstruction of a mammalian circuit across multiple functional brain areas."

An especially intriguing aspect is that the researchers captured the patterns of neural activity while the mouse was viewing various images and movies (generally consisting of natural scenes). This potentially allows for analysis of how the studied brain elements responded due to presented stimuli. Thus, it is one facet to simply gauge what the brain mechanistically contains and a more perhaps illuminating angle of trying to decipher the functional recordings of how the cells responded to the visual stimuli.

Mice might be a crucial pathway toward figuring out the human brain, as mentioned earlier.

Mice might also be a crucial pathway toward devising Artificial Intelligence (AI) in machines.

Say what?

Yes, the more than we can identify how brains work, mice or humans, the better chance we would seem to have toward crafting AI systems. If we can somehow reverse engineer brains, we might be able to create AI systems that do more of what brains do. Some believe that we will simply mimic or simulate the wetware of brains. Others indicate that we might not need to do such mimicry and can instead glean insights to devise AI systems that are able to exhibit intelligent behavior, though they might be made in completely different ways than that of wetware brains.

I've extensively covered these two contrasting trains of thought (a bit of a pun there), namely the bottoms-up versus the top-down theories of how to attain AI.

You can conceive of efforts in AI as racing forward on multiple fronts at once.

There are those that don't especially pay attention to the biomedical efforts of brain reverse engineering. They are fine with such work taking place, but the pace and progress have little bearing on their AI efforts. Absent any hard-and-fast tangible indications from the wetware focus, those AI developers and researchers are forging ahead anyway. No need to wait for the bio side to pin down how the brain operates.

Meanwhile, there are other AI developers and researchers that closely monitor or are directly involved in these wetware examinations. This is then infused into their AI constructions. The AI use of Machine Learning (ML) and Deep Learning (DL) is notably influenced by and tends to use Artificial Neural Networks (ANNs), which are somewhat akin to wetware neural networks, though decidedly less so and not on par (as yet).

The thing is, there is a huge debate about whether having tons upon tons of something that runs on a machine in a computer-based way that mimics neurons is ever going to arise to intelligent behavior in the manner that we construe intelligence. If we don't also come to understand how intelligence arises from the neurons and their interconnections in wetware, we might be doomed to having merely a humongous network of computer-based simulated neurons that aren't particularly overwhelmingly impressive.

Perhaps we might get AI toward parts of intelligent behavior via these massively ANN's and then get stuck. The widespread supposition is that the only way to get unstuck will involve decoding how brains give rise to intelligence in the natural world.

The mighty mouse might be a significant step in that direction.

Where might a better devised AI be used, namely an AI that might be shaped around what we ultimately learn from the brains of mice?

Hold your breath. Get ready to fall off your chair.

Get this: *The seemingly humdrum and shall we say at times unheralded mouse brain could be one of the cornerstones or keys to achieving AI-based true self-driving cars.*

Oopsie, if you fell to the ground, I hope you had a pillow waiting to catch your fall.

Let's talk about self-driving cars.

The future of cars consists of AI-based true self-driving cars. There isn't a human driver involved in a true self-driving car. Keep in mind that true self-driving cars are driven via an AI driving system. There isn't a need for a human driver at the wheel, and nor is there a provision for a human to drive the vehicle.

Here's an intriguing question that is worth pondering: *How might the insights from reverse-engineering the brains of those lovable and clever mice somehow stoke the advent of AI-based true self-driving cars?*

I'd like to first further clarify what is meant when I refer to true self-driving cars.

Understanding The Levels Of Self-Driving Cars

As a clarification, true self-driving cars are ones that the AI drives the car entirely on its own and there isn't any human assistance during the driving task.

These driverless vehicles are considered Level 4 and Level 5, while a car that requires a human driver to co-share the driving effort is usually considered at Level 2 or Level 3. The cars that co-share the driving task are described as being semi-autonomous, and typically contain a variety of automated add-on's that are referred to as ADAS (Advanced Driver-Assistance Systems).

There is not yet a true self-driving car at Level 5, which we don't yet even know if this will be possible to achieve, and nor how long it will take to get there.

Meanwhile, the Level 4 efforts are gradually trying to get some traction by undergoing very narrow and selective public roadway trials, though there is controversy over whether this testing should be allowed per se (we are all life-or-death guinea pigs in an experiment taking place on our highways and byways, some contend).

Since semi-autonomous cars require a human driver, the adoption of those types of cars won't be markedly different than driving conventional vehicles, so there's not much new per se to cover about them on this topic (though, as you'll see in a moment, the points next made are generally applicable).

For semi-autonomous cars, it is important that the public needs to be forewarned about a disturbing aspect that's been arising lately, namely that despite those human drivers that keep posting videos of themselves falling asleep at the wheel of a Level 2 or Level 3 car, we all need to avoid being misled into believing that the driver can take away their attention from the driving task while driving a semi-autonomous car.

You are the responsible party for the driving actions of the vehicle, regardless of how much automation might be tossed into a Level 2 or Level 3.

Self-Driving Cars And The Mouse That Roared

For Level 4 and Level 5 true self-driving vehicles, there won't be a human driver involved in the driving task.

All occupants will be passengers.

The AI is doing the driving.

One aspect to immediately discuss entails the fact that the AI involved in today's AI driving systems is not sentient. In other words, the AI is altogether a collective of computer-based programming and algorithms, and most assuredly not able to reason in the same manner that humans can.

Why is this added emphasis about the AI not being sentient?

Because I want to underscore that when discussing the role of the AI driving system, I am not ascribing human qualities to the AI. Please be aware that there is an ongoing and dangerous tendency these days to anthropomorphize AI. In essence, people are assigning human-like sentience to today's AI, despite the undeniable and inarguable fact that no such AI exists as yet.

With that clarification, you can envision that the AI driving system won't natively somehow "know" about the facets of driving. Driving and all that it entails will need to be programmed as part of the hardware and software of the self-driving car.

Let's dive into the myriad of aspects that come to play on this topic.

We are considering how mouse brains might be useful for making further progress on achieving AI-based true self-driving cars.

First, let's dispense with something that is a bit nonsensical but has to be covered herein else there might be some unfortunate misinterpretations. I am decidedly not suggesting that we could put a mouse in the driver's seat of a conventional human-driven car and ergo suddenly find ourselves with a mighty mouse driver.

Quite unlikely.

Of course, some might bitterly complain that a mouse is not physically capable of driving a car, regardless of whether there might be a mental capacity to do so. A mouse cannot reach the brake pedal and the accelerator pedal, could not seemingly adequately turn the steering wheel and would be unable to sit in the driver's seat and peer over the dashboard and out the front windshield. In that sense of objective constructs, the mouse is at a crucial disadvantage at the get-go.

It is an unfair playing field.

Sigh.

Look here, this is an insipidly transparent concern (sincerely stated?) that can be easily dealt with. We can take that grievance off the table by stipulating that we would craft a set of driving controls that would adequately accommodate the petite size and limbs of a mouse.

Assume that this could be done.

In case you doubt the efficacy of making that possible, I'd like to point out to you the prior efforts that have taken place to see if dogs could drive a car. Yes, dogs. The usual driving controls were modified to accommodate those beloved paws of mankind's loyal companion. The dogs seemed to enjoy the driving and the attention, but they assuredly were not going to be everyday drivers that you would see waving at you during those weekday commutes and weekend go-to-the-park jaunts.

Anyway, the overarching point is that we are focused on the brainpower of the mice, rather than their physicality per se.

Despite the general shrewdness of mice, it seems altogether fair-minded to assert that they could not drive a car, even if we could tap directly into their noggin. When I refer to driving a car, I mean this in the normative sense of what we as humans consider the act of driving. Envision a mouse taking the written exam at your local DMV (Department of Motor Vehicles) and then having to showcase to a driving instructor or tester that the mouse could readily drive on community streets and local highways.

A nice form of dreamy imagery, though not real-world oriented.

If you want to play a wild kind of futuristic outside-of-the-box game, we could possibly do something to mice that could somehow transform them into potential drivers. There have already been efforts of trying to infuse human-related brain cells into those of a mouse. Also, earlier it was mentioned that there are efforts of altering the genes of mice to see what results arise.

To clarify, this notion that mice by themselves could not drive a car is based on the unadorned semblance of today's ordinary mouse brain.

Shifting gears, we ought to get back to the mainstay of the topic.

We can consider this rather vexing question; namely, how do humans manage to drive a car?

There are lots of logical rules that we all agree are presumably at the core of the driving task. You can learn about those rules by reading books about how to drive a car. You can take classes in driving. An instructor can sit with you while you are driving and explain to you what to do. And so on.

It would seem apparent that we know everything there is to know about how humans drive.

The thing is, all of those discernible rules and abundant logic about the driving act are ultimately converted into the human brain. Once the whole kit and caboodle go into your brain, we really do not know what takes place. The brain in terms of turning all that wetware machinations into human thinking is still an abundant mystery.

In short, if studies of the brains of mice could reveal the innermost secrets of how the brain arises to the task of thinking, we might be able to unlock the same as it pertains to human thought. And, if we did that, we would have a much clearer understanding of what goes through the human mind during the driving chore. Some ardently believe that the vaunted and revered Level 5 will not be achieved unless we can first unpack the inner workings of human thought.

That being said, I would not want to imply that the glories of finally figuring out how humans think are going to be used simply to garner autonomous vehicles and self-driving cars. You can bet your bottom dollar that a lot more could be achieved with AI that leveraged or exploited the byzantine complexities of the human brain.

Conclusion

Start small and make our way to something big, really big.

We can welcome and seek to squeeze every ounce of insight from the mapping of the mouse brain. A lot more mapping is going to be needed. Be thankful for those gallant mice that contribute to this grand quest.

A final comment for now.

Remember earlier that the approximate estimated count for the number of human neurons in our brains is around 86 billion, while for a mouse it is something akin to 70 million. Recall too that I described how I obtained a cat, partially prompted to aid in dealing with my mouse problem at home.

The estimate of the number of neurons in the brain of a cat is around 250 million. On a rough comparison, this means that the cat has perhaps three to four times the number of neurons of a mouse. Please note that you have to be careful making any generalizations by the sheer count of neurons alone since (as mentioned earlier) that's not the only factor involved.

But, I'm sure your neighborhood cat indubitably thinks it can readily outsmart those troublesome mice, and the feline is eagerly and earnestly willing to prove to you that by far a cat is heads and shoulders smarter than those annoying mousey freeloaders underfoot.

The race to figure out how to best attain AI is akin to a cat and mouse gambit that we don't yet know how it will play out. It is going to be exciting, that's for darned sure.

CHAPTER 20
STATISTICAL TROLLEY AND SELF-DRIVING CARS

Think about all of those moment-to-moment rapid decisions that you make while driving a car.

Go ahead, do a slow-motion post-driving analysis in your mind. Think about a recent trip to the grocery store or perhaps a driving trek to a local mall.

Whether you realize it or not, there were hundreds upon hundreds or likely thousands of minuscule driving decisions that you made, all part of a larger web of driving decisions in the course of a driving journey. And, notably, they all ultimately encompassed some variant of altogether life-or-death considerations.

How so?

Let's see.

Imagine that you are driving along amid city streets on an otherwise ordinary day.

If you decide to take that upcoming right turn just a bit overly fast there is a heightened risk that you could inadvertently go awry. You might veer into a pedestrian that is standing out at the curb edge. You might swing wide and brush against another car that is in a nearby lane.

Bam, you smack into someone.

In case you are doubtful that these are decidedly life-or-death-related decisions, I have some somber stats to share with you.

There are about 6.7 million car crashes each year in the United States alone. Those car crashes produce approximately 2.5 million injuries and over 40,000 human fatalities. Few of us are contemplating those ominous stats when we get behind the wheel of a car. Nonetheless, they are quite illuminating numbers and worthy of giving due pause whenever undertaking a driving trip.

Now that you are thinking about all of those itsy-bitsy decisions and how vital they are, let's zoom to a more macroscopic perspective. You can envision this like using one of those zoom-in to zoom-out visualizations when looking at the planet earth from the vantage of an orbiting space station. I'm sure that you've seen those before. A person is standing on a city street and the camera pulls back to reveal them standing amidst a city block, which the camera zooms out further to reveal the entirety of the city. This zooming out continues. You next see an entire geographical area and then next an entire continent.

Okay, so we'll do that same kind of panoramic envisioning, but in a different context.

You are one person that is driving on a city street. We zoom out and there are lots of other cars also driving on that same city street. We continue to zoom out and can see lots and lots of cars throughout the entire city, all being driven by a human at the wheel. Keep zooming out and you'll see cars being driven throughout an entire geographical region and then throughout the entire United States.

There are around 250 million registered automobiles in the United States. Of course, at any singular point in time, not all of them are necessarily underway. We do keep our cars parked and ostensibly stationary for about 95% or more of their available usage time. In any case, when we do use our cars, the aggregate number of miles traveled annually is estimated at 3.2 trillion miles (in the United States alone). A typical everyday driver probably drives around 12,000 miles per year, which varies depending upon where you live and what type of work you do.

What does this driving-related zoom-in to zoom-out visioning get us?

The choices that we make as drivers in the microscopic acts of driving are inevitably a virtual kind of collective conglomeration. By adding up all those seemingly minuscule acts, we can begin to potentially detect patterns of widespread behaviors. Those patterns can reveal that the day-to-day moment-to-moment driving decisions might overall be increasing our risks while driving a car or can possibly be reducing our risks, contingent on what choices are being made.

Let's use an example to go from the considered microscopic to the macroscopic. Doing so will provide handy fodder to turn this discussion from somewhat theory-based to one that is imminently practical and provides pragmatic insights for us all.

You are once again at the wheel of a car and driving along in a city that has the usual hustle and bustle taking place. There are other cars around you. Pedestrians are on the sidewalks, and some are jaywalking across the busy streets. Bike riders are amidst all this chaos. The usual zoo of wild and crazy traffic endangerment exists.

Just another day in paradise, as they say.

Being late for getting to work, you are driving with a bit of a strident rush in mind. This does not imply that you are recklessly driving. It is just that you are driving with a certain amount of verve and zest, hoping to shave some time off your daily commute to the office. Perhaps this can be characterized as undoubtedly <u>not</u> driving in a lackadaisical manner. You are driving with a fervently determined goal to try and beat the clock as best you can.

We can now layout a specific driving scenario.

At one point during your driving trek, you are in a major artery of the city that has two lanes going in each direction, making that a total of four lanes (two lanes going southbound, plus two other lanes going northbound). You are in the northbound lanes.

For the moment, you are in the rightmost lane of those two northbound lanes.

Traffic is running along smoothly but busily so. Speeds are around 45 miles per hour. In addition to the lanes of car traffic, there is a bike lane on your side of the street. The bike lane is to your right. Bike riders are actively using that bike lane. The time of day is around rush hour and thus many cars and trucks are flowing along in traffic. Plus, there are lots of bike riders occupying the bike lane.

Hopefully, you've got a pretty good picture in your mind of the driving setting.

Suddenly, you realize that a large truck, one of those massively sized moving vans has incrementally come up beside your car, doing so to your left (and ergo in the northbound left lane). The truck is blocking your view of the southbound lanes, but that's okay since you don't need to see the traffic that is heading in the opposite direction of your travel.

In a sense, you are now trapped in your right lane. To your left is this big lurking truck. There is traffic directly ahead of you in your right lane. There is traffic behind you in your right lane. You have your own little pocket, as it were, sitting tightly squeezed between all those other interlopers.

And there is the bike lane to be considered too.

Please keep in mind that you are flowing along at around 45 miles per hour. Your vehicle is in motion. All the other cars and the truck next to you are also in motion. Turns out that there are bike riders in the bike lane, and they too are in motion.

Here's what comes next.

The moving van is veering somewhat in its lane. The driver of the truck is having a hard time keeping the lengthy and slightly erratic vehicle entirely and solely in its own lane. This is a largely unwieldy truck and the roadway is not the best.

The lanes are slightly askew and the roadway surface is rather rough.

Meanwhile, some of the bike riders decide they are being held back by some slower bike riders ahead of them.

As such, several of these urgently pressing bikers are opting to pass the slower ones. The act of passing them though is going to bunch them all up for a few split seconds, essentially completely occupying the entire width of the bike lane. Indeed, the odds are that some of the bike riders are going to slop over into the regular lane of traffic as they make their dicey and rapid movement around the slowpoke bike riders.

Are you ready to make a snap-driving decision?

The everyday squeeze play has become the ultra-squeeze play.

You can try to stay squarely in the middle of your lane.

In that case, you are hoping that there is sufficient clearance for the swaying truck (coming somewhat toward you, from your left) and enough clearance for those bikes that are bulging out of the bike lane and into your lane of traffic (coming somewhat toward you, from your right).

Or you might decide to ride toward the edge of your lane.

Which edge?

Do you choose to align with the right edge or the left edge of your lane?

By choosing the right edge, doing so would keep you further away from the truck, at least as much as is feasible at this juncture. That truck is an imposing figure and rather painstakingly foreboding. It is extremely bulky and heavy, for which a glancing blow from the truck into your underway car is bound to be grievously problematic, possibly even fatal.

You might be wise to give the most clearance that you can to the wayward truck.

Thus, you aim your car toward the rightmost edge of your lane. This makes perfectly good sense.

Whoa, don't forget about those bike riders!

The bike riders are extremely vulnerable.

The odds are that if you brushed against a bike rider, it would be really bad times for that person. In fact, by striking one of them, there is a notable chance that several of the bike riders would go down to the ground all at the same time, akin to a bowling ball striking bowling pins. Those battered bike riders would undoubtedly get hurt, and there is a chance of fatalities depending upon how things go.

You are now in the proverbial situation of being between a rock and hard place.

One decision entails trying to stay afield of the menacing truck. This is probably safer for you. A collision with that truck is likely to be lethal to you. But you abundantly need to decide between staying afield of those bike riders too. On a somewhat selfish basis, there is little doubt that colliding with the bike riders would probably not be especially injurious to you. Sadly, it would most likely be severely injurious if not fatal to them.

Choices, choices, choices.

Some might assert that it is up to fate to decide. Just stay in the middle of your lane. Whatever happens, is whatever is going to happen. Don't be sweating it. You are rightfully able to be in your lane and by staying in the middle you will always have a clear conscience about what you did.

Maybe so, maybe not.

Suppose you do remain in the middle. It could be that the truck marginally veers into your lane and rams into your car. Had you been just a tad toward the right edge of your lane, the truck and your car would have never touched each other. Because you opted to doggedly be in the middle of your lane, the collision takes place. Bad news for you.

The point is that none of the options are risk-free and nor are any of them outcome-free.

Whichever choice you make, it could turn out to be the "wrong" choice in terms of having an adverse result. Driving is a game of playing the odds, though by referring to the matter as a "game" we need to realize that this is a life-or-death gambit. It is not a playful game. It is a serious contest encompassing probabilities and erstwhile chances that can turn an innocent moment into a heart-wrenching and irreversibly unfavorable one.

Which choice did you make?

I don't want you to be thinking that there is a wrong choice or a right choice per se. That's not what the scenario is trying to portend. The emphasis of this setting is that you are being called upon throughout a driving journey to make essential driving decisions. Those driving decisions are vital. You often make them in a split second. They come and go, like a river that flows endlessly.

Most of the time, those driving decisions are not especially notable. In this case, perhaps you stayed in the middle and everything turned out okay, or maybe you went to the right edge or the left edge, and everything turned out okay. I would dare say that you would not likely remember the next day that you had that precipitous decision to make.

If you tried to remember all the hundreds or thousands of driving choices in each driving trek, you'd probably go bonkers. It just isn't a reasonable thing to do. Sure, some of the more monumental ones will probably stick with you.

For example, this particular scenario could stay in your mindset for a long time, especially if it was a real squeaker and the situation flared to a point of nearly having gotten struck or nearly having struck a bike rider.

Assuming that no one got hurt and there was no collision of any kind, the chances are that this instance would eventually recede in your memory banks. You might recall it from time to time, particularly if telling tall tales about some of your harrowing driving experiences.

Shift gears a little bit and let's zoom-out, akin to the zoom-out notion earlier postulated.

You aren't the only one to have ever been in a situation like this. Being pinned between the wayward truck and those boisterous bike riders is undoubtedly something that happens with some frequency. It happens each day. It happens in your city, and it happens in many other locales.

Consider that daily, zillions of drivers are making the same decision that you were just confronted with. This happens throughout the day. It happens over a period of a year, over and over again. We could end up with zillions upon zillions of those specific decisions being made.

Here is the kicker.

If those drivers all made independent decisions, we would expect that presumably there might be an equal chance of staying in the middle versus going toward the right edge or the left edge. We could look at a statistical distribution and see that in the aggregate there was an equal chance of which way drivers were opting to go.

On the other hand, drivers might have a propensity or specific tendency that would become apparent by examining the aggregated instance. Suppose that the numbers showed that by and large, the drivers went to the right edge. Overall they seemed to be choosing to get away from the truck, though this was simultaneously increasing the risks of hitting the bike riders.

In any real-world sense of things, we do not have any practical means to ferret out this kind of decision-making in the aggregate.

We aren't able to collect the zillions of daily driving decisions being made by each driver, and we cannot then add those up into a convenient database that would show us all of the zillions upon zillions of those itty-bitty driving decisions made by the over 225 million licensed drivers in the United States.

That's a darned shame.

Wait for a second, wave a magic wand, and pretend that we could collect that humongous dataset.

This would enable all sorts of insightful analyses on driving and driver behaviors. We might discover that human drivers are more prone to making one type of decision over another and that this had heightened their risk of incurring a car crash. We could then try to educate drivers accordingly, aiming to change behavior toward being less risk-prone. We might redesign our cars or at least the driving controls, accordingly. We might alter the roadways and our infrastructure, doing so to minimize the bad choices and maximize the good choices.

That kind of data collection and analysis could make a big difference in reducing the number of annual injuries and fatalities associated with driving a car. Sorry to say though that we don't have a magic wand, but we do have something nearly "magical" that is gradually arising, namely the advent of AI-based true self-driving cars.

Let's talk about self-driving cars.

The future of cars consists of AI-based true self-driving cars. There isn't a human driver involved in a true self-driving car. Keep in mind that true self-driving cars are driven via an AI driving system. There isn't a need for a human driver at the wheel, and nor is there a provision for a human to drive the vehicle.

Here's an intriguing question that is worth pondering: *How might driving decisions at the micro-level and also at the macroscopic aggregated level be pertinent to the advent of AI-based true self-driving cars?*

We'll consider quite mindfully this hearty question. First, I'd like to further clarify what is meant when I refer to true self-driving cars.

Understanding The Levels Of Self-Driving Cars

As a clarification, true self-driving cars are ones that the AI drives the car entirely on its own and there isn't any human assistance during the driving task.

These driverless vehicles are considered Level 4 and Level 5, while a car that requires a human driver to co-share the driving effort is usually considered at Level 2 or Level 3. The cars that co-share the driving task are described as being semi-autonomous, and typically contain a variety of automated add-on's that are referred to as ADAS (Advanced Driver-Assistance Systems).

There is not yet a true self-driving car at Level 5, which we don't yet even know if this will be possible to achieve, and nor how long it will take to get there.

Meanwhile, the Level 4 efforts are gradually trying to get some traction by undergoing very narrow and selective public roadway trials, though there is controversy over whether this testing should be allowed per se (we are all life-or-death guinea pigs in an experiment taking place on our highways and byways, some contend).

Since semi-autonomous cars require a human driver, the adoption of those types of cars won't be markedly different than driving conventional vehicles, so there's not much new per se to cover about them on this topic (though, as you'll see in a moment, the points next made are generally applicable).

For semi-autonomous cars, it is important that the public needs to be forewarned about a disturbing aspect that's been arising lately, namely that despite those human drivers that keep posting videos of themselves falling asleep at the wheel of a Level 2 or Level 3 car, we all need to avoid being misled into believing that the driver can take away their attention from the driving task while driving a semi-autonomous car.

You are the responsible party for the driving actions of the vehicle, regardless of how much automation might be tossed into a Level 2 or Level 3.

Self-Driving Cars And The Statistical Trolley Dilemma

For Level 4 and Level 5 true self-driving vehicles, there won't be a human driver involved in the driving task.

All occupants will be passengers.

The AI is doing the driving.

One aspect to immediately discuss entails the fact that the AI involved in today's AI driving systems is not sentient. In other words, the AI is altogether a collective of computer-based programming and algorithms, and most assuredly not able to reason in the same manner that humans can.

Why is this added emphasis about the AI not being sentient?

Because I want to underscore that when discussing the role of the AI driving system, I am not ascribing human qualities to the AI. Please be aware that there is an ongoing and dangerous tendency these days to anthropomorphize AI. In essence, people are assigning human-like sentience to today's AI, despite the undeniable and inarguable fact that no such AI exists as yet.

With that clarification, you can envision that the AI driving system won't natively somehow "know" about the facets of driving. Driving and all that it entails will need to be programmed as part of the hardware and software of the self-driving car.

Let's dive into the myriad of aspects that come to play on this topic.

Driving a car is tantamount to making ongoing life-or-death decisions, as noted earlier in this discussion.

The elaborated example of being squeezed between a large truck to your left and those bike riders to your right was a simple and yet commonly encountered instance of life-or-death driving choices. The lives involved or on the line can include the driver of the car, the passengers that might be in that car, the drivers of nearby cars, the passengers inside those nearby cars, pedestrians nearby, bike riders nearby, and so on.

Some would arguably contend that life-or-death driving decisions are extremely rare.

Their viewpoint is that maybe once in a lifetime as a driver you might come upon a situation that incorporates life-or-death choices. Otherwise, for some 99.999% of your driving experiences, you won't presumably have any such grave matters to consider.

This is an extremely offbeat way to characterize driving a multi-ton vehicle that is able to move at tremendous speeds and convey enormous physical forces. I submit that we indeed are all faced most of the time with life-or-death driving choices. It is perhaps 99.999% of the time that we, fortunately, make the correct or sufficiently apt decisions and avert getting into dire circumstances.

Despite having managed to deviate away from the grim reaper much of the time, the struggle confronting imminent life-or-death while driving, or shall we also say at least the possibility of injury-or-noninjury is a constant one and not an oddball rarity.

There is a famous or some would say infamous mind-bending exercise known as the Trolley Problem that has garnered a great deal of debate and angst in the self-driving car industry and pertains to the weighty decisions involved in driving a car.

Many pundits and vendors in the self-driving car niche are quick to claim that the Trolley Problem is irrelevant to the advent of self-driving cars. They decry the Trolly Problem as purely theoretical, impractical, and a nonsensical distractor from the realities of driverless cars.

Those making such an argument are flat-out wrong.

They either misunderstand how to apply the Trolley Problem to the matter of self-driving cars or they are wishful that it should not be considered applicable. Their wishful thinking at this time allows them to disregard or downplay the issues raised. This in turn can provide a basis for not seeking to encompass Trolley Problem-related solutions into their AI driving systems.

I've predicted that those that take a head-in-the-sand approach to this topic will find themselves and their companies on the legal hook down the road. Eventually, there are going to be gargantuan lawsuits against many of the automakers and self-driving tech firms on their paucity of Trolley Problem considerations. Only then will they apparently take seriously the Trolley Problem, though it will assuredly be the case that they will still fight against it tooth-and-nail, hoping to avoid mega-sized legal losses.

As a quick primer about the Trolley Problem, it is a relatively straightforward thought experiment. Imagine that you are standing at a train track and have access to a control that will shunt a trolley onto one of two forking tracks. On one of the forked tracks is a person that is tied down to the rails and cannot getaway. On the other forked track, there are three people tied down to the rails and unable to escape (the number of people tied down varies by how the setup is envisioned, sometimes five people are mentioned rather than three, etc.).

Which direction do you decide to send the oncoming trolley?

It is a devilish problem. You are either going to choose to kill one person or three people. The inclination by some is that they won't move the switch at all, thereby avoiding having to make a choice. That's not really a means to avoid the issue since the switch is already preset to go onto one track or the other. Your attempt to avoid being involved will nonetheless still produce death.

I won't get into all of the details herein. The main point is that you are at times faced with very difficult life-or-death situations, and you need to make the most horrible of choices.

In a similar way, the example of being squeezed between the large truck and the bike riders was a Trolley Problem-related consideration.

You had to choose from which was more or less unfavorable. The only notable difference per se with the Trolley Problem was that death in this real-world setting was not an absolute certainty. There was a probability of death, and also a probability associated with injuries. Some would contend that this is why the Trolley Problem is irrelevant, due to the thought experiment entailing only sure-death and not a probability of death. That is a rather feeble argument and there are many variations of the Trolley Problem, including the incorporation of probabilities rather than absolute certainties.

Now that I've got you up-to-speed about the Trolley Problem, we can return to the aspects of the microscopic elements of driving decisions and the aggregated macroscopic perspective.

As notably articulated in a research paper "The Trolley, The Bull Bar, And Why Engineers Should Care About The Ethics Of Autonomous Cars" (authored by Jean-Francois Bonnefon, Azim Shariff, and Iyad Rahwan, published in the Proceedings of the IEEE), there is a *Statistical Trolley Dilemma* to be considered and ought not to be unheeded:

"Alas, ignoring the challenges of autonomous vehicles as explicit ethical agents will only postpone the problem. Even if every action of an autonomous car is oriented toward minimizing the absolute risk of a crash, each action will also shift relative risk from one road user to another. The cars may not be making decisions between outright sacrificing the lives of some to preserve those of others, but they will be making decisions about who is put at marginally more risk of being sacrificed."

Upon examining the use case of a driver caught between a large truck and a bike rider, along with implied reference to all sorts of akin driving situations, they saliently point out that: "These are not the dramatic, life and death decisions featured in trolley dilemmas. But once they are aggregated over millions of cars driving billions of miles, these small statistical decisions add up to life and death consequences—and prompt the same questions as the trolley dilemma did."

In a manner of speaking, I would assert that the Trolley Problem does apply to the microscopic day-to-day moment-to-moment life-or-death driving decisions that we make continually while at the steering wheel and that furthermore we need to also recognize the Statistical Trolley Dilemma on a macroscopic scale too.

This is latter aspect is assuredly the accumulation of zillions upon zillions of those day-to-day Trolley Problem instances that add up over time and constitute large-scale aggregated patterns of driving behaviors.

Conclusion

Trying to get human drivers to be contemplative about the Trolley Problem and ergo adjust their driving behavior is a nearly futile dreamy notion. Humans tend to be resistant to change and have a hard time adopting new driving practices.

For the semi-autonomous vehicles such as at Level 2 and Level 3, there is an opportunity to have the assisted driving features attempt to aid a human driver by incorporating Trolley Problem related solving capabilities. The automation providing driving assistance could seek to alert human drivers, possibly even overtaking the driving controls. I've though covered this extensively as a dicey proposition that can lead to a tug-of-war between a human driver and the assisting automation. It is going to be ugly and assuredly a can of worms.

AI-based true self-driving cars are a different matter since there is no human driver at the wheel. This means that we can expect that the AI driving system will be considering Trolley Problem issues. When a car crash or collision occurs involving a self-driving car, we ought to be able to do a full analysis of what the AI driving system was doing and what decisions it made during the incident at hand.

On a large-scale basis, we could accumulate these AI driving system aspects into a centralized database that could be used to study what seems to be working well and what seems to be not quite going so well. Some have suggested that we might need to establish an ethics-oriented oversight board that entails examining the programming of AI driving systems and to what degree the Trolley Problem is being addressed (see my column coverage).

Here's a final remark to give you something significant to ponder. If we could essentially force all self-driving cars to abide by some set of driving rules, such that in the case of being squeezed between say a large truck and a bunch of bike riders, the AI driving system would do as it has been collectively established to do, what would we want that rule to be?

That's the kind of decision that some people would skittishly say is above their paygrade. Maybe so, but it certainly ought to not be left to chance by some semi-random choosing AI algorithm, or be in the hands of some overworked AI programmer that while in the throes of coding up the AI made a life-or-death prior decision about how the AI driving system is going to react. Those are decidedly scary defaults.

I wouldn't and neither should you.

CHAPTER 21
RUNNING NARRATIVE AND SELF-DRIVING CARS

Trying to teach your teenage son or daughter how to drive a car can be quite a dicey activity.

The usual method seems to be that you let your teenager sit behind the wheel of your car and you sit in the passenger seat, during which you proffer sage advice to the newbie about how to drive. The thing is, you are pretty much in the hands of your own offspring at this juncture in the sense that there is little you can constructively do if the teen goes awry inadvertently.

Some parents believe that if needed they could reach over and take control of the steering wheel. This is a possibility but it is not a sure thing. The teen might not relinquish control of the steering wheel or might be panicking and countering whatever steering you might try to desperately apply. In addition, you don't have direct access to the brake pedal and nor the accelerator pedal, thus your only means of trying to affect the driving controls is via grasping at the steering wheel.

Truthfully, you have a minuscule chance of averting a dire car incident by a contortionist attempt to physically overtake the driving effort.

Otherwise, the mainstay of what you can do is tell your teen what to do.

For anyone that has ever tried to tell a teenager what to do, you know this can be extraordinarily problematic. The teen might abide by your wishes or might be rebellious. Whatever you say might be completely ignored.

What you say might go in one ear and out the other, or might be entirely misunderstood and the teen will try to do what they believe you had said to do. The whole interaction can be incredibly messy.

Of course, there's more than just messiness on the line. You are both inside a multi-ton vehicle that has the immense capability of high speed and humongous physical forces. Something really bad can happen if the teen makes a mistake and rams into another car or a pedestrian. A parent sitting in the passenger seat is on pins and needles, as it were, hoping upon hope that the driving trek with the newbie will go well and safely so.

I would dare say that parents that are willing to patiently sit next to their teenager and endure the trauma of watching them learn to drive ought to receive a world-class medal or award of some heroic kind. Your life hangs in the balance and yet nobody will likely ever acknowledge the risky personal sacrifice you made to simply aid your teen in learning how to drive.

Some parents are admittedly lousy at being the passenger that is supposed to provide verbalized assistance to their teen driver. I've seen some parents that berated their child the entire time, as though that is going to make the teen become a good driver. You can usually bet that if the teen and the parent are already on rough terms, the added stress of the driving chore is not going to suddenly make them into the best of buddies. All of the prior angst gets carried straightaway into the driving lessons.

Indeed, some parents will opt to have just one of the parents take on the duty of serving as the driving instructor. Whichever of the parents seems to have the best rapport with the teen is usually tapped for this somber duty. Another selection criterion is the ability of the chosen parent to remain cool and calm while providing driving advice. If a parent is yelling and screaming frantically at the teen driver, you can bet that the driving lesson is not going to be especially productive.

Some parents opt to outsource the driving lessons. This is handy since the third-party driving instructor is presumably going to be steady and proficient in guiding the teen driver. The odds though are that eventually the teen and a parent are going to get into the car and that the teen is going to have to showcase their driving capabilities in front of the parent. In that sense, the use of a driving instructor is more akin to a leg-up rather than a replacement for the parental effort of driving guidance.

We can rachet up the pressure by noting that the parent is not necessarily correct in whatever they might advise the teen driver. You might assume that the parent knows perfectly what to do while driving and they will perfectly instruct the teen accordingly. Not necessarily. A parent sitting in the passenger seat can misgauge what the driving situation consists of. They might falsely believe that the teen is about to hit a car to their left when in fact there is sufficient room for the two vehicles to pass each other without touching.

Okay, so you have a parent that is doling out remarks and commands, and you have a teen that is trying to cope with the driving scene and simultaneously placating their parent. That's a lot for a teen to handle.

Some parents even use a silent treatment approach, whereby the parent remains completely quiet the entire driving journey unless there is some moment that is so catastrophic that verbalization is required. The thinking is that the teen already has enough sensory overload and thus the verbalization from the parent should not be that last straw on the camel's back of overtaxing the newbie.

What about the teen doing verbalization of the driving task?

Yes, that's an approach that some parents invoke.

Upon starting a driving trek, the parent and teen agree that the teen will explain what they are doing. I am starting the car, I am driving down the driveway, I am making a right turn up ahead, etc. Those are the means of the teen soothing the qualms of the parent.

The parent doesn't have to wildly guess at what the teen is going to do. By having the teen plainly state what is happening, the parent can decide whether the driving is going well or the teen is maybe clueless about what they are undertaking.

Some refer to this as performing a running commentary while driving.

Commentary driving is a handy technique.

The person doing the driving is articulating aloud what they are aiming to do. A parent can then detect whether the teen is mindfully doing the driving chore. For example, if the teen doesn't report that a dog is about to run into the street, the parent that has already observed that the dog might do so can then readily alert the teen. Without the commentary taking place, the parent has almost no idea what the teen is seeing, thinking, planning to do, or trying to do.

A significant problem underlying the activity of getting the teen to do a running commentary is that this can be a colossal distractor for them. The teen is already seemingly concentrating with all their being on the roadway and trying earnestly to cope with the terrifying intensity of the driving effort. Having to also explain what they are doing can be an added burden. Some assert that this takes a notable chunk of the thinking activity away from the act of driving per se and devotes it instead to verbalizing what is taking place.

Not a good idea, some claim.

On the other hand, a quick counterargument is that the act of actively generating commentary gets the teen further engaged in the driving task. When the newbie is entirely silent, their mind might not be as engaged. By being forced to explain what is taking place, one belief is that this rivets the attention of the teen and makes them even more so concentrated on the driving activity.

In short, there is the commentary associated with the driver and there is a commentary associated with the parent that is acting as a type of driving instructor. That can be a lot of commentary flying around inside the car. A parent might interrupt the commentary of the teen, due to wanting to point out an urgent matter such as nearing closely to a bike rider. The teen might be talking over the parent since the parent is seemingly blabbering and the teen wants to show that they know what they are doing.

Ugh, the crosstalk and communication woes are potentially troublesome.

Another variant of using commentary while driving entails doing something long before a teen gets behind the wheel of a car. I tried this with my kids. The idea is that you as an adult driver provide a running commentary while driving the car, doing so when the kids are in their pre-teen years or at least early teenager years.

Each time that you take them for a drive, you verbalize what you are doing. You ask them to watch the roadway and pretend that they were driving the car. At some points of a driving trek, you might inquire of the teen as to what they would do if they were at the driving controls. In a sense, you are simulating them driving the car.

You can easily come up with mentally engaging questions. Should I make a left turn or a right turn up ahead? Would it be best to go slower and avoid that truck or try to speed around it? What do you think that red car to our right is going to do next? And so on.

This provides at least a twofold advantage. First, the teen is hopefully garnering the driving act via your verbalizations. You are explaining what you are looking at and how you are handling the driving controls correspondingly. Second, the teen is engaged by the pretense of doing the driving and this gets them to carefully consider what driving consists of.

I sincerely believe this can be a handy exercise.

That being said, if the parent and the youngster are already on bad terms with each other, this could somewhat backfire on everyone involved. The youngster might decide they will do the absolute opposite of whatever the parent is saying. Or the youngster might come to hate the notion of driving, simply because the driving act got mired into the sour relationship between them and the parent.

Anyway, there is no question that the use of commentary while driving is a handy tool that can be used when the circumstances are appropriate to do so.

This brings up an interesting consideration in light of where cars are heading in the future.

The future of cars consists of AI-based true self-driving cars.

There isn't a human driver involved in a true self-driving car. Keep in mind that true self-driving cars are driven via an AI driving system. There isn't a need for a human driver at the wheel, and nor is there a provision for a human to drive the vehicle.

Here's an intriguing question that is worth pondering: *How might the use of commentary while driving be an instrumental factor in the advent of AI-based true self-driving cars?*

I'd like to first further clarify what is meant when I refer to true self-driving cars.

Understanding The Levels Of Self-Driving Cars

As a clarification, true self-driving cars are ones that the AI drives the car entirely on its own and there isn't any human assistance during the driving task.

These driverless vehicles are considered Level 4 and Level 5, while a car that requires a human driver to co-share the driving effort is usually considered at Level 2 or Level 3. The cars that co-share the driving task are described as being semi-autonomous, and typically contain a variety of automated add-on's that are referred to as ADAS (Advanced Driver-Assistance Systems).

There is not yet a true self-driving car at Level 5, which we don't yet even know if this will be possible to achieve, and nor how long it will take to get there.

Meanwhile, the Level 4 efforts are gradually trying to get some traction by undergoing very narrow and selective public roadway trials, though there is controversy over whether this testing should be allowed per se (we are all life-or-death guinea pigs in an experiment taking place on our highways and byways, some contend).

Since semi-autonomous cars require a human driver, the adoption of those types of cars won't be markedly different than driving conventional vehicles, so there's not much new per se to cover about them on this topic (though, as you'll see in a moment, the points next made are generally applicable).

For semi-autonomous cars, it is important that the public needs to be forewarned about a disturbing aspect that's been arising lately, namely that despite those human drivers that keep posting videos of themselves falling asleep at the wheel of a Level 2 or Level 3 car, we all need to avoid being misled into believing that the driver can take away their attention from the driving task while driving a semi-autonomous car.

You are the responsible party for the driving actions of the vehicle, regardless of how much automation might be tossed into a Level 2 or Level 3.

Self-Driving Cars And Digital Commentary Driving

For Level 4 and Level 5 true self-driving vehicles, there won't be a human driver involved in the driving task.

All occupants will be passengers.

The AI is doing the driving.

One aspect to immediately discuss entails the fact that the AI involved in today's AI driving systems is not sentient. In other words, the AI is altogether a collective of computer-based programming and algorithms, and most assuredly not able to reason in the same manner that humans can.

Why is this added emphasis about the AI not being sentient?

Because I want to underscore that when discussing the role of the AI driving system, I am not ascribing human qualities to the AI. Please be aware that there is an ongoing and dangerous tendency these days to anthropomorphize AI. In essence, people are assigning human-like sentience to today's AI, despite the undeniable and inarguable fact that no such AI exists as yet.

With that clarification, you can envision that the AI driving system won't natively somehow "know" about the facets of driving. Driving and all that it entails will need to be programmed as part of the hardware and software of the self-driving car.

Let's dive into the myriad of aspects that come to play on this topic.

First, some assert that self-driving cars ought to include a driving commentary feature or function overall.

The notion is that a human passenger can find out what the AI driving system is doing. This might help human passengers feel more confident in what the self-driving car is undertaking.

You can liken this to the earlier discussion of having a parent ask their teen driver to explain what is taking place during a driving journey.

So far, most of the driving commentary for self-driving cars is nearly entirely visually based via the use of a display or onboard computer screen.

The human passenger can watch the display and see a visual indication of what roadway objects are being detected. Via the use of a range of colors and shapes, the display can overlay where the self-driving car is headed. This can also include blinking indications when something untoward is detected such as another car that is illegally running a red light in front of the self-driving car.

Most of these commentary driving aspects are visually portrayed and only sparingly verbalized. The oral explanations are usually only at key points of a driving trek. Using an Alexa or Siri kind of verbalization, the AI driving system might emit a sentence or two that you are nearing your destination or that there will be a delay in reaching your destination due to heavy traffic.

Some believe that the human passenger should be able to activate a more verbose version of the commentary driving. You might want the AI driving system to report on every itsy-bitsy act it is undertaking. For some passengers, this could be especially reassuring, particularly if they are unable to readily see the display or want to concentrate on the roadway rather than looking at the display.

Some naysayers suggest the verbalization might scare passengers more than comfort them. If the verbalization doesn't seem to cover all the myriad of driving scene aspects, the skittish passenger might become overly worried that the AI driving system is unaware of what is happening. As such, the provision of explaining the driving act should be kept to a minimum.

We'll have to wait and see how this plays out.

The odds are that some automakers or self-driving tech firms will include a rather complete commentary driving capability, while others will restrict their own versions. In the end, it will likely be the human passengers that will determine what is provided since the fleet operators are going to want people to use their self-driving cars and will undoubtedly seek to provide capabilities that the riding public desires. For more on how getting people to use self-driving cars is not necessarily going to be an easy slam dunk.

Shifting gears, slightly, there is a somewhat different reason for the commentary driving of self-driving cars that have been percolating and gradually rising in interest.

Suppose that we could use commentary driving as a means of inspecting the AI driving system and do so to try and ensure that the system is performing the driving chore successfully. Proponents of this approach argue that it could lead to self-driving cars achieving greater safety versus without this type of capacity.

All told, we might require self-driving cars to emit a Digital Commentary Driving (DCD) indication.

The DCD would not necessarily be a vocal verbalization. Instead, the DCD would be a data stream that indicates what the AI driving system is undertaking. By using a data stream, you can avoid the problems associated with having to do verbalization. It is in a sense cleaner and more revealing to have the raw data than to have the vocalized transformation that has been using the data as a basis for making the resulting utterances.

By and large, the AI developers associated with budding self-driving cars are doing something like this already. They tend to use various internal technical tools to get data dumps and find out what the AI driving system was doing during a driving journey. This helps in debugging the AI driving system and can also be instrumental in making modifications and improvements too.

For those that are already doing this DCD, the odds are that it is entirely proprietary. The type of data, the data elements, the values associated with the data elements, are entire of an idiosyncratic nature. Whatever the AI developers happened to come up with, that's what their digitalized commentary contains.

A call to standardize the DCD is being bandied around. This would make life easier for being able to compare different self-driving cars from the various automakers and self-driving tech firms. By having a single standard, everyone would be emitting the same kinds of data and using the same predefined sets of values.

The kicker is that this could be used for regulatory purposes.

Regulators that want to try and ensure that a particular model of a self-driving car is suitable for public roadway use might require that the automaker or self-driving tech firm provide copious amounts of DCD that could be reviewed. The review would go hand-in-hand with the actual roadway results. In the end, a kind of roadway readiness certification might be issued.

A recently released report by the BSI Center for Connected and Autonomous Vehicles (CAV) provides an overview sketch of how a DCD standard might be initiated (the report is entitled "A Review of CAV Safety Benchmarking and a Proposal for a Digital Commentary Driving Technique" and was co-authored by Professor Nick Reed of Reed Mobility, Bryn Balcombe of ADA, Paul Spence of PKSInsights Ltd, Dr. Siddartha Khastgir of WMG, University of Warwick, and Nick Fleming of BSI, Head of Sector Transport & Mobility).

Here's a bit of an overview of their vision:

"Commentary driving is a technique used to train and assess human expert drivers, in which they are required to verbalize relevant information in the driving scene. This is used to determine that they can perceive, prioritize and act effectively when driving. Digital commentary driving (DCD) is proposed as an objective measure of CAV safety performance. DCD does not entail a CAV verbalizing or describing the driving scene in the same way as human drivers, rather, it involves the continuous collection of data from a CAV on its perceptions, decisions, reactions, and feedback whilst driving. This data effectively probes the 'understanding' the CAV has of its environment."

The report points out that not everyone is going to be thrilled with this DCD type of regulatory requirement if one is so divined.

Probably the most notable concern is that the DCD could potentially reveal the inner secrets of the AI driving systems. An automaker or self-driving tech firm that has invested millions or even billions of dollars into their development efforts could be rightfully queasy that the DCD is going to give away their secret sauce. The Intellectual Property (IP) rights issues of devising a DCD standard will be onerous as an attempt is made to avoid veering into IP qualms and yet still ensuring that the DCD is revealing something substantive.

A watered-down DCD is probably not going to achieve the lofty goals of what the driving commentary is intended to produce.

A slew of other concerns is generally less defensible.

For example, there might be a decrying that the shunting of data out of the AI driving system while in the act of driving could end up diluting the use of onboard computing resources. Presumably, you want every ounce of the limited computer cycles to be devoted to making sure that the AI driving system can fully operate. By adding the data export aspects, perhaps this usurps those revered onboard resources.

The counterargument is that you can seemingly devise a pragmatically feasible means to keep the data export aspects from somewhat distracting or overtaxing the onboard processing. Sure, there might be some tinge of an impact, but the aim of attaining the greater good of trying to ensure the overall safety of the self-driving car outweighs that minimal impingement.

One potentially tricky consideration is whether the DCD data exportation might reveal something of a private nature related to the passenger use of a self-driving car. I've noted previously that we are going to enter into an age of the "roving eye" associated with the advent of self-driving cars. This is roving eye notion is a catchy moniker that I use to indicate that we are facing a tradeoff between what self-driving cars beneficially provide and the privacy intrusions that might also result.

Conclusion

There is a somewhat more insidious reason that some might balk at using a DCD approach.

If you aren't fully convinced that your own AI driving system is up to snuff, you certainly would not want it to be baring its soul.

You would prefer to keep things quiet and only known internally. The aspect that you might be forced into revealing the inner workings and perhaps showcase to the entire world that there are incorrect or feeble driving capabilities would strike fear into your heart and those of your investors.

Nobody in their right mind would say this aloud. They would instead stand firmly and overtly on the stance that the highly valued and earnestly earned IP is going to be undercut by the DCD revealing efforts. It might be hard to discern when the resistance due to a legitimate concern about IP is actually hiding the fact that the AI driving system is not yet adequately adroit enough for public roadway application.

But this is something that can potentially be dealt with by adequately defining a standard for DCD that can sufficiently protect the IP considerations.

A final comment for now.

If you got into a car with your teenage newbie driver and they refused to explain what they were doing, this would abundantly give you pause for concern. A parent that continued anyway and let their offspring drive, well, that's either an amazing act of pure devotion and unbridled love toward their wayward teen or something that you might regret the moment that the teen makes a wild turn or perchance runs through a red light.

Being a parent sometimes means employing tough love, including at times asking their teenage driver to provide a semblance of driving commentary (as long as doing so is not overly distracting). As an added plus, the words that your son or daughter utters will always be a memorable part of those days that they first learned to drive and you were there to witness and guide them in this most life-changing of skills.

It is assuredly one of those pivotal parent-child bonding things.

CHAPTER 22
URBAN TOURISM AND SELF-DRIVING CARS

Urban tourism is oftentimes the crucial economic lifeblood that keeps cities humming.

Tourism-related employment is ranked in the top three of largest employers for approximately 60% of the states across America. When tourists make a visit to a particular city, the coffers get filled with those eagerly sought tourism dollars. This flowing money goes in every direction. Businesses do well. People get employed and are able to earn a paycheck. Funding toward city activities gets bolstered. And a veritable trickle-down of buckeroos makes its way throughout the urban setting, spreading delightfully like nourishing rain that springs forth vital economic and societal activity.

In theory, a city should do whatever it can to attract those tourism monies.

Some cities indeed are mindful of trying to allure tourists to their stately lands. They try to roll out the red carpet. Perhaps a city encourages the locals to be especially thoughtful and proactively helpful towards tourists. If you see someone that seems unsure of where the nearest touristy landmark is, gently and with civility point out how to get there. Provide insights about the best places to catch a bite to eat or to soak up the ambiance of the city.

Of course, not everyone necessarily welcomes tourists.

There is a decidedly love-hate relationship that can be had toward tourists. Yes, the tourists are visitors and admittedly adding to the financial bankrolls of the urban area. We should treat them as guests.

But those presumed guests are sometimes quite annoying and there is only so much annoyance that someone can withstand. Having to deal with the wayward tourists that are clueless and boxing up the existing day-to-day living conditions is a bridge too far for some locals.

This can be readily seen in the roadways of a city.

You might realize that historically the emergence of the automobile in the early part of the twentieth century was a humongous boon to tourism throughout the United States. Whereas you normally think of "tourists" as visitors from another country, there is a demonstrative contingent of tourism that comes from fellow citizens that are seeking to be sightseers at cities other than their own. After a while, people tend to get bored with taking in the sights of their own city, so they drive to another one to get a fresh dose of excitement and experience the joys of being on holiday.

They are assuredly tourists in that context.

Anyway, the point is that the use of a car is instrumental to tourism.

There are those people that drive from another nearby city or perhaps from other outer areas and opt to become a tourist in the city of a chosen vacation destination. Some people drive from a faraway locale, such as driving from several states away and come to be a tourist in a seemingly far-flung city. One of the classic adventures for many families entails doing a lengthy family drive across the country and stopping at all the cities they've long relished being able to see while acting in a touristy capacity.

Besides driving a car to an urban locale, some tourists arrive via airplanes or sometimes via cruise ships. The odds are that some of those tourists will opt to rent a car for use during their stay. They become part of the city traffic as they dare to navigate their way around a city that is relatively unknown to them. Sure, they might have a GPS to aid in guiding their path, but this does not mean that the driving act is necessarily smooth and even.

Let's be brutally honest, shall we?

Tourists of any kind that end up driving a car while in your great city are bound to foul up and make a mess of the traffic. These visitors might have the best of intentions. Nonetheless, once they are behind the wheel of a car, all heck breaks loose. They go much too slowly for prevailing traffic. They make crazy U-turns in the middle of busy streets. They turn without showing a blinker or they decide that they want to make a right turn while they are way over in the outskirts of the left lane.

On and on it goes, woefully so.

Locals that drive in a hustling and bustling city are readily able to carp all day long about those touristy drivers. Not only do those nutty drivers from out-of-town produce undue congestion, but there is also a solid chance that car crashes will go up too. The locals are caught off-guard by the wild antics of the tourist drivers. Bam, cars collide and people get hurt.

Some of the tourists probably didn't want to drive to begin with. They would have preferred to walk around, but few cities are walkable in their entirety. The geographic distances are just too much and you cannot readily walk your way from one far-off tourist spot to another one. Furthermore, even if walking is feasible, there is a safety factor that comes to play too.

By safety, I'm referring to the notion that if you are ensconced inside a car, you are seemingly safer overall than if you are walking along on city streets. A person walking here and there is vulnerable to potential attack or other difficulties. Being inside a car is more than just a form of transportation. It is also a protective shield. You can get into your car as a sturdy bubble, plus you can quickly drive away from a situation that is becoming untoward.

This brings us to the usual counter viewpoint that the tourists ought to be using the mass transit options in a city for their traveling needs. Well, yes, that's a good idea.

Unfortunately, many transit infrastructures are set up in a manner that seems baffling to tourists. Seasoned locals might have the transit system figured out, doing so after many years of ridership. A tourist does not want to expend undue time and energy toward deciphering where the transit resources are, where they go, and how to make use of them.

That's not what tourists usually hope to be doing on their days off. The gobbledygook of which stations to use or which benches to sit at are beyond their tolerance and touristy patience. By using a car, you can just get into the car and start driving. This might be less expedient perhaps than using the transit options, but it is easier overall and once again more protective and reassuring.

If you get lost while in the midst of a city transit system, you can feel totally out of whack and highly exposed. Getting lost while driving a car is not much of a problem. You merely turn around and head in another direction. Keep driving and you'll eventually find your way. During those travails, you have air conditioning in case the outside weather is hot, you have heating in case the outside weather is cold, and can be listening to your favorite tunes.

A notable part of the driving equation for tourism includes the use of cabs and ridesharing (the latter is referred to as ride-hailing by some since today's ridesharing is not especially about sharing rides and more so about hailing a ride).

Tourists have flocked to the use of ridesharing.

This makes abundant sense.

Take all of the earlier points about why people would prefer to be in a car, and you can see why using a ridesharing option is a strong allure. Even though the tourist is not doing the driving, they are still consuming the use of a car for tourism purposes. Of course, the trips are usually very short in duration, unlike if you had your own car or rented a car for an entire week of being a tourist.

In any case, a lot of the city traffic that is now taking place can be attributed to tourists that have decided to use ridesharing for their vacation travel needs. The cost though can add up pretty quickly. There is little doubt that in today's city get-around options, using the transit system is certainly less expensive than using a ridesharing service.

Tourists need to weigh the tradeoffs of those choices.

Many choose ridesharing because they figure that the extra cost is worth the ease of getting directly from point A to point B. No need to change busses or switch from one subway train to another. You merely get into a car and it whisks you to where you need to go. You are willing to use up your hard-earned money to ensure that your time as a tourist is focused on enjoying a city and not consumed by having to dreadfully navigate the city.

The nice thing about using ridesharing too is that the tourist does not need to be at the wheel. There is a lot of stress associated with being in a strange city and driving a car. You don't know the roads. You don't know the local driving rules or customs. All of that is readily outsourced by using a local driver via a ridesharing service. The car arrives to pick you up, and a local driver is included. It's a two-in-one package deal, even if just for that short trip from one touristy site to another.

A city that is known for having lousy transit or that has overly pricey ridesharing is often perceived by tourists as being less desirable than other cities that seem to have their act together. The mental calculus by a tourist about which city to visit is ostensibly determined to a great extent by what is there to be seen along with how much pain and suffering you will need to endure to get around that particular town.

Indubitably, you might go to a city on a one-time tryout basis and after experiencing the trauma of getting from place to place, you decide you'll almost never go there again. Once was enough.

On top of this, you might forewarn all your friends and colleagues to avoid that city like the plague, simply due to the high cost of intra-city travel and the byzantine and untenable ways to see what the town has to offer.

On the other hand, if you visit a city that was easy to get around, you might establish that it is now your favorite place to be a tourist. You are happy to go there repeatedly. The sights are worthy of seeing over and again. Plus, the local travel aspects are a breeze. This is something that you are glad to spread the word about.

How might a city then become more touristy traveling friendly?

The answer might seem shocking, so please prepare yourself.

Make use of AI-based true self-driving cars.

This brings up an interesting consideration in light of where cars are heading in the future. You see, the future of cars consists of AI-based true self-driving cars.

There isn't a human driver involved in a true self-driving car. Keep in mind that true self-driving cars are driven via an AI driving system. There isn't a need for a human driver at the wheel, and nor is there a provision for a human to drive the vehicle.

Here's an intriguing question that is worth pondering: *How might cities and city leaders leverage the advent of AI-based true self-driving cars as a tourist-aiming booster?*

I'd like to first further clarify what is meant when I refer to true self-driving cars.

Understanding The Levels Of Self-Driving Cars

As a clarification, true self-driving cars are ones that the AI drives the car entirely on its own and there isn't any human assistance during the driving task.

These driverless vehicles are considered Level 4 and Level 5, while a car that requires a human driver to co-share the driving effort is usually considered at Level 2 or Level 3. The cars that co-share the driving task are described as being semi-autonomous, and typically contain a variety of automated add-on's that are referred to as ADAS (Advanced Driver-Assistance Systems).

There is not yet a true self-driving car at Level 5, which we don't yet even know if this will be possible to achieve, and nor how long it will take to get there.

Meanwhile, the Level 4 efforts are gradually trying to get some traction by undergoing very narrow and selective public roadway trials, though there is controversy over whether this testing should be allowed per se (we are all life-or-death guinea pigs in an experiment taking place on our highways and byways, some contend).

Since semi-autonomous cars require a human driver, the adoption of those types of cars won't be markedly different than driving conventional vehicles, so there's not much new per se to cover about them on this topic (though, as you'll see in a moment, the points next made are generally applicable).

For semi-autonomous cars, it is important that the public needs to be forewarned about a disturbing aspect that's been arising lately, namely that despite those human drivers that keep posting videos of themselves falling asleep at the wheel of a Level 2 or Level 3 car, we all need to avoid being misled into believing that the driver can take away their attention from the driving task while driving a semi-autonomous car.

You are the responsible party for the driving actions of the vehicle, regardless of how much automation might be tossed into a Level 2 or Level 3.

Self-Driving Cars And City Tourism

For Level 4 and Level 5 true self-driving vehicles, there won't be a human driver involved in the driving task.

All occupants will be passengers.

The AI is doing the driving.

One aspect to immediately discuss entails the fact that the AI involved in today's AI driving systems is not sentient. In other words, the AI is altogether a collective of computer-based programming and algorithms, and most assuredly not able to reason in the same manner that humans can.

Why is this added emphasis about the AI not being sentient?

Because I want to underscore that when discussing the role of the AI driving system, I am not ascribing human qualities to the AI. Please be aware that there is an ongoing and dangerous tendency these days to anthropomorphize AI. In essence, people are assigning human-like sentience to today's AI, despite the undeniable and inarguable fact that no such AI exists as yet.

With that clarification, you can envision that the AI driving system won't natively somehow "know" about the facets of driving. Driving and all that it entails will need to be programmed as part of the hardware and software of the self-driving car.

Let's dive into the myriad of aspects that come to play on this topic.

First, you might be wondering why self-driving cars will make much of a difference to urban tourism.

That's easy, the advent of AI-based true self-driving cars is anticipated to bring forth an era of mobility-for-all.

The belief is that self-driving cars will be available at a substantially lower price than a comparable human-driven ridesharing vehicle. This is primarily due to the excising of the human labor component involved in driving a car. The AI driving system will be doing all of the driving. As such, there is no need to provide rest breaks, no need to deal with driving fatigue or tiredness and otherwise be able to do away with the human-related driving woes.

You can add to the benefits that the AI driving system won't be driving while drunk. It won't drive while being drowsy. It won't drive while being distracted from the roadway activity. All in all, a self-driving car will be able to run on a 24x7 basis and will not suffer from the usual limitations and maladies of a human driver.

In short, self-driving cars will be operated at a significantly lower cost than human-driven cars, will be more readily available and usable, and can be volume-wise scaled-up in a manner that trying to do so via hiring or contracting with human drivers is a lot less logistically onerous. This is why the mobility-for-all mantra is bandied around. People that today are mobility disadvantaged will now have an opportunity to make use of cars in ways that heretofore were prohibitive for them to do so.

Getting back to the tourist angle, the notion is that self-driving cars will be the go-to option for tourists.

Upon arriving at your fine city, a tourist will seek out the use of self-driving cars to travel throughout the town. The tourist would undoubtedly use a smartphone app, akin to how ridesharing services are requested today and select a self-driving car as their preferred driving option. This can occur on a ride-at-at-time basis. A self-driving car available on a ridesharing network would get assigned to come to pick up the rider, take them to their destination, and then the autonomous vehicle would continue doing the same with other requested riders.

In addition, it is also envisioned that a tourist might opt to reserve a self-driving car for their exclusive use during their visit.

The nice thing about reserving a self-driving car would be that the tourist can leave their stuff inside the self-driving car while they are on foot or otherwise outside of the self-driving car. When doing a series of disparate pickup requests, a tourist would not be able to leave behind in the autonomous vehicle their various knickknacks and personal gear. By reserving a self-driving car for a longer period, the vehicle becomes their handy-dandy constant companion platform during their touristy activities.

Another welcomed aspect would be that the self-driving car doesn't necessarily need to find a place to park.

If you have a rented conventional human-driven car, you are continually trying to find a legal spot to park your rented vehicle. For tourists, this parking headache is a nightmare since they don't want to get a parking ticket (nor be towed) and are unsure of what is proper when it comes to parking in the city, they are visiting.

As an aside, for cities that rely significantly on revenues from parking tickets and towing, you will need to eventually figure out how to cope with a notably reduced source of revenue. That's why some cities are already discussing or putting in place so-called Zombie taxes associated with self-driving cars.

Self-driving cars are not usually going to be parked for any length of time and will instead be roaming around most of the time. Thus, the tourist can let the AI driving system figure out what is best to be done while the tourist is outside of the self-driving car, namely the AI will opt to drive the autonomous vehicle here and there or might find a parking spot to wait until the tourist becomes in need of a further lift again (the chore of parking is a task then for the AI, not for a human driver).

Okay, it seems pretty clear cut that self-driving cars are a big plus for tourists.

This in turn means that tourists might be more interested in visiting a city that has a lot of self-driving cars available for use. In other words, the benefits to the tourists will in turn attract tourists, which in turn will boost urban tourism for the city that has adopted the widespread use of self-driving cars.

There is also the novelty factor to be included as a bonus of sorts.

A city that has a lot of self-driving cars will possibly be able to promote the fact that the urban setting does indeed have self-driving cars. You could indubitably argue that the self-driving cars themselves will become part of the tourist attraction per se. People might flock to a city that has self-driving cars, partially due to the convenience of local travel, but also for the thrill and excitement of being able to ride in a self-driving car.

It is a twofer!

The combo deal is the ease of local travel that is then combined with the uniqueness and adventure of getting to ride around in self-driving cars.

That being said, over a lengthy period of time the adoption of self-driving cars is likely to eventually even out. A city that once was at the leading edge and was one of the few that had self-driving cars will inevitably become simply on par with other cities that have subsequently done likewise. The availability of self-driving cars will shift from being a novelty to otherwise being a standard expectation.

When that eventually occurs, which admittedly is a bit of time from now, cities that don't have self-driving cars readily aplenty will find themselves at a potential disadvantage when luring tourism. People will be dismayed that the city lacks sufficient self-driving cars. Tourists will decide that they ought to use their vacation time elsewhere, rather than contend with the usual forms of more arduous vehicular options.

Conclusion

Could this all imply that self-driving cars are entirely upside and lack any downsides?

That would be an improper interpretation. As with any form of transportation, there are aspects about self-driving cars that might not be so welcomed in some cities and by some tourists.

For example, some tourists might say that they prefer the human-to-human direct interaction with a human driver. The local driver of a ridesharing service might proffer keen insights about the preferred places to dine or what areas to stay away from. All that localized knowledge about the city is seemingly no longer accessible if you choose to use a self-driving car.

Well, that's not exactly the case.

The odds are that most self-driving cars will eventually have a slew of AI-based components onboard. This is bound to include a locally-focused knowledge base about the city and what to do in the city. Using an Alex or Siri type of interface, a passenger can pretty much get the same kind of insights about the urban setting as they would from a human driver. Indeed, some human drivers are huffy and difficult to chat with, while an AI-based chatbot would presumably be programmed to be either neutral or more favorably responsive.

If you really want that local human interaction, another possibility would be that while inside the self-driving car you could bring up the in-car LED display and make face-to-face contact with a remote human agent. Similar to using Zoom or the equivalent, the person could interact with you during your riding time. This is decidedly better overall than talking with a driver that you might inadvertently be distracting from the driving task itself.

All of that being said, some would still say they will miss having a human driver at the wheel.

This also brings up the qualms about how employment will be impacted in a city due to the advent of self-driving cars. There could be a lot of local city-dwelling human drivers that rely upon driving as a living that will now be displaced due to the use of self-driving cars. This could be bad news for a city, taking away a type of job or work effort that is nearly effortlessly undertaken by locals.

Though this is a serious concern, do keep in mind that it will play out over an extended period of time. The rollout of self-driving cars is going to be gradual, likely taking many decades. There will be a mixture of self-driving cars and human-driven cars on our public roadways for a very long time. We also don't know how readily people such as tourists will take to using self-driving cars, whereas they might have a greater comfort level at using conventional human-driven cars. It might take several generations before enough people become comfortable with riding in driverless cars.

There is another factor that is related to the preceding topic, namely traffic and roadway congestion.

Self-driving cars are anticipated to be driven by AI driving systems in a rather strictly legal manner. They will not go over the speed limits. They will make a full and complete stop at Stop signs. And so on. This certainly seems sensible and you would assume appropriate to do.

The problem will be that human drivers aren't going to like driving amongst these do-gooder driving systems and the cacophony of righteously divined self-driving cars. We've already seen that human drivers get frustrated by self-driving cars that won't go faster than the speed limit or that won't jackrabbit from a stopped position when a red light turns to green.

All told, it could be that the traffic in a city will get even worse as a result of the self-driving cars being utilized. Human drivers will get exasperated and try crazier driving trickery. Meanwhile, self-driving cars might be endlessly roaming, rather than parking and getting off an active roadway, ergo they will be contributing to those massive tie-ups and overwhelming traffic clogs.

A key takeaway for city leaders is that they ought to be planning toward the advent of self-driving cars, encompassing the good aspects and the potential untoward aspects that might arise. And, for those that get there soonest, there is a potential windfall of attracting tourism due to the novelty of having self-driving cars and the ease of providing transportation for urban tourism purposes.

You might need a tune-up or possibly an entire overhaul of your urban tourism transit strategies, making sure to include those someday to be ubiquitous AI-based true self-driving cars. Don't get caught behind the eight ball when it comes to ensuring that lucrative and synergistic tourism for your beloved city.

APPENDIX

APPENDIX A
TEACHING WITH THIS MATERIAL

The material in this book can be readily used either as a supplemental to other content for a class, or it can also be used as a core set of textbook material for a specialized class. Classes where this material is most likely used include any classes at the college or university level that want to augment the class by offering thought provoking and educational essays about AI and self-driving cars.

In particular, here are some aspects for class use:

- Computer Science. Studying AI, autonomous vehicles, etc.
- Business. Exploring technology and it adoption for business.
- Sociology. Sociological views on the adoption and advancement of technology.

Specialized classes at the undergraduate and graduate level can also make use of this material.

For each chapter, consider whether you think the chapter provides material relevant to your course topic. There is plenty of opportunity to get the students thinking about the topic and force them to decide whether they agree or disagree with the points offered and positions taken. I would also encourage you to have the students do additional research beyond the chapter material presented (I provide next some suggested assignments they can do).

RESEARCH ASSIGNMENTS ON THESE TOPICS

Your students can find background material on these topics, doing so in various business and technical publications. I list below the top ranked AI related journals. For business publications, I would suggest the usual culprits such as the Harvard Business Review, Forbes, Fortune, WSJ, and the like.

Here are some suggestions of homework or projects that you could assign to students:

a) Assignment for foundational AI research topic: Research and prepare a paper and a presentation on a specific aspect of Deep AI, Machine Learning, ANN, etc. The paper should cite at least 3 reputable sources. Compare and contrast to what has been stated in this book.

b) Assignment for the Self-Driving Car topic: Research and prepare a paper and Self-Driving Cars. Cite at least 3 reputable sources and analyze the characterizations. Compare and contrast to what has been stated in this book.

c) Assignment for a Business topic: Research and prepare a paper and a presentation on businesses and advanced technology. What is hot, and what is not? Cite at least 3 reputable sources. Compare and contrast to the depictions in this book.

d) Assignment to do a Startup: Have the students prepare a paper about how they might startup a business in this realm. They must submit a sound Business Plan for the startup. They could also be asked to present their Business Plan and so should also have a presentation deck to coincide with it.

You can certainly adjust the aforementioned assignments to fit to your particular needs and the class structure. You'll notice that I ask for 3 reputable cited sources for the paper writing based assignments. I usually steer students toward "reputable" publications, since otherwise they will cite some oddball source that has no credentials other than that they happened to write something and post it onto the Internet. You can define "reputable" in whatever way you prefer, for example some faculty think Wikipedia is not reputable while others believe it is reputable and allow students to cite it.

The reason that I usually ask for at least 3 citations is that if the student only does one or two citations they usually settle on whatever they happened to find the fastest. By requiring three citations, it usually seems to force them to look around, explore, and end-up probably finding five or more, and then whittling it down to 3 that they will actually use.

I have not specified the length of their papers, and leave that to you to tell the students what you prefer. For each of those assignments, you could end-up with a short one to two pager, or you could do a dissertation length paper. Base the length on whatever best fits for your class, and the credit amount of the assignment within the context of the other grading metrics you'll be using for the class.

I mention in the assignments that they are to do a paper and prepare a presentation. I usually try to get students to present their work. This is a good practice for what they will do in the business world. Most of the time, they will be required to prepare an analysis and present it. If you don't have the class time or inclination to have the students present, then you can of course cut out the aspect of them putting together a presentation.

If you want to point students toward highly ranked journals in AI, here's a list of the top journals as reported by *various citation counts sources* (this list changes year to year):

- Communications of the ACM
- Artificial Intelligence
- Cognitive Science
- IEEE Transactions on Pattern Analysis and Machine Intelligence
- Foundations and Trends in Machine Learning
- Journal of Memory and Language
- Cognitive Psychology
- Neural Networks
- IEEE Transactions on Neural Networks and Learning Systems
- IEEE Intelligent Systems
- Knowledge-based Systems

GUIDE TO USING THE CHAPTERS

For each of the chapters, I provide next some various ways to use the chapter material. You can assign the tasks as individual homework assignments, or the tasks can be used with team projects for the class. You can easily layout a series of assignments, such as indicating that the students are to do item "a" below for say Chapter 1, then "b" for the next chapter of the book, and so on.

a) What is the main point of the chapter and describe in your own words the significance of the topic,

b) Identify at least two aspects in the chapter that you agree with, and support your concurrence by providing at least one other outside researched item as support; make sure to explain your basis for disagreeing with the aspects,

c) Identify at least two aspects in the chapter that you disagree with, and support your disagreement by providing at least one other outside researched item as support; make sure to explain your basis for disagreeing with the aspects,

d) Find an aspect that was not covered in the chapter, doing so by conducting outside research, and then explain how that aspect ties into the chapter and what significance it brings to the topic,

e) Interview a specialist in industry about the topic of the chapter, collect from them their thoughts and opinions, and readdress the chapter by citing your source and how they compared and contrasted to the material,

f) Interview a relevant academic professor or researcher in a college or university about the topic of the chapter, collect from them their thoughts and opinions, and readdress the chapter by citing your source and how they compared and contrasted to the material,

g) Try to update a chapter by finding out the latest on the topic, and ascertain whether the issue or topic has now been solved or whether it is still being addressed, explain what you come up with.

The above are all ways in which you can get the students of your class involved in considering the material of a given chapter. You could mix things up by having one of those above assignments per each week, covering the chapters over the course of the semester or quarter.

As a reminder, here are the chapters of the book and you can select whichever chapters you find most valued for your particular class:

Companion Book By This Author

Advances in AI and Autonomous Vehicles: Cybernetic Self-Driving Cars

Practical Advances in Artificial Intelligence (AI) and Machine Learning

by

Dr. Lance B. Eliot, MBA, PhD

This title is available via Amazon and other book sellers

Companion Book By This Author

Self-Driving Cars:
"The Mother of All AI Projects"

by Dr. Lance B. Eliot, MBA, PhD

Chapter Title

This title is available via Amazon and other book seller

Companion Book By This Author

Innovation and Thought Leadership on Self-Driving Driverless Cars

by Dr. Lance B. Eliot, MBA, PhD

Chapter Title

This title is available via Amazon and other book sellers

Companion Book By This Author

New Advances in AI Autonomous Driverless Cars Self-Driving Cars

by Dr. Lance B. Eliot, MBA, PhD

Chapter Title

This title is available via Amazon and other book sellers

Companion Book By This Author

Introduction to Driverless Self-Driving Cars

by Dr. Lance B. Eliot, MBA, PhD

Chapter Title

This title is available via Amazon and other book sellers

Companion Book By This Author

Autonomous Vehicle Driverless Self-Driving Cars and Artificial Intelligence

by Dr. Lance B. Eliot, MBA, PhD

Chapter Title

This title is available via Amazon and other book sellers

Companion Book By This Author

Transformative Artificial Intelligence Driverless Self-Driving Cars

by Dr. Lance B. Eliot, MBA, PhD

Chapter Title

This title is available via Amazon and other book sellers

Companion Book By This Author

Disruptive Artificial Intelligence and Driverless Self-Driving Cars

by Dr. Lance B. Eliot, MBA, PhD

Chapter Title

1 Eliot Framework for AI Self-Driving Cars

2 Maneuverability and Self-Driving Cars

3 Common Sense Reasoning and Self-Driving Cars

4 Cognition Timing and Self-Driving Cars

5 Speed Limits and Self-Driving Vehicles

6 Human Back-up Drivers and Self-Driving Cars

7 Forensic Analysis Uber and Self-Driving Cars

8 Power Consumption and Self-Driving Cars

9 Road Rage and Self-Driving Cars

10 Conspiracy Theories and Self-Driving Cars

11 Fear Landscape and Self-Driving Cars

12 Pre-Mortem and Self-Driving Cars

13 Kits and Self-Driving Cars

This title is available via Amazon and other book sellers

Companion Book By This Author

State-of-the-Art
AI Driverless Self-Driving Cars

by Dr. Lance B. Eliot, MBA, PhD

Chapter Title

This title is available via Amazon and other book sellers

Companion Book By This Author

Top Trends in AI Self-Driving Cars

by Dr. Lance B. Eliot, MBA, PhD

Chapter Title

This title is available via Amazon and other book sellers

Companion Book By This Author

AI Innovations and Self-Driving Cars

by Dr. Lance B. Eliot, MBA, PhD

This title is available via Amazon and other book sellers

Companion Book By This Author

Crucial Advances for AI Self-Driving Cars

by Dr. Lance B. Eliot, MBA, PhD

Chapter Title

This title is available via Amazon and other book sellers

Companion Book By This Author

Sociotechnical Insights and AI Driverless Cars

by Dr. Lance B. Eliot, MBA, PhD

Chapter Title

This title is available via Amazon and other book sellers

Companion Book By This Author

Pioneering Advances for AI Driverless Cars

by Dr. Lance B. Eliot, MBA, PhD

Chapter Title

This title is available via Amazon and other book sellers

Companion Book By This Author

Leading Edge Trends for AI Driverless Cars

by Dr. Lance B. Eliot, MBA, PhD

Chapter Title

This title is available via Amazon and other book sellers

Companion Book By This Author

The Cutting Edge of AI Autonomous Cars

by Dr. Lance B. Eliot, MBA, PhD

Chapter Title

This title is available via Amazon and other book sellers

Companion Book By This Author

The Next Wave of
AI Self-Driving Cars

by Dr. Lance B. Eliot, MBA, PhD

Chapter Title

This title is available via Amazon and other book sellers

Companion Book By This Author

Revolutionary Innovations of AI Self-Driving Cars

by Dr. Lance B. Eliot, MBA, PhD

Chapter Title

Companion Book By This Author

AI Self-Driving Cars
Breakthroughs

by Dr. Lance B. Eliot, MBA, PhD

This title is available via Amazon and other book sellers

Companion Book By This Author

Trailblazing Trends for **AI Self-Driving Cars**

by Dr. Lance B. Eliot, MBA, PhD

Chapter Title

Companion Book By This Author

Ingenious Strides for
AI Driverless Cars

by Dr. Lance B. Eliot, MBA, PhD

Chapter Title

This title is available via Amazon and other book sellers

Companion Book By This Author

AI Self-Driving Cars
Inventiveness

by Dr. Lance B. Eliot, MBA, PhD

Chapter Title

This title is available via Amazon and other book sellers

Companion Book By This Author

Visionary Secrets of AI Driverless Cars

by Dr. Lance B. Eliot, MBA, PhD

Chapter Title

This title is available via Amazon and other book sellers

Companion Book By This Author

Spearheading AI Self-Driving Cars

by Dr. Lance B. Eliot, MBA, PhD

Chapter Title

This title is available via Amazon and other book sellers

Companion Book By This Author

Spurring
AI Self-Driving Cars

by Dr. Lance B. Eliot, MBA, PhD

Chapter Title

This title is available via Amazon and other book sellers

Companion Book By This Author

Avant-Garde
AI Driverless Cars

by Dr. Lance B. Eliot, MBA, PhD

Chapter Title

1 Eliot Framework for AI Self-Driving Cars

2 Linear Non-Threshold and AI Self-Driving Cars

3 Prediction Equation and AI Self-Driving Cars

4 Modular Autonomous Systems and AI Self-Driving Cars

5 Driver's Licensing and AI Self-Driving Cars

6 Offshoots and Spinoffs and AI Self-Driving Car

7 Depersonalization and AI Self-Driving Cars

This title is available via Amazon and other book sellers

Companion Book By This Author

AI Self-Driving Cars
Evolvement

by Dr. Lance B. Eliot, MBA, PhD

Chapter Title

This title is available via Amazon and other book sellers

Companion Book By This Author

AI Driverless Cars Chrysalis

by Dr. Lance B. Eliot, MBA, PhD

Chapter Title

This title is available via Amazon and other book sellers

Companion Book By This Author

Boosting
AI Autonomous Cars

by Dr. Lance B. Eliot, MBA, PhD

Chapter Title

This title is available via Amazon and other book sellers

Companion Book By This Author

AI Self-Driving Cars Trendsetting

by Dr. Lance B. Eliot, MBA, PhD

Chapter Title

This title is available via Amazon and other book sellers

Companion Book By This Author

AI Autonomous Cars Forefront

by Dr. Lance B. Eliot, MBA, PhD

Chapter Title

This title is available via Amazon and other book sellers

Companion Book By This Author

AI Autonomous Cars Emergence

by Dr. Lance B. Eliot, MBA, PhD

Chapter Title

This title is available via Amazon and other book sellers

Companion Book By This Author

AI Autonomous Cars Progress

by Dr. Lance B. Eliot, MBA, PhD

Chapter Title

This title is available via Amazon and other book sellers

Companion Book By This Author

AI Self-Driving Cars Prognosis

by Dr. Lance B. Eliot, MBA, PhD

Chapter Title

This title is available via Amazon and other book sellers

Companion Book By This Author

AI Self-Driving Cars Momentum

by Dr. Lance B. Eliot, MBA, PhD

Chapter Title

This title is available via Amazon and other book sellers

Companion Book By This Author

AI Self-Driving Cars Headway

by Dr. Lance B. Eliot, MBA, PhD

Chapter Title

This title is available via Amazon and other book sellers

Companion Book By This Author

AI Self-Driving Cars
Vicissitude

by Dr. Lance B. Eliot, MBA, PhD

Chapter Title

This title is available via Amazon and other book sellers

Companion Book By This Author

AI Self-Driving Cars Autonomy

by Dr. Lance B. Eliot, MBA, PhD

Chapter Title

This title is available via Amazon and other book sellers

Companion Book By This Author

AI Driverless Cars Transmutation

by Dr. Lance B. Eliot, MBA, PhD

Chapter Title

This title is available via Amazon and other book sellers

Companion Book By This Author

AI Driverless Cars Potentiality

by Dr. Lance B. Eliot, MBA, PhD

Chapter Title

This title is available via Amazon and other book sellers

Companion Book By This Author

AI Driverless Cars Realities

by Dr. Lance B. Eliot, MBA, PhD

Chapter Title

This title is available via Amazon and other book sellers

Companion Book By This Author

AI Self-Driving Cars
Materiality

by Dr. Lance B. Eliot, MBA, PhD

Chapter Title

1 Eliot Framework for AI Self-Driving Cars

2 Baby Sea Lion and AI Self-Driving Cars

3 Traffic Lights and AI Self-Driving Cars

4 Roadway Edge Computing and AI Self-Driving Cars

5 Ground Penetrating Radar and AI Self-Driving Cars

6 Upstream Parable and AI Self-Driving Cars

7 Red-Light Auto-Stopping and Self-Driving Cars

8 Falseness of Superhuman AI Self-Driving Cars

9 Social Distancing and AI Self-Driving Cars

10 Apollo 13 Lessons and AI Self-Driving Cars

11 FutureLaw and AI Self-Driving Cars

This title is available via Amazon and other book sellers

Companion Book By This Author

AI Self-Driving Cars Accordance

by Dr. Lance B. Eliot, MBA, PhD

Chapter Title

This title is available via Amazon and other book sellers

Companion Book By This Author

AI Self-Driving Cars
Equanimity

by Dr. Lance B. Eliot, MBA, PhD

Chapter Title

1 Eliot Framework for AI Self-Driving Cars

2 AI Oligopolies and AI Self-Driving Cars

3 AI Intent and AI Self-Driving Cars

4 "Life On Wheels" Film and AI Self-Driving Cars

5 Murder Hornet Spread and AI Self-Driving Cars

6 Simons Sight Research and AI Self-Driving Cars

7 NASCAR Car Racing and AI Self-Driving Cars

8 Ballot Harvesting and AI Self-Driving Cars

9 Apollo 12 Lessons and AI Self-Driving Cars

10 Running Over Shooter and AI Self-Driving Cars

11 Grimes Soul Selling and AI Self-Driving Cars

12 Cyber-Hackers Make Money and AI Self-Driving Cars

This title is available via Amazon and other book sellers

Companion Book By This Author

AI Self-Driving Cars Divulgement

by Dr. Lance B. Eliot, MBA, PhD

Chapter Title

This title is available via Amazon and other book sellers

Companion Book By This Author

AI Self-Driving Cars
Consonance

by Dr. Lance B. Eliot, MBA, PhD

Chapter Title

This title is available via Amazon and other book sellers

Companion Book By This Author

Revelatory AI Self-Driving Cars

by Dr. Lance B. Eliot, MBA, PhD

Chapter Title

This title is available via Amazon and other book sellers

Companion Book By This Author

Edifying AI Self-Driving Cars

by Dr. Lance B. Eliot, MBA, PhD

Chapter Title

This title is available via Amazon and other book sellers

Companion Book By This Author

Apprising AI Driverless Cars

by Dr. Lance B. Eliot, MBA, PhD

Chapter Title

This title is available via Amazon and other book sellers

Companion Book By This Author

Improving AI Self-Driving Cars

by Dr. Lance B. Eliot, MBA, PhD

Chapter Title

Companion Book By This Author

Progressing AI Driverless Cars

by Dr. Lance B. Eliot, MBA, PhD

Chapter Title

This title is available via Amazon and other book sellers

Companion Book By This Author

AI Self-Driving Cars Imminence

by Dr. Lance B. Eliot, MBA, PhD

Chapter Title

This title is available via Amazon and other book sellers

ABOUT THE AUTHOR

Dr. Lance B. Eliot, Ph.D., MBA is a Stanford Fellow and a globally recognized AI expert and thought leader, an experienced executive and leader, a successful serial entrepreneur, and a noted scholar on AI, including that his Forbes and AI Trends columns have amassed over 4.5+ million views, his books on AI are frequently ranked in the Top 10 of all-time AI books, his articles are widely cited, and he has developed dozens of advanced AI systems.

He currently serves as the CEO of Techbruim, Inc. and has over twenty years of industry experience including serving as a corporate officer in billion-dollar sized firms and was a partner in a major consulting firm. He is also a successful entrepreneur having founded, ran, and sold several high-tech firms.

Dr. Eliot previously hosted the popular radio show *Technotrends* that was also available on American Airlines flights via their in-flight audio program, he has made appearances on CNN, has been a frequent speaker at industry conferences, and his podcasts have been downloaded over 100,000 times.

A former professor at the University of Southern California (USC), he founded and led an innovative research lab on Artificial Intelligence. He also previously served on the faculty of the University of California Los Angeles (UCLA) and was a visiting professor at other major universities. He was elected to the International Board of the Society for Information Management (SIM), a prestigious association of over 3,000 high-tech executives worldwide.

He has performed extensive community service, including serving as Senior Science Adviser to the Congressional Vice-Chair of the Congressional Committee on Science & Technology. He has served on the Board of the OC Science & Engineering Fair (OCSEF), where he is also has been a Grand Sweepstakes judge, and likewise served as a judge for the Intel International SEF (ISEF). He served as the Vice-Chair of the Association for Computing Machinery (ACM) Chapter, a prestigious association of computer scientists. Dr. Eliot has been a shark tank judge for the USC Mark Stevens Center for Innovation on start-up pitch competitions and served as a mentor for several incubators and accelerators in Silicon Valley and in Silicon Beach.

Dr. Eliot holds a Ph.D. from USC, MBA, and Bachelor's in Computer Science, and earned the CDP, CCP, CSP, CDE, and CISA certifications.

ADDENDUM

AI Self-Driving Cars Imminence

Practical Advances in Artificial Intelligence (AI) and Machine Learning

By
Dr. Lance B. Eliot, MBA, PhD

For supplemental materials of this book, visit:

www.ai-selfdriving-cars.guru

For special orders of this book, contact:

LBE Press Publishing

Email: LBE.Press.Publishing@gmail.com

Made in the USA
Monee, IL
09 November 2026

67997597R20226